Witch Camps and Witchcraft Discourse in Africa

Witch Camps and Witchcraft Discourse in Africa

Critiquing Development Practices

Matthew Gmalifo Mabefam

LEXINGTON BOOKS
Lanham • Boulder • New York • London

Published by Lexington Books
An imprint of The Rowman & Littlefield Publishing Group, Inc.
4501 Forbes Boulevard, Suite 200, Lanham, Maryland 20706
www.rowman.com

86-90 Paul Street, London EC2A 4NE

Cover photo taken by the author: Gnai Refuge Community: Footpath Leading to Gnani-Tindang

British Library Cataloguing in Publication Information Available

Library of Congress Cataloging-in-Publication Data
Names: Mabefam, Matthew Gmalifo, author.
Title: Witch camps and witchcraft discourse in Africa : critiquing development practices / Matthew Gmalifo Mabefam.
Description: Lanham, Maryland : Lexington Books, 2023. | Includes bibliographical references and index. | Summary: "This book explores how local development interventions related to witchcraft in Africa intersect and conflict with globally accepted development practices. It argues for expansion and diversification of development practices and problematizes international development practices that can jeopardize the well-being of the people it seeks to support"-- Provided by publisher.
Identifiers: LCCN 2023027035 (print) | LCCN 2023027036 (ebook) | ISBN 9781666918496 (cloth) | ISBN 9781666918502 (ebook)
Subjects: LCSH: Witchcraft--Social aspects--Africa. | Witch hunting--Africa. | Older women--Crimes against--Africa. | Social isolation--Africa. | Non-governmental organizations--Africa.
Classification: LCC GN475 .M334 223 (print) | LCC GN475 (ebook) | DDC 306.4096--dc23/eng/20230606
LC record available at https://lccn.loc.gov/2023027035
LC ebook record available at https://lccn.loc.gov/2023027036

Contents

Preface

In my natal community, as elsewhere in Africa, a cultural ideal often expressed is that the elderly are wise and should be respected. Close interaction between the young and the elderly is likewise encouraged and presumed to be the primary mode for youth to gain wisdom. However, this cultural ideal may not necessarily reflect the reality of either the position of the elderly or the nature of interactions between the young and old. In my case, however, I had a particularly strong bond with my uncle and each time we had a conversation I was in awe of him. Not only did he seem wise to me, but he was also the only member of my extended family who was relatively rich. He seemed to own so much in comparison with other family members: cattle, goats, sheep, motorcycles, and many other valuable items. During one of our conversations, I asked him why he was rich while other family members had so little. He simply said, "I am only a custodian of most of the things; they are not mine." My uncle was rich because other family members gave their things to him. This led to many more questions on my part, but the most puzzling one seemed to me the issue of why people would give their things to a "custodian" when they had so little. My uncle provided the answer to this question simply by saying that people, especially the young, were afraid that they would be bewitched if others realized that they were wealthy. The fear of witches doing harm to them, destroying their property, and even potentially killing them was so strong that it hindered opportunities to enjoy what they had achieved. That is, there is a presumption that one's social and economic advancement arouses spite and envy. Moreover, the explanation offered by my uncle about his role as a custodian clearly rested on the belief that age was an important anecdote to potential bewitchment: "Witches are afraid of me because I am old."

Indeed, within many communities, as with my own family, elderly people are assumed to have gained wisdom about how to fortify themselves and those that they love against witchcraft. As discussed in this book, however, the "old" are not always respected nor perceived as capable of spiritual fortification. Further, in the case of women, who are the predominant number of individuals resettled in communities of refuge in Ghana, Burkina Faso, or Benin on the basis of witchcraft, being old and a woman presents a double conundrum. Firstly, elderly women are often not viewed in the same way as elderly men such as my uncle. Elderly women are less likely to be obligated to have the power of spiritual fortification, and even if they are thought to have spiritual powers, women are accused of using such powers to bewitch others. And secondly, the overwhelming number of individuals living in the communities of refuge are women, be they old or relatively young. For women, in other words, there are greater challenges grounded in cultural norms and values that discriminate against them.

To give another example from my own experiences, I moved to the town of Chamba in 1996 to further my studies. Not long after I arrived, an "old" woman was accused of witchcraft and asked to leave the community. She left her marital home and had nowhere to go because no one would accept her. The woman's only option was to live in the bush as a lone settler. Her new settlement was located on the outskirts of town close to my school. As students, we could see her house and it was daily pointed out and referred to as "the witch's house." Occasionally, we would see her walk past the school and head toward town. She appeared to me very lonely with little engagement or support except for the occasional visits she made to my landlord's mother's house. The two women had been friends in their youthful days and though they had lost touch, they had become reacquainted following the accused woman's resettlement near the town. The renewed contact between the women, however, was cautiously navigated because of the fear and prejudices associated with individuals who are accused of witchcraft and the potential that those that associate with them may also find themselves suspected or accused and, possibly, ostracized.

Indeed, the problems encountered by the woman living alone and ostracized on the outskirts of the town were undoubtedly exacerbated by the general fear and prejudices associated with individuals accused of witchcraft. Instructions for dealing with "witchcraft" and avoiding contact with those accused of witchcraft abound. For instance, rumors abounded in Chamba while I lived there of some places and sites as being a haven for ill deeds, with people accused of engaging in the occult practice to create wealth (relatively many people were considered rich in the suburb). Children in the township were often warned by their parents and relatives not to make friends with any school children from particular places, such as one particular suburb presumed to be a hub for such practices. Understandably, with such deep-seated prejudices, everyone feared the people of this suburb. If one were to visit the suburb, warnings were given against drinking, and eating while visiting, the parents advised, was strictly forbidden. This was particularly difficult for me, as two of my very closest school friends lived in this suburb. Though I would occasionally visit my friends, I too was influenced by the warnings given about how best to navigate interactions. Thus, I politely declined the food that was offered to me, claiming that I was not hungry. Eventually, my cousins warned me to cut ties with my friends and as I lived with my cousins, I felt obliged to respect their wishes. I could not sever the links completely, however, and thus I minimized the number of times I visited my friends.

Needless to say, my subsequent scholarly interest in witchcraft and communities of refuge arose out of my personal experiences and the manner in which the issues around this phenomenon form a significant component of everyday life in Africa. It was only when I commenced tertiary studies and undertook fieldwork with a local nongovernment organization (NGO), however, that I understood the extent of the problems for individuals accused of witchcraft. Located in Bimbilla in northern Ghana, Grameen Ghana worked with individuals that were accused of being "witches" in the Kukuo community. The most memorable aspect of my visits to the community is the extent of the injustice and deprivation experienced by the individuals accused, all of whom were older women. Though among all communities of refuge, as I would later learn, Kukuo appears to be the one where it is difficult to differentiate persons and dwelling places on the basis of witchcraft accusations. However, due to NGOs' focus on such women, they were often the center of our meetings and thus easy to identify them. Though challenges abound for many residents in Kukuo, cut off from their families and ostracized from their communities, the individuals that were accused of witchcraft faced enormous challenges in meeting their basic needs. Notwithstanding the impact on the individuals accused, it was also clear that there was a significant threat to the fabric of family and kinship identities and relations. Many of the accused individuals also had ongoing family responsibilities such as the care of dependent children and grandchildren.

Indeed, the issue of witchcraft accusations in parts of Africa, the banishment of people (mostly poor old women) from their communities, and the existence of the communities of refuge despite some efforts by the government and NGOs for their disbandment (in the case of Ghana), or creating the shelters themselves (Burkina Faso), prisons (Benin, Cameroon, etc.), points to an ongoing problem for differently positioned actors (governments, NGOs, human rights watchdogs, etc.) depending on the angle that it is viewed and thus merits closer academic attention. In presenting a detailed and nuanced case that specifically focuses on the experiences and lives of individuals accused and subsequently sought refuge in other communities, the book highlights the complexities inherent in the intersections between culture and development, and further, calls for the need to pay greater attention to where cultural beliefs and practices such as witchcraft are situated within the discourses and approaches to development. Overall, the book highlights an opportunity to call for a rethinking of the mainstream approaches to development that nominally include culture and yet do not delve into the nuances of what this entails and how engaging with local epistemologies might better inform more culturally appropriate development discourse, policies, and strategies.

Figure 0.1. A bedroom for a woman accused of witchcraft. Photo taken by author. Typical one-bed round mud and thatch house for a person accused of witchcraft and residing in Gnani-Tindang.

Acknowledgments

This book would not have become a possibility without the generous support of many people and institutions. I would like to thank the people of Gnani for allowing me to live and learn from them. In particular, I want to thank all the people accused of witchcraft and evicted from their communities who have sought refuge in Gnani. Although I'm unable to mention your names, the stories and conversations we had about your lived experiences are the foundation of this book. I also want to thank government officials from the various departments and institutions who sacrificed parts of their valuable time to share helpful information for this book, particularly officials from the Ghana Police Service, the Commission on Human Rights and Administrative Justice and the National Commission on Civic Education. Again, I thank the staff of the NGOs who agreed to discuss issues of witchcraft and development with me, especially the staff of ActionAid Ghana, Songtaba, and Humanist Service Corps.

I would like to express my profound gratitude to the University of Melbourne for offering me an academic home and supporting the research that led to this book. I also use this opportunity to thank my academic mentors and colleagues at the University of Melbourne whose pieces of advice influenced the writing of this book. In particular, Dr. Violeta Schubert, Associate Prof. Kalissa Alexeyeff and Prof. Tamara Kohn deserve special thanks for their diverse roles. In addition, Associate Professors Lan Hoang, Bina Fernandez, Monica Minnegal, Hans Baer, Simon Batterbury, Dolly Kikon, Debrah McDougall, Dr. Erin Fitz-Henry, and Dr. Anne Decobert offered pieces of advice anytime I asked for one. This book has benefited immensely from such pieces of advice and would not have become what it is without their support.

I owe debts of gratitude to Drs. Emmanuel Awoh Lohkoko, Adam Orlando, Tom McNamara, Bibiana Huggins, Kennedy Mbeva, Denisse Rodriguez Quinonez, Lesley Champion, and Jai Patel, all colleagues at the University of Melbourne for their companionship and friendship during the period of

xi

writing this book. I also thank Prof. Mavis Dako-Gyeke of the University of Ghana, Dr. Dominic Dagbanja of the University of Western Australia, Dr. Kirsty Wissing of CSIRO, Dr. Festus Muasun of the University of Regina, Dr. Charles Gyan of McGill University, and Dr. Samuelson Appau of University of Melbourne, all of whom I have discussed some rough ideas about this book with at some point and received valuable input.

The African Studies Group at the University of Melbourne also deserves special commendation. Since arriving in Melbourne, I found a "home" and intellectual community in the African Studies Group. The group provided an enabling platform for informative and supportive collegial discussions. I got the opportunity to share my formative ideas with colleagues and received constructive feedback. I say thank you to all mentors, colleagues, and friends who have provided me with companionship over the years. In particular Franka Vaughan, Jean Pierre Ndabakuranye, Kofi Bediako, Moses Mensah, Issa Wumbla, and Vincent Dogbey among many others.

Furthermore, I thank the editorial office team, Sydney Webush and Emilia Rivera, who took time to work with me from the beginning till this book became a reality. Your attention to detail through the copyediting process and crosschecking of all files are well appreciated. I acknowledge the anonymous review comments and thank the reviewer for investing their precious time and intellectual labour to provide detailed constructive feedback. I must say that I feel lucky to have had this book sent to someone who is not only very special-ised in the topic but also very conversant with the study area. Your insights directed me to review and rewrite some portions of this book. If this book is any better, then it is because of your constructive feedback. Thank you.

Finally, I am thankful to my family who unconditionally allowed me to go to school and has had to bear so many years of my absence from home. Though education is considered a right for many, for me it was a privilege, and I was one of the lucky ones. And to my beloved wife Chengetai Julia Jera who unreservedly supported me in writing this book, I say thank you.

Chapter 3 of this book is derived in part from my article "Limitless Opportunities for Wealth? Witchcraft as a Strategy for (In)Equality and Economic (Dis)Empowerment" published in Forum for Development Studies (2023) with copyright © Norwegian Institute of International Affairs (NUPI), reprinted by permission of Taylor & Francis Ltd, http://www.tandfonline.com on behalf of Norwegian Institute of International Affairs (NUPI).

All the names of people who participated in this study have been anony-mized to protect their identity, however, all the stories and experiences shared with me remain valid. Also, despite the support I received from many people during the writing of this book, I take full responsibility for any errors and shortcomings that this book might contain.

List of Abbreviations

AAG	ActionAid Ghana
CHRAJ	Commission on Human Rights and Administrative Justice
DANIDA	Danish International Development Agency
DOVVSU	Domestic Violence and Victims Support Unit
FGDs	Focus Group Discussions
GSS	Ghana Statistical Service
HND	High National Diploma
IMF	International Monetary Fund
ISSER	Institute of Statistical, Social and Economic Research
LEAP	Livelihood Empowerment Against Poverty
NCCE	National Commission on Civic Education
NGOs	Non-Governmental Organisations
NPP	New Patriotic Party
UNESCO	United Nations Educational, Scientific and Cultural Organization
UNDP	United Nations Development Programme
USAID	United States Agency for International Development

Introduction

"Witches Are Falling from the Sky": Problematizing Witchcraft Beliefs and Practices in Africa

Witchcraft beliefs and practices are important to the social, spiritual, and economic life in many parts of Africa. A Gallup poll conducted in 2009 indicated that on average 55 percent of people in selected Sub-Saharan African countries who responded to their survey held a belief in witchcraft (Tortora, 2010). If we disaggregate the respondents into individual countries, the degree to which people believe in witchcraft varies, with some very high and others low. From the Gallup poll, Ivory Coast (95 percent), Senegal (80 percent), Ghana (77 percent), Mali (77 percent), and Cameroon (75 percent) occupy an unenviable position when it comes to witchcraft belief (Tortora, 2010).

Let's take Ghana for example and interrogate it a bit further. A study by ActionAid (2008a) estimated that 90 percent of Ghanaians believe that witchcraft exists, and further, that it has affected their lives in some way. Ghanaians refer to witchcraft by many names. For example, among the Akans of southern Ghana, witchcraft is referred to as *bayi*, among the Dagombas of northern Ghana, *sotali*, while the *Bikpakpaam*[1] of northern Ghana call it *kisook*. Although the terms are varied, as are the practices and articulations of what belief in witchcraft entails, it is generally understood as referring to a supernatural power possessed by an individual and used for their benefit to harm others or influence them against their will (see Richter, Flowers, and Bongmba, 2017; Goody, 1970; Nukunya, 2003; Tembo, 1993). Witchcraft, as a (*un*)conscious and purposive act used by individuals, coexists with notions of its social nature, of it being a phenomenon that affects some people in some way, and that there is a need for individuals to pay attention to regulating their conduct and relationships with others to ensure that they do not become potential targets (See Forsyth, 2016, p. 332).

The embeddedness of beliefs in witchcraft and the presumption that there are people who practice the craft is profound. In both rural and urban sites alike, the landscape is scattered with anti-witchcraft shrines (Adu-Gyamfi and Owusu-Ansah, 2014; Lentz, 2000; Martin, 2014; Parish, 2003). Parish (2003), for example, asserts that Akan anti-witchcraft shrines are often located in remote rural villages. Further, Parish explains the importance of anti-witchcraft shrines as follows:

> At these shrines the ritual knowledge possessed by shrine priests is often envisaged as made up of unchanging elements within what is seen as a tightly bounded epistemological framework of the real/unreal, visible/invisible, and natural/ supernatural. (2003, p. 18)

In this "tightly bounded epistemological framework," to borrow Parish's phrase, anti-witchcraft shrines play a crucial role in Ghana as a mode of protection for people so that they do not become targets of witchcraft and to cleanse those who believe that they have already been targeted (see also Martin, 2014). In addition, such shrines also serve as places where people go to seek wealth and fertility (see Lentz, 2000; Martin, 2014; Parish, 2003). For an illustration of anti-witchcraft shrines in urban Ghana, there is documented evidence that notes that Korle We (the shrine to the Goddess of the Lagoon), Nai We (the shrine to the Goddess of the Sea), and Sakumo Tsoshishi (the shrine to the God of War), all in Accra, the capital of Ghana, hold important transcripts on witchcraft trials (Roberts, 2014). Further, alongside anti-witchcraft shrines, Christian prayer camps are present across Ghana, purporting to ward off witchcraft and save people who are believed to be bewitched (see Onyinah, 2002).

The extent of the embeddedness of witchcraft beliefs and practices is also evident in the enormous attention that witchcraft receives in the media. In a survey of several Ghanaian newspapers that I undertook in 2016, I found discussions of witchcraft issues to be prevalent across different media, including in reputable national daily newspapers such as the *Daily Graphic* and the *Daily Guide*. To give an example, on August 6, 2016, an article by Ohene read, "Witches Are Falling from the Sky in Ghana" (see Darko, 2016). Ohene's article reports that the witch fell off because she was electrocuted by electricity wires while flying at night (Ohene, 2016). This was reported to have happened in a suburb of Kumasi (Akyeremadi), the second-largest city in Ghana. Earlier in the same week, another incident of a "flying witch" was reported in Tema, an industrial city in southern Ghana (Heerde, 2016; Searburn, 2016).

The reporting of sightings of "flying witches" is undoubtedly sensationalist in tone and has been critiqued, if not condemned, for the lack of due diligence on the part of journalists (see Adinkrah, 2019; Igwe, 2016a). Accordingly, such sensationalist reporting is condemned for evoking or exacerbating the fear and panic associated with the existence of witchcraft beliefs, practices, and accusations. Nonetheless, media attention, especially sightings of "witches," are frequent and reflect the ongoing cultural saliency and interest in issues relating to witchcraft.

Alongside the frequent (and sensationalist) attention given to "flying" and "crash-landing" witches, the media landscape has also proven to be an important avenue for public debate around witchcraft beliefs and practices in Africa. The rise of public debate and media attention indicates a growing concern among Africans about how witchcraft impacts lives and their self-identity as a modern society. With growing skepticism among some members of African societies, some openly proclaim that they do not believe in witchcraft or are at least beginning to challenge this belief (See Tortora, 2010; Onyinah, 2002). For example, it was reported that 21 percent of people who partook in the GALLUP survey did not believe in witchcraft in Ghana. The percentage of people who disbelieve in witchcraft is even higher in countries such as Uganda (85 percent) and Rwanda (83 percent) of their participant population (Tortora, 2010). The high percentage of people who disbelieve in witchcraft both in Ghana and elsewhere will be interesting to unpack although that lies outside of this book. However, there is a paradox in that although the public debate is growing and people are endeavoring to distance themselves from such beliefs, there is often a continuing concern with witchcraft. Africans are thus often caught between belief in witchcraft, practices, and accusations and the social shame associated with holding onto "primitive" or "irrational" beliefs and practices that are not in keeping with ideas of themselves as educated and modern people (See Mesaki, 1993, pp.1–2 for Tanzania; Parish, 2003). To a great extent, the ongoing presence of the communities of refuge in some African countries has undoubtedly brought to the surface the cultural sensitivity around the constructions of modern African identities as requiring a reckoning of sorts with seemingly "archaic" or "traditional" beliefs and practices.

However, the growing public discourses and debates about the impact of ongoing witchcraft beliefs and practices cannot compare to the problems and challenges experienced by individuals who are accused of witchcraft (see Mutaru, 2022; Mabefam and Appau, 2020). Returning to the alleged crash landings of witches, Adinkrah (2019) analyzed ten cases of alleged crash-landings of witches reported in the Ghanaian media over a twelve-year period. Adinkrah notes that "the alleged witches were overwhelmingly female, elderly, and poor, and suffered from grave psychopathological conditions" (2019, p. 1). Adinkrah's analysis is especially worth highlighting here as it speaks to the core of the concerns in this book, of the experiences of individuals who are accused of witchcraft and their removal from their local communities and their intersections with development practice.

One such area where there is an alignment of the government of Ghana's efforts and other development actors' agendas is the closure of communities of refuge as an intervention. Although much has been done in this area the different actors rarely delve into the key problem that accused individuals who are expelled from their communities face. To be clear, communities of refuge provide vital basic needs and services necessary for their capacity to survive (see Mutaru, 2022; Mutaru and Sekyi, 2023; Mabefam and Appau, 2020). Though aware of the plight and the situations of the people accused of witchcraft, government and NGOs who call for the closure of communities of refuge grounded in the argument of the violation of human rights and thus argue that it is wrong to banish people from their communities (ActionAid, 2008a, 2008b, 2014; Government of Ghana, 1998; NCCE, 2010). There is no doubt that banishing people from their communities based on witchcraft is an abuse of their rights. However, the urgency of asking those people to return to their communities without any efforts to protect them, I argue, is risky and exposes them to more danger, and deserves a second thought.

It is based on the risk or danger involved in the closure of communities of refuge without any sustained protection mechanism for the victims of witchcraft accusations that some scholars, including myself, argue against closing such communities. This is because their communities may not want them back, and until structures are put in place to protect them, sending them back to their communities and ignoring the looming danger that awaits them is a conundrum. The murder of ninety-year-old Madam Akua Denteh on Thursday, July 23, 2020 in broad daylight at Kafaba in the East Gonja Municipality of the newly created Savannah Region in the public on the basis of a witchcraft accusation without anyone including the security personnel coming to her rescue is a case in point. Although this line of thought is unpopular within development practice in Ghana, I'm not alone in taking that stance. For instance, on August 22, 2016, Leo Igwe (2016a), an academic specializing in witchcraft in northern Ghana and a human rights activist, wrote an influential article, "Do Not Close Down 'Witch Camps' in Northern Ghana." Igwe asserts that witch camps are a "safe haven" for displaced women accused of witchcraft and closing down such communities exposes them to more risk (see also Riedel, 2017).

Moreover, where witchcraft beliefs and practices are enmeshed in cultural norms, there are enormous implications for how modernity and socioeconomic development are understood, navigated, and experienced. That is, the tensions between the perceived wisdom about social and economic development—poverty alleviation, gender, justice, and equity—and the way that cultural beliefs and practices might frame understandings and approaches to development differently is especially evident in relation to witchcraft beliefs and practices. Indeed, for a long time, the perceived "problem" of witchcraft beliefs and practices was directly linked to a lack of modernity and development and presumed to disappear alongside societal advancement (see Green and Mesaki, 2005; Mair, 1964; Mayer, 1954; Mesaki, 1993; Stenberg, 2010). The problem of such normative views has been extensively critiqued and as explored in the following chapters (chapter 3) a number of scholars have particularly delved into the nuanced intersections between witchcraft and modernity. Moreover, witchcraft beliefs and practices appear to be on the rise and find different expressions alongside socioeconomic development (see Richter, Flowers, and Bongmba, 2017; Kyriakakis, n.d.).

In the development field, issues of witchcraft beliefs, practices, and accusations and how they are enmeshed in the broader social-economic structures and processes have received some attention, especially in relation to the protection of individuals accused of witchcraft (see Powles and Deakin 2012). But much of the attention is directed toward development professionals, NGOs and agencies concerned with improving their practices. While this book contributes to informing development practice, it argues that the issue of witchcraft beliefs and practices, and especially the presence of communities of refuge and the banishment of people (mostly poor old women) from their communities also merits more nuanced academic exploration of how development is conceptualized and approached in specific contexts. Overall, the book contributes to the decolonization of development epistemes, knowledge, and practices.

WHAT IS IN A NAME? NAMING COMMUNITIES AND THE POLITICS OF DEVELOPMENT INTERVENTION

As noted above, witchcraft beliefs and accusations are common across many societies in Africa. Due to the perceptions of the role of witchcraft in these societies, victims of witchcraft accusations face various alienations or exclusion from their communities. Such exclusions usually include social, physical, economic, or psychological (See Mabefam and Appau, 2020; Barbier, 2020). In Ghana, some villages have become known as places that provide refuge to people banished from their communities. It is important to emphasize that some of these villages were not created for this purpose. Rather, they are already existing communities that have chosen to provide such refuge as a local protection mechanism to people who would otherwise have been lynched. Communities that provide refuge, especially in the case of Ghana, I would argue have become a local development intervention or approach to provide protection and ensure the well-being of individuals who have been alienated from their societies. These villages can sometimes offer both permanent and temporary accommodation, food, and a sense of community and belonging while efforts are made to help them transition to making such places their homes if such individuals choose to.

The above conceptualization of communities of refuge is not universal. For example, development actors in Ghana describe such communities as "witch camps" (see Mutaru, 2019, 2022). The naming of such communities as camps, I would argue, presents a new challenge that needs to be dealt with. That is, such renaming denies the original identity of the communities and activates an action such as closing that might not be necessary. A similar conclusion has been reached by a recent anthropologist, Shaibu Mutaru, who noted that "during my fieldwork, locals referred to the places that accommodated accused 'witches,' mostly women, by names semantically different from the western notion of a 'camp'" (2019, 14). However, due to the conceptualization of such communities as camps, which are loaded with prejudice, there have been calls for action to be taken. The most radical of such actions is the closure of such communities.

In her recent article, "What Is in a Name: How Colonial Patriarchies Have Contributed to Breaking Relationship between Humans and Nature" (2022, 1), Tahmina Rashid noted that

> naming practices are reflective of prevailing power structures and hierarchies; creating new identities by erasing previous identities; creating new relationships and histories. . . . These naming practices have pedagogical implications for the discipline of Social Science in general and Development Studies as it intersects with development practice. Naming systems have patriarchal and colonial legacies and continue to influence Development Studies especially in terms of "what" and "who" is valued and what is worth "preserving" in terms of norms, values, cultures and traditions. (Rashid, 2022)

Reconceptualized as "witch camps," the government's position is that there is no need for witch camps and thus existing ones should be closed (see ActionAid, 2014; Riedel, 2017). In line with the government's position, many development professionals are also working toward the closure of "camps" (ActionAid, 2008a, 2008b, 2014; Forsyth, 2016; Mutaru, 2019; Naboo, 2017; Riedel, 2017). There is however a contradiction in this line of thought and action, which is further telling not only of the "name" but also of who is doing the naming. This relates to the ideas contained in Rashid's quote above—*the power behind the naming.* I will draw on Burkina Faso, Cameroon, and Benin to illustrate and shed light on the contradiction.

Unlike in Ghana, in Burkina Faso, NGOs established "shelters," in fact, eleven of them, to accommodate people banished from their communities based on witchcraft (Ouédraogo, 2012). Despite the prejudicial label of communities as camps in Ghana that warrants their closure, on the flip side, they are being encouraged in Burkina Faso as a development intervention. *What accounts for the differences in the approach to witchcraft intervention in Burkina Faso and Ghana?* The simple answer is embedded in the actors offering the intervention and the inherent power such actors have. In Burkina Faso, it is perceived the NGOs are doing something good to protect the lives of the evicted women based on witchcraft. In Ghana, the local communities providing refuge for the evicted individuals are condemned because it is the local communities that offer such an intervention. The experiences of real victims of witchcraft accusations are at times in danger of becoming a mere footnote to the argument, especially in Ghana, if relentless efforts are committed to emptying such communities. In the broader scheme of things, the discourse in the two countries seems to be about power more than the welfare of the individuals. This book thus centers on the experiences of individuals accused of witchcraft and banished from their societies.

WITCHCRAFT INTERVENTIONS IN SELECTED AFRICAN COUNTRIES

In this section, I give a brief overview of Africa and then highlight the existence of different communities of refuge in selected African countries. This will help us put things in a broader perspective for comparison purposes and also serve as a way of advancing my argument in the book.

Benin

Benin is one of the countries that is noted to have had witch prisons in Africa as it embarked on a nationwide anti-witchcraft crusade to rid the country of witches as a way of "modernising" itself (Kahn, 2011). Dating back to the 1970s and 1980s, Kahn (2011) notes that Benin embarked on a nationwide witchcraft eradication program using occult groups. This program was meant to identify, accuse, and incarcerate those found guilty of practicing witchcraft. However, Kahn argues that the very act of engaging occult groups to hunt down witches as a way of modernizing Benin was self-defeating and rather heightened the very practice it tried to exterminate (2011, p. 6). Though numbers are not given, it has been reported that people who were accused of witchcraft, usually widows and childless women had filled up the prisons to the extent that huts were constructed to further contain the overflowing numbers. The irony, however, is that the state officials and the general populace knew that witchcraft cannot be contained by merely imprisoning the so-called witches (Kahn, 2011). Khan (2011, 26) emphatically stated that "Government Council officials and other state employees from the bottom to the top of the administrative hierarchy were fully aware of the imperfections in the quarantine method and feared violent reprisals by imprisoned witches." This is where Kahn asserts that by trying to end the practice of witchcraft in Benin, the officials were caught in a complex web of paradoxes, that is, drawing on the same powers of witches to protect themselves.

Burkina Faso

Burkina Faso is a country in West Africa and one of the countries that has witch "shelters." The belief in witchcraft is high in Burkina Faso and permeates most parts of their socio-economic lives. People fear witches and hold a belief that witchcraft can be used to destroy or harm others. As a result, individuals who are accused and confronted as witches face stringent punishment from those who see themselves as victims of their bewitchment. This has led to a score of people accused of witchcraft being banished from their societies by an angry mob or village elders. It is reported that several scores of women in particular have been banished from their communities from such accusations and are now being supported in 11 shelters that have been established by NGOs (Barbier, 2020; Ouédraogo, 2012). To illustrate, Barbier (2020) notes that two centres that were the focus of her study alone welcomed over 250 women. She argues that the conditions in such shelters are deplorable and do not augur well for the well-being and dignity of women in such a society. She attributes such treatment to women due to the patriarchal and hierarchical nature of Mossi society, which was the focus of her study. However, in comparison to the danger such women would have been exposed to back in their societies, witch shelters are an alternative place to be.

Cameroon

In Cameroon, there has been evidence of state officials trying and sentencing people accused of and confirmed as witches to a prison term. The prevalence of witchcraft belief in Cameroon is considered high as 75 percent of the people hold a belief in witchcraft (Tortora, 2010). Unlike Benin or Burkina Faso or elsewhere where there is a linguistic gap regarding the knowledge of witchcraft in the Anglo-Saxon scholarship, Cameroon is probably different and thus there is much knowledge both in English and French, the two official languages of the state. Geschiere (1997, 2005) notes that both local and national politicians in Cameroon have drawn on witchcraft to champion their cause. Paradoxically, some of the people who are accused of witchcraft are reprimanded while others are not. As one accused witch is standing trial, others are called on as experts to assess the guilt of a person accused of witchcraft (Fisiy and Geschiere, 1990, p. 135). Geschiere notes that witchcraft issues are "a minefield of ambiguities and shifting meanings," highlighting the lack of clarity, certainty, or consistency (2005, p. 94). In post-independent Cameroon, the state acknowledged the existence of witchcraft. It thus was determined to punish those found guilty of the crime of practicing it, including imprisonment of no less than ten years.

Gambia

Another country that has had a nationwide anti-witchcraft crusade, arrest, and torture is Gambia. Unlike Benin, which can be said to be in the historical past, the Gambia example is quite recent. President Yahya Gemeh in 2009 ordered a nationwide anti-witchcraft campaign and sporadic ones in the years following to cleanse the country of witches (Hayden, 2018). Reports say this move was due to the death of his aunty and he suspected that witches were responsible. During these campaigns and searches, people were compelled to confess their engagement with witchcraft-related activities by forcefully injecting a hallucinating substance into them. Related family members revealed that once they extracted these confessions, the victims were left to go but they died shortly afterward, which they believe was a result of the hallucinating substance that was injected into their bodies (Hayden, 2018).

Ghana

Ghana is an independent state located in West Africa. It was formerly known as the Gold Coast due to its large gold deposits. Ghana is geographically situated in the middle of three other West African countries. To the north, it shares a border with Burkina Faso, to the east with Togo, to the west with Côte d'Ivoire, and the south with the Gulf of Guinea. It has a total land size of 239 thousand square kilometers (Sasu, 2023).

The primary research site for this book where I conducted an ethnography is the Gnani community in the Northern Region. In the above map, villages with stars next to their names are the places which provide refuge for people accused of witchcraft and evicted from their communities. Though the Northern Region was the largest in terms of land size, it has low population density, with fewer than 2 million inhabitants, due partly to emigration. Further, over 75 percent of the Northern Region population is involved in agriculture. In 2018 the Northern Region was split into three administrative units: Savanna, Northeast, and Northern. Some parts of the Northern Region of Ghana are also characterized by higher rates of poverty than the national average (Cooke, Hague, and McKay, 2016).

From a different perspective, the current development profile of Ghana points to significant advances since independence in 1957. Though it is

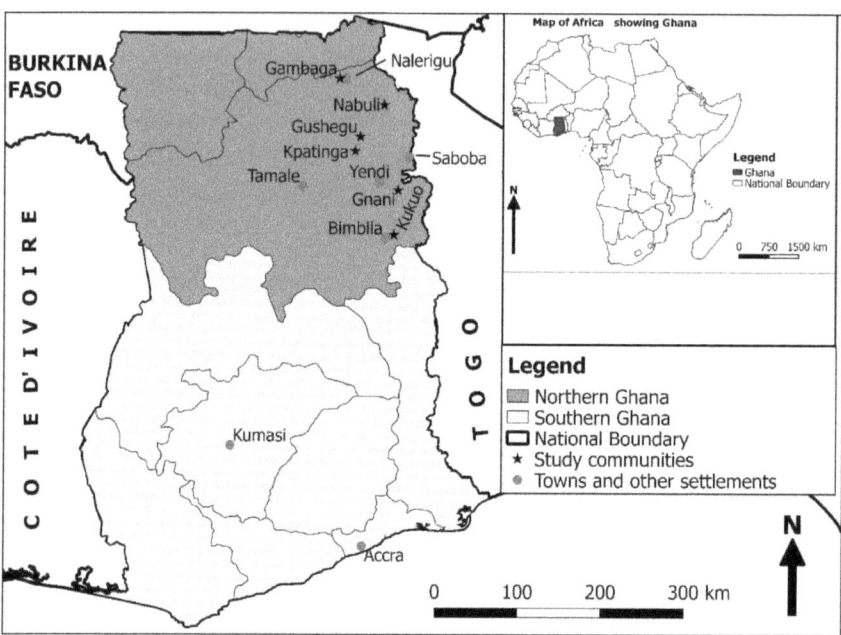

Figure 0.1 Map of Ghana showing the various communities of refuge. Source: Adapted from Saibu Mutaru's thesis (2018).

beyond the scope of this book to do justice to Ghana's social, economic, and political development, it is nonetheless important to provide a brief contextual overview of its key features. Politically, Ghana was the first sub-Saharan Africa to gain independence from the British on March 6, 1957. Though Ghana has experienced its share of upheavals and challenges, it is nonetheless viewed as one of Africa's leading nations, with relative political stability. Since 1992, when the Fourth Republic began, Ghana has had a working multiparty and principled democracy that has successfully and peacefully changed governments seven consecutive times through elections. In a more recent analysis of the human development index, as noted in the UNDP Country Report for Ghana, the country's position is in the medium human development category and "above average" for countries in Sub-Saharan Africa (2019, p. 4). Likewise, the multidimensional poverty index (Alkire et al., 2015) shows that the basic indicators of development such as education, health, and living standards have improved significantly in the last few decades.

But the country also has its share of ongoing development problems and challenges. For instance, though social and economic advances have been made, in terms of economic development Ghana continues to face challenges and is ranked as a "lower middle income" country by the World Bank

(2019). In particular, there are significant urban-rural differences as well as regional variations in social and economic development. Northern Ghana has been especially plagued by lower-than-average economic development and higher levels of poverty relative to the southern regions (FAO, 2012). According to the Food and Agriculture Organization, Ghana continues to be a predominantly rural society, and, in the northern region, 80 per cent of the population is classified as rural (FAO, 2012, p. 12). That is, the northern part of the country is not only rural but also has the highest levels of poverty (Kambala, 2022).

Moreover, in relation to the gender and development indicators, there are many advances evident in promoting gender equity overall in the country but nonetheless, there continue to be significant gender disparities and inequalities, and Ghana is ranked 133 out of 166 countries (UNDP, 2019, pp. 5–6). In a similar vein, the challenges faced by women in northern Ghana are notable in terms of education, work, and ability to sustain livelihoods (see FAO, 2012).

In short, various aspects of navigating modernity and social and economic development coalesce with issues of gender disparity, discrimination, and the inability of some to access the advances that have obviously been made in society. In particular, issues of gender disparities and the plight of women in northern Ghana who are accused of witchcraft are intimately entwined. Moreover, those accused and subsequently resettle in communities of refuge including Gnani are often disadvantaged not only by cultural values and norms relating to the position of women in their families, rural communities, and the society more broadly but also highlight the comparative position of Ghana as a society vis-a-vie other societies in the global social, economic, and political arena. Importantly, the problem of women, especially older women, who are accused of witchcraft needs to be understood from a broader societal context, in terms of what it speaks to about the tensions and challenges associated with both local and global development and how they intersect within Ghanaian society.

Furthermore, the management of issues of witchcraft by governments of developing societies such as Ghana leads to both internal and external criticisms. Witchcraft beliefs, practices and accusations are undoubtedly prevalent in many African communities. However, the strategies for dealing with people accused of witchcraft vary across different contexts. In some societies, violence, murder, victimization, and ostracism are prevalent. In the Northern Province of South Africa for instance, Comaroff and Comaroff (1999a), Niehaus (2005), Mavhungu (2012), among others, have provided detailed analyses of the crimes committed against people accused of witchcraft and the social context of significant changes in post-apartheid society. The large-scale witchcraft allegations and violent killings in South Africa, especially in the 1990s, motivated the government to establish a Commission of Inquiry, led by Professor Ralushai, to investigate this sensitive matter and make recommendations to the government. Likewise, across many African societies, such as in Cameroon, the problem is even more pronounced as the state has codified the supposed criminality of witchcraft activities and people accused of witchcraft are now being prosecuted in courts (see Ciekawy and Geschiere, 1998; Geschiere, 2005; Mavhungu, 2012).

There are many strategies for dealing with witchcraft in Ghana, though manifested in different ways in different parts of the country. The strategy that stands out and has attracted the most global attention is the issue of communities of refuge in northern Ghana. Though the term "witch camp" is usually used by NGOs and government, I am aware that it is not neutral and thus is politically contested (see Mutaru, 2019, p. 127). That is, "witch camp" is a term coined by development actors and magnified by the media to refer to where people accused of witchcraft and banished from their communities seek refuge. For my personal preference, I will adopt communities of refuge. This is important to highlight as it brings out conceptual differences in how different actors view such communities. On my part, I do not consider such communities as camps and neither do the communities consider themselves as such. As part of my endeavor to give weight to the voices of the community, I will refer to such communities as I heard them call themselves while conducting fieldwork.

There are five communities that offer refuge to people accused of witchcraft and banished from their communities in Ghana at the time of my fieldwork in 2016. With the exception of the Gushegu community of refuge (known to locals as "Leli-dabari"), the rest of the communities are known to have anti-witchcraft shrines or powerful persons perceived to possess the ability to neutralize witchcraft by leading the accused through specific rituals. Such communities are usually headed by an *Utindaan (Likpakpaaln) /Tindana (Dagbani),* the English equivalent is the landowner. *Bitindam (Plural of Utindaan)* are often assisted *by Uwadaan (Pl. Biwadam)*-shrine priests. In some instances, the same person could occupy both positions as was the case of Gnani at the time of my study. *Uwadaan* constitutes a local court of the community's shrine, through which certain rituals can determine the culpability of the accused and pass judgement.

In terms of process, people accused of witchcraft enter these communities mainly through two pathways—people accused of witchcraft are either forced by the community into such communities or they move there on their own (see also Baba, 2013; Mutaru, 2019). Some of the people accused of witchcraft, mostly old women, "run" to any one of the communities named above when such accusations are made against them. There are many reasons for women voluntarily seeking to go to such communities, such as the fear of mistreatment and the need to thus seek refuge (see Palmer, 2010; Baba, 2013). Some of the women leave even before they may experience mistreatment or threat to their safety, including hearing gossip about them in which they are accused of witchcraft. In contrast, the majority of individuals are compelled or even forced into such communities by community members or the accusers, who are mostly family or kin members (Musah, 2013; Palmer, 2010).

Available data on the number of people residing in the communities of refuge in Ghana suggest that there has been a decline (AWACC-Ghana Field Monitoring 2015 as cited in Riedel, 2017). Several plausible reasons could account for this supposedly decreasing rate of people in various communities. For instance, the issue of age may play a factor in the decreasing numbers since most of the individuals are elderly and may pass away with time. Or the decrease could also be due to reintegration programs embarked on by different organizations where some people are made to return home and may or may not need to return if the reintegration is not successful. Riedel (2017) offers another explanation for the case of Gambaga, commenting that "the total number declined from 400 individuals in the late 1980s to 81 in 2009. Numbers bounced back to 120 in 2016 due to a lack of resources for the Go Home Project and then increased according to Samson Laar. The decrease in numbers from the 1990s was mainly the result of resettlement campaigns of the Go-Home-Project." However, some studies suggest that such statistics are manipulated and do not reflect reality on the ground (Riedel, 2017). During fieldwork in Gnani, I noted that the number of people (615) in the Gnani community was higher than the number (184) provided by the NGOs working to reintegrate the accused back into their various homes.

Furthermore, it may also appear as if communities that provide refuge are a relatively new phenomenon. However, although there is no accurate record of when communities of refuge began, there is some evidence that they have existed in northern Ghana for about two-and-a-half centuries. The following are the dates when the communities started receiving people displaced as a result of witchcraft accusation: Gambaga, 1870 (as recorded by Truxler, 2006); and Gnani, 1918 (first recorded by Cardinall, 1918). There were unknown exact years of the establishment of others such as Gushegu, Kpatinga, Nabule, and Kukuo, Bonyase. However, Riedel, an anthropologist who has conducted the most up to date historical analysis of "witch camps" in northern Ghana hints that they probably existed before the end of the nineteenth century (Riedel, 2018). Stromberg (2011), for instance, points to such communities being present since the nineteenth century. Bekoe argues that they have been present much longer, saying that

the Gambaga witch camp in the Northern Region of Ghana is believed to have been established in the 18th century in an attempt to provide shelter for women

who were accused of being witches. It is said to have been a place that witches
would go to have their powers neutralized by the local gods. (Bekoe, 2016, p. 7)

Truxler provides a far more specific date of when witch camps began: "the
·witch camps of northern Ghana were established in 1870 when a Muslim
Imam of Mamprugu sent a woman suspected of witchcraft to Gambaga where
she allegedly lived as a "refugee" (Truxler, 2006, pp. 49–50).

The reasons for the establishment of these communities of refuge in the
past appear to be varied, but I suspect that in keeping with the findings
of this research of the contemporary context, the community fears around
witchcraft, the closing of doors and hearts to those accused that leads to
banishment or ostracism continue to play a role in the formation of alternative spaces to accommodate individuals beyond the extremes of putting such
people to death.

Unlike development practitioners, in fact, for many locals, the existence
of communities of refuge is justifiable, as those who are accused and "confirmed" as witches have little if no recourse to protection or livelihoods in
their natal communities. For instance, from the perspectives of the chiefs, the
main reason for opening their communities to the people accused of witchcraft and banished from their communities was to provide a "safe haven"
for women who would have otherwise been killed, lynched, discriminated
against, and abused within their communities (see Musah, 2013; Palmer,
2010; Mutaru, 2022). There is undoubtedly evidence of violence and threats
to individuals who are accused of witchcraft in Ghana, including lynching,
destruction of properties of the accused, and murder (ActionAid, 2008a;
Adinkrah, 2015). Thus, alongside most of the NGOs and advocates that focus
on the rights of the individuals who are accused and subsequently resettled
(discussed in the below section), some local actors reframe the issue in terms
of a balance between community needs and individual rights. Some of the
Bitimdam argue that they provide a vital refuge to people accused of witchcraft and the communities. Those in favor of communities of refuge such
as the *Biwadam* or *Bitindam* often argue that maintaining peace in the community (or at least reducing conflict) is enabled through such spaces being
available. That is, the communities of refuge, to some degree, are indicative
of the managing and containing witchcraft allegations and the fears associated with the presence of "witches" from becoming more extreme for both
individuals and the communities. Thus, communities of refuge mitigate and
manage conflicts in the broader society.

In short, the debates relating to the communities of refuge amplify the
point that witchcraft is a culturally sensitive issue and highly politically
charged. Indeed, it is clear that witchcraft beliefs and practices are implicated
in politics at various levels and highlights the fact that there are multiple,

if not contesting, views about their meanings and significance. Further, the meanings and significance attached to witchcraft beliefs and practices also highlight more broadly the experiences and concerns relating to development as well as the engagement of development actors in contemporary African societies.

COMMUNITIES OF REFUGE AND ENGAGEMENT BY DEVELOPMENT ACTORS

Though there are undoubtedly divergent views of communities of refuge and what they contribute to individuals who are accused (or the community that the accused come from), what is clear is that there has been increased visibility of them both within Ghanaian society and more globally. In particular, the increased visibility of such communities in Africa is notable due to the advocacy and attention garnered in the media by NGOs and religious organizations, especially in the 1990s. Development and human rights advocates have highlighted those scores of women and some men who have been ostracized from their communities and live as "prisoners" or "cultural refugees" in Ghana's Northern region (ActionAid, 2008a, 2008b; NCCE, 2010). The revelations of various NGOs and advocates have attracted public debate, at both the local and global levels and have had varying impacts on policy. In 2003, for instance, Ghana's Commission on Human Rights and Administrative Justice (CHRAJ) reported that though the number of people in these communities of refuge were growing, it suggested that the government disband them (see Mutaru, 2019; Palmer, 2010; Riedel, 2017).

From a different perspective, the mention of witchcraft in an African context automatically raises judgments regarding beliefs and practices associated with "tradition," if not "primitive" practices and thus is perceived as problematic. For example, in participating in conferences and other presentations relating to communities of refuge in Ghana, I am invariably faced with questions such as "Are there people who still believe in witchcraft?," "Where is that?," and "What period are you looking at?" In 2018, I was invited as a guest lecturer to present my research to a third-year undergraduate class at an Australian University. After my lecture, a student stood up and said that it was "ridiculous that people still believed in witchcraft." He added that "such beliefs must be a thing for Africans." For more than thirty minutes, he tried to convince me that there was no witchcraft and that the world in its entirety has moved beyond such belief systems. The inferences, at least to me, from such questions and comments are that witchcraft stands opposed to modernity and development, that it speaks to the "exotic," or that it is the stuff of "other" people.

Such stereotypical associations or perceptions of witchcraft as being "backward" and in need of eradication is also evident in much of the development actors' engagement with witchcraft beliefs and practices, especially in the arguments presented for labeling local communities in Ghana as "witch camps" and thus the need for their closure. There is, however, a contradiction here. As in the case of Ghana where arguments abound that "witch camps" are an abuse of the rights of those accused, a suggestion perhaps that there are problematic issues about the advancement of rights in the society (ActionAid, 2008a, 2008b; NCCE, 2010), at the same time, NGOs establish witch shelters in Burkina Faso to accommodate women banished from their communities based on witchcraft accusation. It does seem to me that it is an act of intervention when external actors have been involved to save but an act of abuse when local actors intervene with a similar approach. Though the reasons for witch shelters in Burkina Faso and Ghana are similar, the debates and conversations are not the same.

To give an example, ActionAid's Ghana country director, Sumaila Abdul, stated at the *National Conference on Witchcraft Accusations in Ghana* held on December 10, 2014 that "having witch camps is a national embarrassment: tourists and international media visit Ghana to see the witch camps" (ActionAid, 2014, p. 3).

In such contexts, the perceptions of witchcraft as posing a conundrum for modernity and development are most pronounced. As an "embarrassment," as the ActionAid director phrases it, one can see the influence of hegemonic Western constructs during the colonial era, which continued into the postcolonial context. Moreover, such perceptions highlight the nebulous distinction between "developed" and "underdeveloped" societies and the problems associated with backwardness, lack of education or modernity (see Stenberg, 2010).

As explored in the next chapter, western scholarship on witchcraft beliefs and practices has also influenced such perceptions. For a long time, the hegemonic framing of witchcraft as encountered in non-Western contexts is that it speaks of some kind of backwardness of thought, practice, or social development. Indeed, there has been extensive scholarly debate around witchcraft beliefs and practices *vis-a-viz* modernity and social development that still capture public and scholarly attention today Ciekawy and Geschiere 1998; Comaroff and Comaroff 1999b, 2001 2002; Geschiere 1997; Parish 2003, 2005, 2011; Stenberg 2010). However, in the last few decades, there has been a significant shift in Western scholarship and a critique of the past theorizing, debates, and hegemonic framing of witchcraft. Nonetheless, the relationship between modernity and witchcraft continues to be an important scholarly leitmotif.

Many scholars have especially argued that witchcraft is an aspect of modernity and cannot be viewed simply as a relic of beliefs and practices that continues in some way to the present (Comaroff and Comaroff, 1993, 1999a, 1999b, 2000; Geschiere, 1997; Smith, 2008). For example, in unpacking their conceptualization of occult economies to depict the deployment of witchcraft as a tool for economic success in South Africa, Comaroff and Comaroff (1999a, 1993, 1999b) have convincingly argued that witchcraft speaks to how people struggle to adjust to modernities. The shift in attention from witchcraft as being about how people navigate, adjust, and make sense of modernity has many merits. It shifts the discourse away from witchcraft being some kind of manifestation of irrationality or a relic from the past.

Furthermore, there is often an unnecessary divide between "West and the Rest," to borrow Hall's (Hall and Gieben, 1992) phrase, in which the extent of the use of witchcraft to facilitate economic enhancement and wealth-making is evident not only in societies such as in Africa but also in European contexts. In the "commodification of witchcraft," as Ezzy refers to it, the new form "facilitates an ideology of consumption by attempting to manipulate people's decisions about their spiritual practices for the purposes of selling commodities such as books of spells and bottles of lotion" (Ezzy 2001, p. 31). This has been captured by others as occult forces that people draw on to make wealth (see Geschiere, 1997; Niehaus, 2005). I found similar assertions made by opinion leaders in Ghana that occult force/power, which sometimes is akin to witchcraft, is innovative; and some individuals such as businesspeople and politicians have adapted and integrated it into their transactions to create more wealth and protect their property and people (see Geschiere 1997; Niehaus, 2005). Indeed, it could be argued that the witchcraft of today should be seen as a modern technique, the stuff of modern individuals engaged with local and global ways, rather than a remnant of traditional practices.

As argued in this book, there is a need to integrate the different strands of theorizing and research across different contexts, as there is a need to shift the attention in development studies toward a better understanding of what witchcraft says about the way that development is understood and navigated by differently situated peoples. Likewise, witchcraft cannot be easily relegated to "alternative" or a *reaction* to modernity. Although it undoubtedly encompasses some, if not all, of these elements, witchcraft is an important avenue for exploring sociopolitical relations and people's positions in society.

In short, the ongoing presence of witchcraft beliefs and practices relates to how individuals perceive themselves and are perceived by others, as development subjects. Importantly, local imaginaries of development highlighted in this study, it is not simply about navigating, managing, or making sense of uneven change. Indeed, witchcraft belief and practice are presumed to be at the core of the ability of some to exceed their social, economic, and political positionalities and circumstances. That is, witchcraft is perceived as a technique to access development resources. However, the concern is with those that cannot tap into the advances of society and because of their socioeconomic position, gender, or age are susceptible to victimization and accusation of witchcraft by others. That is, witchcraft speaks directly to development in many ways, and thus how development engages with witchcraft matters.

A CRITIQUE OF DEVELOPMENT
PRACTICE AND SCHOLARSHIP

In this section, I provide an overview of different theoretical frameworks that have influenced development practice in Africa, and elsewhere. In particular, the section contextualizes the key development studies' theories that inform the field (namely, modernization, dependency, and neoliberalism, "post-development") and decolonization approach and the rationale for decolonization as central in shaping the theoretical framework and logic that inform this book. Concomitant to the decolonial paradigm, there has been a call for development to pay closer attention to culture, local epistemologies, and uneven power relations. In fact, the post-development paradigm for instance signaled the "cultural turn" and is a relatively recent shift in development scholarship. The call to pay closer attention to culture, values, and practices in a more nuanced and meaningful way emerged as significant to the various anthropological works that have contributed to development studies, particularly in the ethnographies of aid (see Eves and Forsyth, 2015; Lewis and Mosse, 2006; Pieterse, 1995, 2001). Indeed, one of the advantages of the broad post-development perspective is that it enables a recognition of "plurality," fluidity, and multiplicity of perspectives and experiences of development (see Pieterse, 1995).

Though as explored in this section, there is a discernible shift in theorizing about witchcraft, there are two points that need to be highlighted about the ongoing influence of previous scholarship in shaping contemporary perceptions of development practice. Firstly, past intellectual and societal perceptions continue in some ways to be present, and indeed, are influential in various ways. For instance, there is a common thread throughout past and current literature that witchcraft beliefs and practices tell us something about societal development; be it a "cultural survival" or indicative of the alternative ways that some people navigate modernity (and societal change more broadly). In this, uncertainty, insecurity, inability to navigate relationships or societal change is presumed to be at the core of ongoing witchcraft beliefs and practices. So too, in some strands of scholarship there is still a strong evolutionist element, of relegating such beliefs and practices to less developed (evolved) ways of thinking and doing things. Of equal importance, in the field of development studies attention to witchcraft is relatively under-explored theoretically and typically approached from the perspective of development intervention in which there is often a perception that witchcraft poses a "problem" that needs to be solved. But, as highlighted here, this scant focus on local epistemologies and practices by development is itself problematic. For development scholars and practitioners, in other words, there is a need to engage more deeply and critically with witchcraft in Africa.

Though a number of development theories have emerged, particularly in the post–World War II (WWII) period with the introduction of international development projects across a number of countries, post-development and decolonial paradigms are especially relevant for this book. One of the seminal works that is attributed to post-development theory is Arturo Escobar's (1995) *Encountering Development*, where he argues that development policies meant to engender development became mechanisms of control that were just as pervasive and effective as their colonial counterparts. As discussed below, there are in fact many scholars that have critiqued the post-WWII framing of development and each, in their different fields, call for development to be questioned, if not rejected as a model that had failed (see Esteva, 1992; Sachs, 1992). While the idea that development should be rejected sounds radical, the post-development theory refers to the post-WWII project and not development in general. In post-development scholarship, the predominant view is that the failure of post–World War II development theory is something that cannot be improved or corrected within the same framework (Pieterse, 2000, p. 176). Before delving further into post-development theory and its utility for this book, it is important first to contextualize the dominant paradigms and theories of development. The key theories of development are *modernization*, *dependency*, *structuralism*, and *human dependency* among a number of others. As discussed below, post-development diverges significantly from these main theories but has nonetheless emerged as a critique of them.

Post-WWII development has hegemonically been framed as an economic project driven by the modernization thesis, which needed to spread to other parts of the world. Regardless of whether the modernization thesis was problematic or effective, the importance of it here is that it has set an agenda for development and the ramifications continue to be felt today. However, modernization theory's implementation was fraught with challenges across the "third world countries." This is because the diagnosis of why such places were underdeveloped was found to be a problem of lack of an understanding of those trying to intervene on what the real issues were. The theory rested on the idea that the West was once undeveloped but followed a pathway that led to their developed status, and that this provides a universal solution. For example, Rostow (1960) as one of the main theorists of modernization

theory argued that before development could happen, societies needed to follow the five stages he proposed. The five stages include traditional society,
preconditions for take-off, take-off, drive to maturity, and age of high mass
consumption.

Modernization theory was limited by the idea that while a lack of development was the problem of the undeveloped society, the outside influence was
needed to facilitate development, often without the input of the society being
developed. The modernization thesis often focused on what the third-world
countries did not have. This can be conceptualized as the "deficit model,"
(Muchie, 2004) and the theory becomes characterized by a list of propositions as to how to fill such deficits. Of course, as pointed out quite strongly
by dependency theorists (Gunder, 1969; Kothari, 2005a; Walter, 1972) the
"deficit" that modernization theory sought to fill was a creation of colonial
advantage and power that continued to exploit third-world countries in the
post-colonial era, a creation that was neither acknowledged nor accounted for.

Dependency theory is also important for this book in the sense that it
deepens an understanding of failure of standardized development approaches
at the local levels. Dependency theory is generally associated with two seminal papers written in 1949 by Hans Singer and Raul Prebisch, where each
of them in their respective papers observed that the economic exchanges
between the west and third-world countries were exploitative and unfavorable
to the underdeveloped world. Dependency theory therefore highlights the
unevenness and unfair relationships between developed and underdeveloped
countries as resources are exploited and carted to developed countries, leading to further impoverishment of the former (see Kothari, 2005b; Prebisch,
1949; Singer, 1949). The theorists argue that the kind of relationship existing
between the former colonized and the colonizer post-independence states still
mimicked the colonial logic, where resources are flown from the colonized
to the colonizer states leading to underdevelopment of the colonized places
(Gunder, 1969; Walter, 1972). The seminal book of Rodney Walter, *How
Europe Underdeveloped Africa*, is an example of dependency theory, offering an explanation of the power dynamics behind the struggle to develop.
He makes it clear that dependency theory does not discount the existence of
"underdevelopment," but rather provides an explanation for it in uneven economic relationships. Dependency theory is therefore not so much about lack
of development as much as it is about uneven development (that is, development is there but below the belt, under the belt, or not satisfactory). However,
the problem is that the hegemonic framing of development is not concerned
with nor interested in what is "under."

Dependency theory is often used to analyze the relationship between different states (macro-level). However, it can also be applied for theorizing
relationships within a state, where similar exploitation can be found at the

local levels in relationships between urban and non-urban areas, as in the case of Africa. It informs local explanations of the reasons as to why development does not take place in certain communities as compared to other communities. It gives voice to the local people to comment on their development issues and expose how their relationship with urban traders and government is exploitative and imbalanced. In this case, it is useful to my book as both people accused of witchcraft, the accusers, and other local actors begin to interrogate how national and international arenas of development have framed the local people as the problem.

Though dependency theory attracted much criticism, the idea of modernization as an economic project continues to dominate other development models such as neoliberalism. Neoliberalism can be argued to be the extension of modernism, seeking to reassert the importance of economic growth and freedom. However, the two differ significantly in the sense that while modernization emphasized the role of the state, neoliberalism argued for the opposite, that state intervention should be kept to the barest minimum (Harvey, 2005).

There is a belief that the ways people have attempted to adapt to modernity, heavily influenced by the ideals of neoliberalism, have led to an increase in the beliefs and practices of witchcraft. The contribution from John and Jean Comaroff about the use of witchcraft to adjust to modernity, detailed later in this chapter, makes clear links to neoliberalism. In this regard, Harvey too asserted that neoliberalism

> is in the first instance a theory of political economic practices that proposes that human well-being can best be advanced by liberating individual entrepreneurial freedoms and skills within an institutional framework characterized by strong private property rights, free markets and free trade. The role of the state is to create and preserve an institutional framework appropriate to such practice. (Harvey 2005, 2)

If we recall that the discussion of modernization centered on the idea of deficit, the neo-liberal paradigm made it clear that what was lacking was an open and competitive market economy. Many critiques of neoliberalism have pointed to the extent that there is an assumption of a level playing field for everyone to compete to meet their needs. But the issue with such a framing is that due to structural disadvantages and lack of equal opportunities for people to access goods and services, such a level playing field for everyone cannot be justified. According to neoliberalism, inclusive growth, equality, and positive discrimination could help ameliorate, to some extent, the structural disadvantages but still should be left outside the domain of government direct intervention.

Even in dependency theory, which emerged from the global south, the focus was on the economic performance of states, and the competition between states brought about the prominence of statism as a central actor in development, leading to terms such as developmentalism. Dependency nonetheless concerned in a similar vein with the role of the state, only Marxian framing of production, economic development, and the relationship between different states that ensued dependency. The issue of culture was either omitted altogether or seen as a "problem." It was rarely delved into and employed as a strength to improve development. That is where post-development theory becomes crucial due to its central focus on culture, and its belief that this could be used as a strength.

As Escobar notes, from the early postwar years to the 1970s, "development was chiefly a matter of capital, technology, and education and the appropriate policy and planning mechanisms to successfully combine these elements" (Escobar, 1992, p. 20). In the imagination of the superior knowledge, technology, and approach coming from the West and applied to the "Third World," "under-developed" or "developing societies" there was little consideration of "alternatives" to this model, nor the questioning of power or resistance to these interventions. Indeed, the post-development theory emerged in the 1980s and 1990s at a time when significant critique was gathering momentum following the failure of development interventions in developing countries and the limitations of previous development theories that are often described as "obsolete or bankrupt" (Matthews, 2004, p. 373). Indeed, Matthews argues that "the practice of development has done more harm than good" (2004, p. 373). He justified his argument in regard to the crumbling nature of development, which he suggests has caused some sort of disillusionment.

Although a number of scholars have critiqued post-development as not being a pragmatic or feasible theory (Edelman, 1999; Kiely, 1999; Ziai, 2004), my understanding is, in fact, the opposite. That is, post-development theory essentially speaks to the idea that what does not work is not improvable. Further, in the critique of how development is conceived and implemented, post-development provides an analytic framework that takes into account, as Matthews aptly describes, "the diversity of experiences, needs and aspirations of those it claims to assist" (2004, p. 379). Further, as Matthews adds,

> [a] dismissal of the PWWII development project must not mean an end to attempts to solve the problems it purported to be able to address (such as poverty, deprivation and inequity), but rather the pursuit of alternative ways to address these problems. (2004, p. 379)

That is, the utility of post-development theory is that it captures the nuances of the conceptualizations of development as well as the relational dynamics and the nature of uneven power relationships that it brings forth. In particular, post-development theory enables a focus on development as an agenda or project in itself that needs to be interrogated (see Escobar, 1992, 1995, 1999; Esteva, 1992; Ferguson, 1994; McGregor, 2009; Pieterse, 2000; Ziai, 2007). This is especially important in the case of Africa.

Furthermore, with the emergence of post-development theory, there has been a greater focus on culture and the extent that it has been predominantly missing from development theory and approaches. Post-development theorists value development and argue for a model of development that can advance the well-being of people within their societies. They asserted that people should be given the opportunity to "change the rules and contents of change, according to their own culturally defined ethics and aspirations" (Rahnema and Bawtree, 1997, p. 385). That is, cultural freedom and sensitivity should be given priority, thus focusing more on local epistemologies. This has been termed as the "cultural turn."

The "cultural turn in development" became a key component of the post-development theory in framing this study. The cultural turn in development is a distinct strand of discourse that champions the fact that culture has a place in the development industry. The cultural turn is viewed as the fourth pillar of development (Pieterse, 2001; UNESCO, 2012). It argues that in an age of polycentrism, different cultures offer strengths that can be enablers of development and a potential resource that should be reconsidered in development and scholarship. For example, Pieterse argues that the scholarship and debates surrounding the "culture-free" paradigm of development and modernist discourse are rarely actually culture free themselves, as these ideas embody cultural elements from the West that are seemingly invisible due to their dominance in the literature (Pieterse 2000, p.178). If that is the case, the development of necessity should include, or pay greater attention to, other cultures and draw from their strengths to champion development, rather than follow a monolithic Western-centric approach that seems no longer sustainable in this globalized era (see also Pieterse, 2001).

To some degree, the cultural turn has in fact infiltrated development approaches. For example, according to UNESCO,

culture-led development also includes a range of non-monetized benefits such as greater social inclusiveness and rootedness, resilience, innovation, creativity and entrepreneurship for individuals and communities, and the use of local resources, skills, and knowledge. Respecting and supporting cultural expressions contribute to strengthening the social capital of a community and fosters trust in public institutions. (2012 p. 4)

This book responds to this call by extending the discourse on culture and development, as encouraged by UNESCO. Moreover, it raises the question of how we might pay attention to specific cultures in developing contexts where development takes place. The argument presented in this book is that it is insufficient to simply "include" culture in an analysis. Taking culture into account needs to be deeper and more detailed accounting for the intricacies and complexities that it comes with. That culture is inherently both political and changing is something that development practitioners often omit from consideration, assuming that culture is fixed and needs to be "changed" by them, rather than being in a state of perpetual adjustment. As argued here, knowledge is culturally informed if not governed, and a researcher is also a cultured being. This is especially the case for someone like me, who is studying my own culture. Karen Wells's words are important in the way they highlight the relevance of paying attention to culture in development:

> If development studies were to engage fully with the cultural turn it would have to repudiate its historical origins in the colonial project and colonial technologies of government and recognise development as a discursive practice that constitutes the object about which it claims to speak. If development studies views its interventions as the refinement and application of expert knowledge to specific problems, then the challenges of the cultural turn threaten to entirely disassemble the discipline. (Wells 2012, p. 111)

That is, it is not enough to just "add culture and stir" (Pieterse, 2001, p. 68). Pieterse's caution here is crucial because most development agencies—in response to the cultural turn—assume that it is enough to simply include culture in some way. However, they do not interrogate the inherent connection between culture and politics or power. Ignoring this strong connection between politics and culture, some development strategies insert reflections of culture as if this is a strategy to depoliticize what is inherently political, rather than recognizing that politics is within, rather than outside culture (Pieterse, 1995; 2001, p. 68). In Eric Wolf and Silverman Sydel's book—*Pathways of Power: Building an Anthropology of the Modern World* (Wolf and Silverman, 2001, p. 321)—they argue for "taking stock of ideas" as a "critical evaluation of the ways that we pose and answer questions." Although Wolf and Silverman were discussing anthropology, I would suggest this is also pertinent for development studies.

Despite the criticisms leveled against the post development theory as being too radical and does not provide any solution in a methodical way, Nustad asserts it should not go unheard (Nustad 2001). What I draw from such an argument is that post development may not have an exact answer as to how things should be done, but it sets an agenda for practitioners and scholars to work toward a hitherto unrealized desired version of development. In short, post development theory calls for a rethinking of development in various ways and enables a more expansive purveyance, the inclusion of multiple ideas and perspectives, reflexivity, and further, the role that culture plays in how development is conceived and experienced. This book also contributes to the ongoing pursuit of alternatives to development, especially in the case of Africa, where many aspects of understanding and approaches to culture are implicated, especially in relation to witchcraft.

In contrast to other development theories, such as modernization and dependency, which focus on the state, the contribution of a post-development theory is also evident in the focus on the grassroots and how enabling the agency to individuals, communities, and societies is envisaged relative to their cultural contexts and their lived experiences (Escobar, 1995, 1999; Matthews, 2004). This "bottom-up approach" is important for my book as I interrogate the place of different actors in development in relationship with witchcraft and how each manages to navigate their positions, as well as the conflicts that might emerge as a result. It also applies to people accused of witchcraft as they share their lived experiences of how they navigate their everyday existence and the role of development in this narrative.

Certainly, the anthropology of development, especially aid ethnography, has brought to the fore not simply the issue of uneven development, but how important it is to consider culture. Culture, in this sense, relates not simply to the essentialist notion of ethnic or national culture, but, more importantly, functions as a nuanced way of capturing the different views, points of value, exchanges, experiences that shape human experience in a given context. Irrespective of the various theoretical orientations and debates, post development theory enables more nuanced attention to uneven power dynamics and relationships that typically overemphasized power and politics from the perspective of the state or economics over culture and local epistemologies.

The theoretical framework for this book also draws on a number of key theorists of witchcraft. Thus, it pays particular attention to the contributions of Evans-Pritchard (1937), a number of individuals as well as coauthored works by John and Jean Comaroff, Peter Geschiere (1997), and James Smith (2005, 2008) who have particularly focused on the intersections between witchcraft, development, and modernity. I am mindful of the fact that anthropological theories, despite their strengths, also have their limitations, as Tucker points out below:

> a range of research methodologies such as ethnography, participant observation, and fieldwork which focused on "localities" and face-to-face encounter or what is now called the lifeworld." . . . However, with a few notable exceptions, the

theoretical and methodological significance of the global processes which are present in every local situation were not considered. (Tucker 1996, p. 11)

Nonetheless, the contribution of anthropology to the study of witchcraft is significant and in relation to the charge by Tucker that it often lacks consideration of the "global processes" in the methodological approach of the discipline, in the anthropology of development it is undoubtedly strong. For example, the work of Ferguson (1994) is based on ethnographic fieldwork of development in Lesotho, where his attention to the local context enables a broader understanding of broader and global development processes and approaches. I seek to add to the body of scholarship that is typically referred to as the anthropology of development by exploring the space of communities of refuge from both a local as well as global perspective. By doing so, I seek to build on post-development and decolonial theories. In particular, I draw on the decolonial paradigm as an analytical tool for the future of development practice.

ETHNOGRAPHY OF COMMUNITIES OF REFUGE: REFLEXIVITY, POSITIONALITY, AND THE ISSUE OF VOICE

The book is deeply informed by my own experiences growing up in Ghana and working in some of the communities that offer refuge to banished people. Furthermore, the book is based on extended ethnographic fieldwork (2016–2017) in one of the communities that provide refuge for people who have been banished from their communities. The primary data collection involved participant observation during fieldwork in the Gnani community, as well as interviews with community members, staff of nongovernment organizations and several government officials engaged at the local level with such communities. Secondary data analysis, including government reports and media accounts, highlighting the divergent views of and tensions associated with the so-called "witch camps" also complemented the ethnographic data. While the emphasis in this book is on providing a nuanced account of the divergent views of witchcraft and witchcraft accusations, significant attention is also paid to the lived experiences of those who have sought refuge. Women, most of whom are elderly and poor, are disproportionately accused of practicing witchcraft and compelled to seek refuge due to ostracism or alienation, livelihood insecurity, and, in some cases, the threat to life. Understanding their life circumstances is especially important for highlighting how gender, age, socioeconomic development, kinship, and social relationships are implicated in witchcraft accusations.

This book utilizes a qualitative methodology to capture the unique experiences of individuals who are impacted by witchcraft. The qualitative approach enables attention to the knowledge that is socially constructed and most appropriate to adopt to collect and interpret data about the multiple realities of the social world. Although there are several alternatives to designing and embarking on qualitative research, I approached this study primarily from an ethnographic perspective involving participant observation and included a number of other techniques such as semi-structured interviews. Anthropologists such as Whitehead (2004), and O'Reilly (2012) shaped the direction of my research approach. Adopting an ethnographic approach for data collection was appropriate, as the issue of witchcraft is an entrenched cultural practice that can only be understood while living and observing activities within the host community through "immersion" (O'Reilly, 2012). Immersion is a situation where a researcher chooses to live in a community for research purposes and engages in everyday life within the host community. In such circumstances, the researcher aims to achieve a point where he or she is no longer considered a stranger, but a member of the host community. Immersing myself within the host community created the opportunity to understand people both as an "insider" and "outsider." Brown noted that with an ethnographic approach, "the ethnographer immerses himself or herself in the field so that they come to see how life and the phenomena under investigation are viewed by the social group and/or organisation" (Brown 2014, p. 171).

This is important because cultural patterns may be ideal or real, tacit or implicit, such that what people express as their culture may differ from how they experience it. It is only by living among people that one is able to understand these dynamics and probe into possible ambiguities that may exist (Brown, 2014; Reeves et al., 2013; Whitehead, 2004). This is particularly salient in relation to issues that are deemed cultural taboos such as witchcraft. Indeed, there is a marked difference often between the public discourse of witchcraft in Ghana and the more intimate or personal understandings and experiences. Further, many Ghanaians discuss witchcraft among themselves but very often find the topic difficult to discuss with outsiders. As one researcher noted, Ghanaians consider the belief and practice of witchcraft as a black spot on the country's image and do not want to be ridiculed as primitive or archaic for these beliefs (Palmer, 2010, p. 15), and thus requires that the researcher is able to live among the people they study and to establish relationships in which they became enmeshed in various ways.

There are some things that I knew had to be done in order to gain access to the research site, Gnani. Gaining access to a research site is a journey in itself. I had to prepare for this journey cognizant of the cultural expectations and modes of going into place. Getting access to the community was dependent on introduction and guidance by a respected community member.

I set off from Yendi, riding through the dusty winding road to Gnani with a friend. We arrived at about 5 p.m., after a forty-five-minute motorcycle ride. We looked dirty and exhausted as the road was untarred and full of potholes. Since neither of us had been to Gnani, we asked for directions to my contact person's home. We were offered some water to drink. Offering water to a stranger is an important cultural element in northern Ghana, and Gnani was no different. I was informed that to refuse offered water has dire consequences on one's acceptance into the community and the level at which people would open up. It is also considered an act of kindness, where people are encouraged to be kind to one another, especially strangers. It is believed in the area that spirits, ancestors, and even gods can transform into human form just to test how good someone is. This is especially important if it has been alleged that the person has been wicked or mean.

My contact person was a former assembly member of the Gnani electoral area. This position is a political post one occupies after having been voted for by the electorate. An assemblyman or woman is the bridge between the community and government authorities. They are opinion leaders in the community and are influential; through their assistance, they can contribute to the success of one's research. After introducing me he explained that it would be problematic to enter the community through him. He suggested that the current assemblyman would disapprove of his interference, and by extension, my research. His guess was based on an experience where the current assemblyman had asked some officials from the Ghana Health Insurance Office to stop working in the community. His reason was that the resident former assemblyman was trying to usurp his powers. To prevent this from happening to me, he directed us to the new assemblyman.

It is important to note that entering a new community as a researcher is a political activity that one must be conscious of, and Madden (2010) is particularly useful in drawing researchers' attention to such politics as they embark on ethnographic studies. Madden asserts that "the fact that applied ethnography is typically produced in political, legal, economic and personal circumstances that constrains the nature of the research is important to note" (2010, p. 4). Turning a blind eye to local community politics can also be dangerous to the researcher and could damage the quality of the research. Mindful of this, I approached the issue of politics and considered how best to navigate engagement with local communities. Through understanding cultural protocols and deploying appropriate behaviors I negotiated access to communities, adapted to the local politics of the Gnani community and how best to work with the systems of authority and power, and navigated discussions of witchcraft, which is a culturally sensitive issue.

Suffice it to say that navigating fieldwork is not a one-off event; it is a process that continues through the entire fieldwork period. To give an example, while I was interviewing an elderly man at his home, Jato, his motor interjected, saying, "My son is still a child. He does not know anything about witchcraft. Where is this man from and why is he asking a lot of questions about this sensitive matter?" The man (Jato) was over fifty years old. Jato was a council member of the *Ukpakpaanbɔr* (chief) and an *Ubɔa* (soothsayer) at the same time. As *Ubɔa,* he consulted for both the public during funerals and private individuals. An *Ubɔa* is a spiritualist who foretells people's futures. The *Ubɔa* is also responsible for determining the cause of every death among the *Bikpakpaam* ethnic group. This was why I chose to speak with him. Taking his background into consideration, I found him knowledgeable, particularly regarding issues of witchcraft. But I sensed that the mother's presence was deliberate, to censure the kind of information he revealed to me. I was still considered a stranger and thus the mother felt it was inappropriate for her son to present himself as someone with knowledge of witchcraft. I was later told that she worried that this knowledge would lead to accusations of witchcraft.

Moreover, I had arranged for an interview with Jato at his residence after meeting him in the chief's palace and learning that he was an *Ubɔa* and a member of the council of elders. I had at the time asked that our conversation be private (as part of ensuring ethical research). As mentioned above his elderly mother became engaged in our conversation but there were in fact many others. Alongside his mother, many of Jato's relatives also joined us. Soon, there were many people listening to our conversation. This is a common challenge in undertaking fieldwork. The strong kinship ties between family members and their neighbors often resulted in people participating in the affairs of others; for example, when one welcomed a stranger into their home.

Upon noticing that the environment was no longer conducive to us having a more intimate or detailed conversation, I switched from the topic of witchcraft to more general issues, which led to the others sharing their opinions. Although those present also spoke about witchcraft, I sensed that the fact that I was a stranger made it difficult to share more sensitive information.

Nevertheless, it was important to find time to speak individually with Jato. As we got to know each other better (building trust and confidence), we had another conversation and this time his mother was absent. During one of our conversations, he said, "We are telling you all these because you are one of us. We would not ordinarily tell strangers these things." By that time, the community members had learned more about me, especially where I had come from and my ethnicity (which was the same as theirs). This highlights my position as a Ghanaian and one from northern Ghana where my study was based. I was perceived as an insider on the one hand and as an outsider on the other. Both identities had positive and negative aspects in terms of my positionality as a researcher.

In short, the authenticity, credibility, and uniqueness of research depend on the soundness, rigor, and appropriateness of the methodology adopted by the researcher and the extent that they are transparent about the choices that they make. The methodological strategy adopted for this study arose from the nature of the research questions and the sensitivity of the subject under study. As is typical within ethnography, conscious efforts were made to build trust and gain the confidence of the people I was studying. These efforts were key to gaining access to the community and collecting worthwhile data for my study. Building trust during fieldwork is not automatic. It needs to be planned, with effort invested (Hosokawa, 2010; O'Reilly, 2012) so that valid data may be gathered.

Reflecting on my position as a Ghanaian studying my own society is important here, as some measure of the efficacy of the data and its interpretation is undoubtedly affected by this. I am a Ghanaian from Northern Ghana, and am literate in *Likpakpaaln,* which is one of the main local languages spoken in Gnani and its surroundings. Gnani and its environs are the primary fieldwork sites where I conducted my research over a ten-month period. I grew up in an environment where people were very sensitive to issues of spirituality, including witchcraft. I was aware of such sensitivities and was guarded by a high sense of circumspection, taking into consideration the subtle and overt consequences of witchcraft allegations, beliefs, and practices. Young people's fear of witches, for instance, made them put every property they had in the family head or elder's names as was captured in the introduction of the book. I realized that witchcraft had a remarkable impact on people's way of life (i.e., on their psychological, social, and economic modes of being) and their relationships with others.

Until I became an undergraduate social work student undertaking an internship at a social agency, I had never heard of, nor been to, a community of refuge. Both my undergraduate and masters courses of study attached importance to fieldwork with social agencies and government departments that deal with social issues. In 2009, I attached myself to three NGOs that had partnered at the time to improve the well-being of people accused of witchcraft and seeking refuge in the Kukuo in the Nanumba South District of Northern Ghana. These NGOs are pro-poor, human rights-based, and work with people in rural communities to improve their well-being. Through my attachment to these NGOs, I was exposed to the issue of the communities of refuge phenomenon in Northern Ghana. I visited many communities, including the Kukuo community of refuge on several occasions. I was struck by the extent to which they were gendered. In fact, all the accused living at Kukuo were all women as were most of the children and grandchildren who stayed in the community of refuge as caretakers.

To give a brief of the situation at the communities of refuge in Northern Ghana, Stromberg (2011, p. 2) reported that about two thousand to six thousand accused witches, together with their caretakers or dependents, resided in the seven communities of refuge across Ghana's Northern Ghana. The grandchildren of those accused of witchcraft were sent to the communities of refuge to assist the elderly women with services such as cooking, fetching water, and gathering firewood, for the grandmothers were no longer capable of doing so on their own. From that point, I began to realize the enormity of the problems associated with witchcraft in Ghana. Although I was merely an observer at the time of my undergraduate fieldwork placement and did not play an active role in the fight for women's rights, the situation fueled a desire to especially understand why women seemed to be predominantly resettled and whether this related to their gender identities and positionalities in the society. This motivated me to choose communities of refuge as a place of study for my book. I hoped that I would better understand the phenomenon of witchcraft accusations and such communities in Ghana.

After reading about such communities in literature, news articles, and NGO reports, I settled on the Gnani community. The choice of field site was made precisely because I did not have familiarity or experience, and further had no kin besides the Kukuo when I was doing my field placement or social links to individuals living in the communities of refuge. The choice of this site, however, brought forth various aspects that are typical of researchers studying their own society: tensions between familiarity and strangeness, being considered an insider in some contexts and an outsider in others. Moreover, I was not a resident of the communities of refuge, nor did I have an official role or function with the organizations and government agencies present and typical of non-local actors who enter the communities. However, it was possible for some of the residents in any of the communities of refuge to know me since our nature of work with the NGOs brought them together for advocacy work. I was even prepared for the unlikelihood of someone recognizing me as the intern who had visited the community many years ago. In such a likelihood I considered how I would explain my position as a student then as well as now in relation to my capacity and power to offer any support, services, or resources.

Further, the issue of my gender and marital status required consideration in terms of how I navigated relationships and interactions. As a Ghanaian male with a different socioeconomic background (with regard to education), relatively young and unmarried, I was concerned with the potential challenges of building relationships with significantly disadvantaged women. Aside from the fact that no woman residing in the communities of refuge had completed even basic education, I was sensitive to the fact that the women were not only "rejected" by their communities but also victims of various kinds of prejudice because they were women and more likely predisposed to accusations due to multiple factors.

I considered how my gender, experiences, and positionality might influence my ability to engage with various members of the community. For instance, being educated, a researcher coming from a university, could be a positive given the value attached to education and afforded respect because of it. But it could also restrain more intimate engagement in the sense of people feeling uncomfortable about speaking openly with me. And, because of my positionality as an educated person, there might be expectations placed upon me to provide help where I might not be able to do so. The term *borga*, which in Ghanaian parlance refers to someone who has traveled or experienced life outside Ghana, captures my position—as an insider, perhaps on the surface, and yet fundamentally shaped by foreign influence. Perceived as a *borga*, and thus touched by the influence of the outside world, I was initially viewed with trepidation and ignored. However, over time, through interactions, building relationships, and participating in local activities, those perceptions changed, and I was accepted. All names used in this book are not the real names of the people who participated in the study. However, their stories remain valid despite their being anonymized.

NOTES ON NOMENCLATURE AND ORTHOGRAPHY

In northern Ghana, there are many contestations of who can claim indigeneity in relation to specific local areas. This has sometimes led to intense debates and tensions among the various ethnic groups that reside there. Before embarking on my ethnographic fieldwork, I was fully aware of these contestations. My knowledge of these contestations derives from not only my study of northern Ghana but also from my lived experience as I hail from there. I was born and raised in the region, and it is home to me. During fieldwork in Gnani and my movement within the region, I witnessed several instances of these contestations.

However, this book does not in any way engage with any of the region's political and cultural contestations of indigeneity. Thus, my usage of one language or another does not in any way make a contribution to such debates either. My linguistic approach is instead premised on two propositions; first, my disciplinary approach obligates me to highlight the voices of the research participants as a form of their representation and identity; and second, my intentions to decolonize development policy, practice, and scholarship. I mostly use *Likpakpaaln*—the language spoken by the *Bikpakpaam* ethnic group in Ghana. Where possible, I have also drawn on *Dagbani*, the language spoken by the *Dagbamba* ethnic group in Ghana. These were the two main ethnic groups to which my research participants belonged. I justify this approach below.

First, as a scholar who uses ethnography as a methodological approach, I stayed among the Bikpakpaam (colonially referred to as the Konkombas) ethnic group for my fieldwork. My everyday observations, encounters, conversations, and interviews were mostly among Bikpakpaam, and the modalities of these interactions were in Lipakpaaln. The majority of women and men I interacted with were also Bikpakpaam and spoke mainly Likpakpaaln. As an illustration, out of the total number of thirty participants who were accused of witchcraft and partook in my research, 66 percent belonged to the Bikpakpaam ethnic group while 34 percent belonged to the Dagbamba ethnic group. As I try as much as possible to capture the rich ethnographic account of what happened in the field, I have used Likpakpaaln and refer to Dagbani where possible. For example, the specific name of the community where people accused of witchcraft reside is called Gnani-Tindang (Dagbanli term). I have also referred to the custodian of the settlement as *Utindaan* (referring to the landowner*)* who also doubled as *Uwadaan* (shrine priest) during the period of my *fieldwork*, both Likpakpaaln terms, as he referred to himself during my numerous encounters with him.

Second, this book is also decolonial in nature and thus has been very critical of the interventions of development actors in northern Ghana. My decolonial approach is not only in ideas and arguments presented but also in terminologies used. In particular, I challenge some of the adulterated colonial names of ethnic groups and other communities that have continued up to date. These names have therefore misrepresented the identity of the people and their communities. For example, the ethnic group who were mostly my research participants refer to themselves as Bikpakpaam as I highlighted above. Their neighbors called them *Kpakpamba,* later translated to *Konkomba* by the colonialist. The term Konkomba has now been widely used by scholars and other official policy documents in Ghana and elsewhere. This has misrepresented the people's identity and takes explanations to let Bikpakpaam understand they are being referred to as Konkombas when attending official documents, events, or processes. Since many of my research participants self-identify as Bikpakpaam, and our daily interactions or encounters were in Likpakpaaln, I have therefore stuck to capturing them as the way they prefer to be identified, which does not deny representations made by Dagombas.

In sum, my commitment to capturing the ethnographic richness of data and my decolonial approach to development have informed my usage of the

Likpakpaaln language in this book, and other terminologies that challenge the conventional usage.

CONCLUSION

This chapter introduces the book's main argument and the theoretical approach that underpins it. It starts with the scene of witchcraft accusations, sighting of witches, lynching, and the problems that emerge from there. Specifically, I make the case that there are tensions between development actors' approach to dealing with witchcraft, people accused of witchcraft, and places of refuge in both how they are conceptualized and approached and the local framing and dealing with the same issues. I draw on social science scholarship, especially anthropology, sociology, gender, legal, and development studies. In this chapter, I also present the methodological approach to the research that informed this book, the overview of the book and the theoretical contribution that the book makes.

NOTE

1. In this book, I use the term Bikpakpaam to refer to the ethnic group colonially labeled as Konkomba. This is because they self-identify as Bikpakpaam, and I have stuck to their wish.

Chapter 1

Who Is a Witch?

Judgement, Facts, Truths and Knowledge

In this chapter, I present a detailed analysis and information on the identities of the individuals who are accused of witchcraft, thus responding to the question, *who is a witch?* I situate the discourse on the identities of the people accused of witchcraft within the broader context of kinship/community. The mode of kinship and the structure of social relatedness form a cultural landscape that fundamentally shapes the nature of interactions within African societies. Kinship and other relationships are central to informal social support systems and bonding. Discord, nonetheless, is present. In this chapter, I argue that the escalation of conflicts in kinship relationships is crucially implicated and leads to the context in which witchcraft allegations, accusations and confrontations emerge.

Expanding on the above assertion, I delve deeper into the broader range of issues that give rise to witchcraft accusations. Here, I argue that within the contexts of most African societies, although not unusual, witchcraft accusations seldom happen among people who are unrelated. Thus, the epicenter of witchcraft accusations is within the family, clan, or ethnic group or community. As such, in this chapter, I argue that witchcraft accusations reflect locally specific ideas built on shared knowledge and experiences. But accusations are always contested and given that the accusers are likely to be part of the intimate or social world of the individual accused, a neutral and independent "expert" is called in to assess the case. I draw on the knowledge and experiences of the local actors deemed to be experts in relation to adjudicating and assessing witchcraft accusations in Benin, Burkina Faso, Cameroon, and Ghana.

THE PERSONA OF A WITCH

This section presents attributes that are often considered as the identity of individuals accused of witchcraft. This section, although limited to the ethnicities where my ethnographic study took place—and in other analyses, I draw from other scholars, though that should be limited to those contexts—they also have broader implications for other contexts. There are commonalities across different societies, and I highlight that in the following pages.

Starting with Ghana, out of the total number of thirty-eight participants whom I interviewed, 66 percent belonged to the *Bikpakpaam* ethnic group while 34 percent belonged to the *Dagbamba* ethnic group. Regarding the relationship between the accuser and the accused, all of the thirty-eight participants reported that their accusers were related to them. That is, they were either part of the nuclear family, extended family, or the same clan or ethnic group or resided within the same community. This suggests that witchcraft accusation happens within kinship or within a familial relationship. In terms of the gender of the people accused of witchcraft, the analysis shows that the majority, 84 percent, of the people accused of witchcraft were women, while 16 percent were men. In terms of religion, 50 percent of the people accused of witchcraft also identified as Christian, 34 percent as Muslim, and 16 percent identified as Traditional African Religion (ATR).

In terms of age, it was difficult for people accused of witchcraft to tell their exact ages as they were often not documented during their birth. However, based on the description of certain events in Ghana and their knowledge at the time, the people accused of witchcraft would typically make an estimate of their age. The majority, 79 percent, reported that they were aged forty to fifty at the time of arrival in the Gnani community, 16 percent were aged fifty-one to sixty, and 5 percent were above sixty years. In terms of the number of years spent in Gnani community, 50 percent of the people accused of witchcraft said that they had spent between sixteen to twenty years, 32 percent reported that they had been in the community for eleven to fifteen years, 15 percent reported they had spent more than twenty years while 3 percent said they had spent five to ten years in Gnani. Many of the participants, 84 percent, reported that they had been in polygamous relationships in their lifetime, while 16 percent said they were in monogamous relationships at the time of their accusation. In terms of the reasons for which people were accused of witchcraft, 79 percent reported that they were accused because of the death of a relative, 13 percent said it was due to illnesses, 9 percent were blamed for their perceived successes or failures of other people, while 3 percent said it was a result of dreams. In some instances, accusations were a combination of all the above factors, which have built up over time.

Table 1.1 Socio-demographic Characteristics of People Accused of Witchcraft

Variable		Frequency (N=38)	Percentage (%)
Ethnicity of Participants	Bikpakpaam	25	65.8
	Dagbamba	13	34.2
Gender of Participants	Female	32	84.2
	Male	6	15.7
Religion of Participants	Christianity	19	50
	Islam	13	34.2
	ATR	6	15.8
Age of Participant at the Point of Accusation	40–50	30	78.9
	51–60	6	15.8
	61–70	2	5.3
No. of Years Participants Spent in the Camp	5–10	1	2.6
	11–15	12	34.2
	16–20	19	50
	21 and more	6	15
Marital Status of Participants	Widowed	21	55.5
	Separated	7	18.4
	Married	5	13.2
	Divorced	5	13.2
Type of Relationship Participants	Polygyny	32	84.2
	Monogamy	6	15.8
Cause of Accusation	Death	30	78.94
	Illnesses	5	13.2
	Failure/success	2	5.3
	Dreams	1	2.6
Are you Related to the Accuser?	Yes	38	100
	No	0	0
Whether the Accused has a Caregiver	Yes	18	47.4
	No	20	52.6
Living Arrangement	Living with others	31	81.6
	Living alone	7	18.4
Child Status	Yes	37	97.4
	No	1	2.6
Employment Status	Self employed	14	36.8
	Unemployed	24	63.2
Educational Status	Not been to school	38	100
	Been to school	0	0

Author Created

Regarding marital status, 56 percent of the accused persons *interviewed* reported that they were widows at the time of their accusation, while 18 percent reported they were separated from their partners following the accusation and banishment. Thirteen percent reported that they were married at the time of their accusation, while 13 percent said they were divorced. In terms of caregivers, 47 percent had a relative, usually a grandchild staying with them and helping with errands and house chores, while 53 percent reported they did not have anyone helping them as caregivers. Regarding living arrangement, 82 percent of people accused of witchcraft lived with others, while 18 percent lived alone. Regarding child status, 97 percent reported they had given birth to children, while 3 percent said they had never given birth. With regard to employment with a formal job, none of the people accused of witchcraft were employed. However, 37 percent reported they were self-employed, while 63 percent of the people accused of witchcraft said they were not and lived their lives on the goodwill of others. None of the people accused of witchcraft had ever been to school.

The characteristics highlighted in my fieldwork among *Bikpakpaam* and *Dagbamba* are common across other African societies. Let's look at a few examples. According to Barbier (2020) who studied the Mossi ethnic group in Burkina Faso, the majority of people accused and banished from their communities were often elderly women and widows, and although they had children, many of them had also had some of their children die. She reported that only 2 percent of them never gave birth. Similar characteristics were found in the study by Kahn (2011) in Benin, especially those who were arrested and imprisoned according to the state's new legislation to "police" evil in society. Kahn, like any of us, makes a case that the above characteristics that make up the identity of a witch are common in many other places and have been used to accuse people of practicing witchcraft. That is, they have used their witchcraft to cause their own barrenness, to kill their own children or that of others, or to bewitch their husbands and hence why many of them were widowed. In each of these societies, it is not that men are never accused of witchcraft, they are, except that they are either given a free pass due to the patriarchal nature of such societies (Barbier, 2020) or they migrate to different communities (Kahn, 2011) or in an exceptional case also sent to the communities of refuge as I found in Gnani. Similar characteristics have also been found in South Africa, Ivory Coast, Nigeria, Uganda, and Tanzania among many other countries. Let's now turn our attention to how individuals accused of witchcraft are authenticated.

WITCHCRAFT TRIAL DEBATES

There exists a body of scholarship that examines the process by which people accused of witchcraft have their cases assessed and adjudicated (see, for instance, Agyekum, 2004). While reviewing literature for this study, I found three sets of scholarship assessing and adjudicating witchcraft accusations. The first refers to the family, clan, and chiefs of the community. This category

of adjudicators is the first point of call whose roles are to provide an opportunity for both the accused and the accuser to dialogue to find out how they
will be able to resolve the issues that led to the accusation. Wumbla studied
the Gambaga community in northern Ghana and notes that people accused
of witchcraft have had their cases adjudicated within the communities before
being banished (Wumbla, 2017, p. 34). Although Wumbla acknowledges the
first-level adjudicators and the roles they play in providing an opportunity for
hearing, he presents the accused persons as docile persons who are denied
any opportunity of hearing, and thus, the preface of his paper "*Condemned
without hearing.*" A similar argument is made by ActionAid (2012) in their
provocative report titled, "Condemned without Trial: Women and Witch
Camps in Ghana." Such prefaces suggest that people accused of witchcraft,
especially women, are not given the opportunity for a hearing.

The contrast, however, is that both Wumbla and ActionAid's narratives
detail how witchcraft cases are assessed and adjudicated by their families,
clan heads, and chiefs of their communities. However, it is only when such
accusations are still contested after the outcome from family heads and
chiefs that an opportunity is provided for the accusers and accused to seek
the services of local experts that are mandated to deal with spiritual issues.
That being said, both of these works draw on provocative titles that can be
sensational and may undermine the relevance of local processes of providing
opportunities for hearing, or they do not consider such hearings as proper. It
seems to me that what both authors in their respective works consider proper
is a hearing conducted in formal state institutions such as courts, police,
NCCE (National Commission on Civic Education) and CHRAJ (Commission
on Human Rights and Administrative Justice), leading us to the second level
of assessment and adjudication. Such positioning as seen in both authors
seems to ignore and delegitimize local interventions and processes and only
focus on state avenues as the only channel through which such deliberations
should be held. If I am correct in this assumption, then, there is a contradiction of a sort; that is the state recognizes local authorities and even has specific mandates in the constitution for them. Thus, what they do would appear
to be legitimate and within their mandates. Perhaps, such a philosophical
stance and blatant efforts to ignore the authority of local authorities is something that needs further investigation.

In Ghana, although witchcraft trials have occurred in both traditional
and formal courts starting from the colonial era to now, there has been little
scholarly attention on witchcraft trials and their implications in Ghana (see
Adinkrah, 2015). To fill the gap in scholarship established, Chapter 6 of
Adinkrah's book, *Witchcraft, Witches and Violence in Ghana* (2015, pp.
183–207), is devoted to examining witchcraft trials in the Ghanaian courts,
drawing on four cases. Adinkrah refers to two key works that have dealt with

witchcraft trials, but in the instances of the two works, only Gray's doctoral dissertation focused on formal court systems. In sum, Adinkrah argues "that witchcraft trials are of enormous significance in the purveyance of witchcraft ideas in society, playing a role in fueling violent witch hunts in society." The existence of witchcraft trials in the Ghanaian courts, as revealed by Adinkrah, complicates the position of Wumbla and ActionAid, which highlight the lack of opportunity for adjudication in the formal court. They two would seem to favor an opportunity in the court setting rather than within the community. However, the very essence that an opportunity is provided, Adinkrah rather finds it problematic as such information, in his view, perpetuates witchcraft beliefs and fuels witch hunts in Ghana. The lacuna in court trials of witchcraft cases as I found in Adinkrah's work was not about finding out whether the people involved were witches or not, but a defamation suit, which was the case before the court.

Igwe (2016b) pointed out that witchcraft studies have always presented people accused of witchcraft as passive in their accusation, without any form of agency to challenge and reject such accusations. However, Igwe finds that such narratives are one-sided and expose a gap in scholarship. Igwe studied witchcraft among the *Dagbamba* of Ghana and argues that in contrast to the passiveness of people accused of witchcraft, "alleged witches were active participants in the accusation process because they accepted, rejected, challenged, protested, resisted, redefined and contested imputations of occult harm" (2016b, p. v). People accused of witchcraft relied on state institutions as a medium of resolving witchcraft accusations. However, the cases of witchcraft accusations that are tried by state institutions are minuscule in comparison to the cases being tried in the communities by local experts. This then leads us to the third level of witchcraft accusation trials in Ghana.

I extend the scholarship of Igwe and Adinkrah, but here, I focused on local experts and their adjudicatory mechanisms rather than formal court systems. I note that Igwe has touched on this a bit in his writing too. This is necessary because many people rely on local experts to assess and adjudicate matters of witchcraft accusations, and they are seen to have the "power" to do so. I also highlight and place value on the local assessments and adjudicatory frameworks because they are the predominant form in the context of the research sites. Also, some participants do not believe that the state institutions have the capacity or the expertise to delve into witchcraft accusations. For example, Mabru, a forty-year-old male farmer in Gnani said that he would not take any person accused of witchcraft to court. He asserted that magistrates and lawyers do not have the capacity to delve into witchcraft cases. Rather, he preferred to take the accused to the local experts in Gnani, Kukuo, or Gambaga for assessment and adjudication. Based on the lack of trust in the state institutions as a medium of resolving witchcraft accusations, my attention is focused on the more commonly used local experts, and make the point that people accused of witchcraft are not passive when they are accused, but instead are active participants in the whole process, using different local media such as family heads, clan heads, and chiefs. When such issues are not able to be resolved, both accusers and accused seek the services of local experts such as *Uwadaan (Biwadam-plural)*, *Ubɔa (Bibɔab-plural)*, and *Unyɔkdaan (Binyɔkdam-plural)*, to make an assessment of accusations.

The significance of focusing on local experts cannot be understated. As Crampton asserts, witchcraft

> [is] an evolving form of cultural practice linking global audiences to local contexts that cannot simply replace local moralities and social response. What has been more effective advocacy is to work from within cultural norms through informal conflict mediation among family and community systems. (Crampton, 2013, p. 200)

The informal conflict mediations and community systems Crampton refers to are the family, clan, chiefs, and broader community mechanisms such as the experts I have alluded to, who have the knowledge to adjudicate witchcraft accusations, and thus contributing to the local epistemology of handling and managing witchcraft accusations. This approach, as I argue, contributes to paying attention to indigenous knowledge by exploring linkages with the expertise of local authorities and their intersections with development actors in dealing with complex and sensitive issues such as witchcraft.

AUTHORITY OF AN EXPERT: JUDGEMENT, FACTS, TRUTHS, AND KNOWLEDGE

During the fieldwork period, I witnessed five cultural expert assessments of witchcraft accusations. Out of the five, the assessment of three of the cases were conducted in the Gnani community by the *Uwadaan*. The first of the cases saw fifteen men brought in a car from a suburb of the Kpandai community over the death of a young man. One of the men was found guilty after the assessment ritual. The second case was about an elderly woman who was accused of witchcraft in Duuni. She was not found guilty after the assessment. And lastly, three women were accused of witchcraft in Tamale and brought into Gnani for assessment. Again, one of the women was found guilty while the other two were pronounced innocent. The assessment of the last two cases was conducted outside of Gnani community by different local experts *(Bibɔab).* The fourth case was an inquest into the death of a young woman that took place in Sakpei a neighboring community to Gnani where

I was resident. The fifth case was likewise related to death, but in a different village (Chamba), and concerned the death of an elderly man. For the purposes of this chapter, I focus on three cases. The three cases below are chosen because they detail witchcraft assessments by different local experts that help to deepen the discussion of the reasons for which they were accused and the strategies being employed.

Case One: Uwadaan's Assessment and Adjudication of Witchcraft Accusation (Dagbamba)

It was a Friday, late afternoon, when two rusty taxi cabs overloaded with people drove into Gnani community with six people in each. The two taxi cabs headed toward the *Uwadaan's* residence. The residents of Gnani were unsurprised by this common sight. At the time, I was in a conversation with a group of young people concerning which political party was going to win an upcoming election. National and local elections were just a few weeks away. Upon seeing the taxis, it was clear to everyone (except me) that someone had been accused of witchcraft and they had come for the assessment process at the shrine in Gnani.

While in Gnani, I had anticipated a moment like this one. I was told by some community members that assessment rituals were quite common. I was yet to experience the process to gain insights and firsthand experience into assessment; the length of period the process takes, what words are said, and what actually happens at the shrine. I thus immediately headed off to witness the proceedings. When I got to the *Uwadaan's* residence, the taxi passengers and the local community members were already in the shrine ready for the assessment ritual to commence. The case involved three elderly women of *Dagbamba* ethnic descent who had been accused of witchcraft in Tamale, northern Ghana's capital. The women were accused of bewitching people and inflicting illness and death. They were also accused of bringing bad luck to other people in their community. The accusations followed the recent death of a boy and the subsequent context of the three women being confronted about being implicated in it. The women denied any involvement in witchcraft. They were therefore brought to Gnani to assess whether they were witches. It is interesting to note that though there were regional and district courts in Tamale and Yendi that the accusers had bypassed them to come to a local shrine in Gnani for assessment and adjudication. This is probably because the accusers do not trust that such institutions in Tamale and Yendi have the capacity to handle witchcraft accusations and cleansing.

The whole assessment process was quite short. It happened within an hour of their arrival. It was open to the public and was witnessed by many in the community. The *Uwadaan* slaughtered a chicken for each of the three women. In the end, one of the women was pronounced guilty while the other two were pronounced innocent. The accusers who had accompanied them looked unfriendly as they returned to their taxis, murmuring some words to one another. The women looked worried and exhausted, with the one found guilty pleading her innocence. I had approached her to ask a few questions, but she declined, noting that it was getting dark, and they had to get back home to report to the elders what they had found. However, I had an extensive conversation with the *Uwadaan*, especially regarding how he navigated his role and made use of his expertise in determining who was a witch and who was not. The *Uwadaan*, Materi, is forty-two years old and a farmer. He is a family man with a wife and seven children. Materi was one of the first persons the assemblyman took me to seek permission to study in Gnani. I chose to interview him because he is influential in the community, being the *Uwadaan* and also doubling as *Utindaan* of the Gnani community. The encounter at the assessment ritual was my second time interacting with him.

Although in principle Materi had told me what he does as *Uwadaan*, the case of the assessment of the three women was an important moment to gain a better understanding of what such a role entails. Materi reaffirmed that he is the spiritual overseer of the Gnani community. Though this was common knowledge, Materi's narrative accentuated his knowledge and authority and the fact that he is responsible for verifying witchcraft accusations, purifying people who are accused of witchcraft, and making sacrifices to the gods and other spirits on behalf of the community. He also explained the work that this entails such as, for example, convening a meeting of community elders to make contributions to appease the gods and ask for the intervention of the gods for the rainfall. He described tasks such as receiving the contributions of communities, making necessary purchases for the ritual, and then following up with conducting the sacrifice of appeasement. He also told me he is responsible for providing every accused person who comes into the community with temporary and sometimes permanent accommodation and feeding until they have their own structures. While the conversation was ongoing, Materi let me know he had to attend to other family issues, and that I could come back at another date to continue our chat.

On the following day, I arrived at his residence to continue the discussion. Materi told me that when people are accused of witchcraft and brought to the community for the assessment ritual, he has enormous responsibility for the individual; he will cleanse them of the witchcraft and resettle them if they are rejected by their communities or let them go back home if they choose to.

> Our rule is that if anyone is being accused of witchcraft and rejected by their community members, and they come to us, we must accept and resettle them according to our culture. You don't reject people who need places of refuge. But

we can only do this when they agree to go through the verification and pacification process if they were found guilty of the accusation.

Materi states that there are two complementary ways of doing the assessment. First, any person accused of witchcraft is presumed to be a witch until he or she goes through what is locally termed as *"ti buen ti nyu liwal"* (which means "let's go and drink from the water of the shrine") or *"ti buen to gii ikobi"* ("let's go and slaughter a chicken for verification"). The drinking of the water of the shrine' *("liwal aa nyu pu")* is a ceremony conducted to confirm or refute an accusation against an accused. At Gnani, one way to determine whether an accused is a witch is for the *Uwadaan* to sacrifice a chicken *(likobi giil),* after a series of questions is posed to the accused. He starts by saying:

> This person (mentions the name of the accuser) has accused you of being a witch and has brought you here. If you are innocent, please the gods reject her chicken, but if you are not, the gods please accept her chicken.

Materi then cuts the throat of the chicken and drops the blood on the stone-like symbol, representing god in the physical realm, and drops the chicken on the ground. In the case of the three women I had witnessed, two of them had their chickens facing up while the third woman's chicken landed facing down. An accused person whose chicken dies while facing down is declared "guilty," while the person whose chicken dies while facing up is declared "innocent." So, in the case of the three women, the "third woman" was declared a witch.

After the chicken sacrifice, the accused can still claim innocence. In such instances, the accused would be asked to drink a concoction *("nyunn bi liwal")*. This forms the second part of the assessment and purification processes. Here whether the accused is guilty or not, they may choose to drink from the shrine water. The most important thing is the kind of words that are being said and the meaning behind them, Materi told me. If an accused is guilty or knows he or she has witchcraft and goes ahead to drink the concoction without admitting guilt, he or she is said to die. On the other hand, if the accused accepts that he or she has witchcraft, the same concoction will cleanse him or her of the witchcraft.

Materi told me that some people do not believe in the prowess and authenticity of the assessment process and have accused him of poisoning his victims or forcing them to confess that they are witches. But he narrated to me that if this were the case, everyone who drinks the water would have died. Furthermore, he performs the ritual in public and does not always know the people accused of witchcraft until they are brought to him. It, therefore, baffles him as to why he will poison some of the accused and leave others alive.

I further enquired from Materi at what point in time people stay in the community. This was because in all the cases I witnessed in the community, the people accused and assessed returned home the same day. Materi told me that a lot of people go home to tell the community what had happened. The community then gathers either at the chief's palace or at the eldest of the community and a decision leading to banishment is made. The chances that the woman who was found guilty will return to live in Gnani or go elsewhere, he told me, was high. This is an example of a local assessment of witchcraft accusations from *Uwadaan,* the ritual custodian of Gnani-Tindang.

Case Two: An Inquest into the Death of a Young Woman at Sakpei

The second case involves the spiritual assessment of the causes of death as opposed to the assessment by a community "expert" discussed above and involves different and multiple actors such as the *bininkpiib* (elders), *bibɔab* (Soothsayers), *bibɔrib* (chiefs) and *bidichandam* (family heads). Case 2 also typifies the range of community assessments but is substantially different in process and implications. For example, in case 1, the people suspected to be witches were already identified by their accusers and brought to the Gnani for assessment. In case 2, as well as the third case following, it is the *bibɔab* who are brought into the community and required to make a community assessment of the probable cause of the deaths. In the end, if witchcraft is suspected, then accusations will be made. Such accusations may be subject to further assessments by *biwadam* of the various shrines in Ghana if the accused deny the charge. A difference between *Biwadam* in the communities of refuge and *bibɔab* is that *bibɔab* are mobile and are often invited.

Among the *Bikpakpaam* ethnic group in Gnani and elsewhere in Ghana, any time a person dies; it is incumbent on the part of their relations to bring in a *ubɔa* at the funeral to identify the cause of death. I had the opportunity to observe this in the Gnani community and its surroundings. It is usually a public event where anyone who attends the funeral can observe and listen. As I have been informed and witnessed, there are stages and certain background activities that take place before the *ubɔa* is public with his revelation. As a Ghanaian, even before my study, I had witnessed this several times. The difference this time though was to turn an academic lens on my observations as well as a critical introspection of my previous experience.

Below is an account of how it was done when I attended the funeral celebration of a woman, Pigri, who had died during childbirth. Pigri was twenty-eight years old when she died. Pigri had home delivery of a baby with the assistance of local birth attendants. However, the afterbirth (placenta) remained in her womb. They rushed her to the Gnani community clinic, but unfortunately, she died before the nurses could attend to her.

In tandem with the Bikpakpaam culture, there was also the need for social and spiritual assessment to find out the cause of her death. The spiritual assessment of the death normally takes place during the funeral performance. I was invited by my landlord and his other relatives as the woman was related to them. My research associate, landlord, and some of their relatives were residents in Sakpei before moving to Gnani. Her funeral was scheduled for June 3, 2016, at Sakpei, a village that was about a fifteen-minute motorcycle ride from Gnani. At the funeral ground, this is what I observed.

Everyone was gathered at the house of the dead woman. Men were seated outside while women and children remained in the yard. The men sat in a semicircle. There was complete silence. Two elderly men came into the center of the sitting arrangement; they were *Bibɔab* who were called to make a spiritual inquest into the death of Pigri. After greeting the people, one of the *Bibɔab* went into the bush briefly before returning to report what the spirit of the dead person had told him. The *Ubɔa* described the person who had bewitched the Pigri. No name was mentioned, but cues were given. However, after a while in the case of Pigri, the first *Ubɔa* shook his head and said he wasn't going to beat about the bush. He revealed that the cause of death of the woman was her parents. Her parents were unhappy with the clan she married into, and her parents insisted the husband return their daughter to them. The parents had threatened that if the husband refused, they were going to curse her. According to the *Ubɔa,* the parents did curse her and that was what caused her death. Her mother had given birth to four girls who got married to the same clan. *Ubɔa* concluded by saying that "the parents were not happy about the refusal of the husband to return their daughter. It was these contestations between Pigri's parents and her husband that led to her death."

As the first *Ubɔa* finished, the second *Ubɔa* regurgitate and summarized what the first had said. This act of regurgitation authenticates the spiritual authority and expertise in death inquests and also reinforces the findings of the ceremony. At the end of the second *Ubɔa's* regurgitation, elders of the community met separately with the *bibɔab* to ask further questions. This is because the parents had denied bewitching their daughter or cursing her as the *Ubɔa* had proclaimed. The purpose of the elders' meeting with the *Bibɔab* was to make further follow-ups into the death of Pigri.

The elders put three different sticks and earmarked each stick with a description. The first *Ubɔa* moved away to a distant area. He was then called to come and show the cause of Pigri's death. After these final revelations with the elders, the exact person was known. Everyone then dispersed. I was not privy to the final part, as strangers or visitors or people who do not belong to the clan are denied participation. After the ceremony, I was told the community would convene a meeting later to determine the fate of the parents, and the possibility of going to Gnani or elsewhere for further verifications was high if they continue to deny knowledge of bewitching their daughter.

Case Three: An Inquest into the Death of a Ukpakpaanja

The third witchcraft accusation assessment surrounded the death of a businessman. Waja was considered a successful businessman who migrated from northern Ghana to Accra, the capital city of Ghana. He was a polygamous man with two wives and eleven children. He sold building wares such as cement, roofing zinc, and building poles among other things. He also had cargo cars that carted goods from the north to the south and vice versa. He built three houses in Accra and several other buildings back in the north. By all standards, he was considered a rich man by all those who knew him. When he eventually fell sick, his family suspected the hand of a witch.

I visited Waja at the hospital. Upon my arrival, I found that his relatives—children, wives, and brothers of Waja—were outside. There seemed to have been an argument. The family members were talking in hushed tones, and it was as if they did not want people to hear them. Everyone was quiet and pretended as if nothing was happening when I entered their midst. I greeted the family. One of the wives had moved upstairs to where the husband lay in the sick bed. I followed. While in the sick room, a man of about thirty-five years came in. He looked very unkempt and was messily dressed. The man was later identified as *Unyɔkdaan* (juju man). The children followed me into the room too. The man brought out some concoctions and put these into a cup for Waja to drink. He chanted and commanded the sickness to vanish while Waja was given the concoction by one of his wives. The juju man claimed someone had dug a hole (spiritual plot) that he had fallen into. That was why he was sick, meaning Waja was bewitched. He told the family he had the ability to undo the spiritual plot and heal him.

There was a divided view of *Unyɔkdaan* giving concoctions to Waja while he was in the hospital. Some relatives contended that no one knew him, and they were not sure the concoction was safe to drink. Some of the family members advanced this argument by pointing out that the concoction could be poisonous and that everyone could be in trouble, including the medical team, the family, and even the *Unyɔkdaan*. In contrast, some family members held the view that since it was the sick man who invited him, it was safe for him to drink the concoction. The children and the wives agreed for the man to go ahead while an extended family member objected to it. The *Unyɔkdaan* made a case that he could not poison Waja because he was his friend. Waja had invited him to visit him before falling sick and losing his ability to speak. Besides, he consumed some of the concoction himself to prove that it was not poisonous. In the end, Waja was given the concoction.

What struck me most about the whole episode was the distrust of the medical team. The family believed that the sickness had a spiritual cause rather than a medical one. I was baffled by the fact that the very people who took Waja to the hospital harbored doubts about the efficacy of the medical team. I would come to realize later that the children had plans to take their father out of the hospital to the herbalist/spiritualist precisely for this reason. The other relatives, however, stopped the children's plot. The relatives that challenged the idea of the children argued that it was improper to take Waja out of the hospital while he was being attended to. Their reason was that the medical team could find out what was wrong clinically and could administer appropriate treatment. Further, it would be appropriate to request a transfer to a higher facility if the hospital did not have an efficient team and resources to cater to him, rather than take him to the spiritualist. In the end, he was transferred to a well-equipped hospital.

The medical team found that Waja had suffered a severe stroke. His ability to speak was impaired because of the stroke. The right side of his body was inactive, and no signs of movement were observed. My enquiries with the head of the medical team at the hospital revealed that the patient was only to be managed. The medical team could not restore normal functioning after the illness. Waja eventually died at the second medical facility.

I attended the funeral to listen to the spiritual assessment of his death. The *Ubɔa* indicated to the populace that the man had been bewitched. *Ubɔa* revealed that it was the elderly wife and the firstborn who had bewitched their father.

Indeed, there were some tensions among the family members. Waja lived with his two wives and children who initially sent him to the hospital when he felt ill. They took care of Waja for a few days before letting the external family members know about his illness and that he was being sent to the hospital. My arrival at the hospital coincided with the arrival of the *Unyɔkdaan* who claimed that he was invited by Waja to visit him before he felt sick. At this point, Waja could no longer speak and hence neither could he verify the *Unyɔkdaan's* claim. Taking into consideration that the *Unyɔkdaan* was a total stranger, some of Waja's family members resisted his treatment because they felt that they could not trust him, while the others were easy to trust and asked him to go ahead, claiming that "if you are sick, you try all medications. You never know which one can cure your illness." Therefore, there was ambivalence due to differing approaches by various members of Waja's family.

WHAT DO WE MAKE OF THE ABOVE CASES?

In this section, I present the themes emerging from the cases I have presented above and discuss them in detail and as well as their relationship to broader scholarship in Ghana and in Africa.

Folk Discourses of Causative Factors

Drawing from the cases presented above, causative factors refer to the perceived facts of the cases that lead to the accusation. They form the basis of evidence when an individual is accused of witchcraft. These factors usually include but are not limited to, misfortunes such as death, illness, and failures. Causative factors are not only manifested in negative phenomena such as the ones mentioned above, but also in positive occurrences where individuals are considered too successful, confident, assertive, wealthy, or live longer than usual (see Adinkrah, 2015). I tackle the positive stories of witchcraft suspicion in chapter 4 of this book. Beliefs in witchcraft are informed by local knowledge, which teaches that all lives should be fairly equal; thus, people who fall from the average are considered abnormal. Some of these abnormalities could be equated to witchcraft (the people are the best judges of which abnormality is and which is not), with the very poor or very rich being vulnerable to the accusation.

Suspicious Deaths, Cause for Investigation

Every death among the *Bikpakpaam* is investigated. But not every investigation will lead to an open accusation of witchcraft or, relatedly, the banishment of an accused individual. To corroborate my findings, Tait, an early anthropologist who studied witchcraft in northern Ghana among the *Bikpakpaam* similarly found that "before the arrival of the Germans in Togoland all deaths were investigated on the day of death . . . and the sorcerer was killed on the spot (954: 73)." Today, the sorcerer or witch is not killed but banished from the community. Some of the people who are banished find themselves in communities of refuge such as Gnani or elsewhere.

The *Bibɔab* are acknowledged experts in assessing deaths and in most cases, witchcraft is implicated in their assessment of the cause of death and required trials to be conducted. In the first case, the death of a child triggered accusations, in both the second and third cases too, inquests into the deaths of Waja and Pigri also triggered witchcraft accusations. These trials bring into focus the expert knowledge of different local actors who are contracted either by the accusers, the accused themselves, or the entire community. These trials are normally public in the sense that anyone can attend but rules are strictly enforced in relation to taking photographs, recording, where you stand, and what you can and cannot say or do.

Adding onto the analysis of the cases presented here, I asked the thirty-eigth participants accused of witchcraft in Gnani why they were accused. Death was one of the main causes of accusations. Sixty-eight percent (68 percent) of my participants said that they were accused of killing someone through witchcraft. I had asked one of the people accused of witchcraft in Gnani why she was accused, and she had this to say:

> I wasn't even at home. I was in Accra, and he died. The community brought one spiritual woman and she came and revealed to them that I was the one who bewitched the child. Upon arrival in the village, the community told me that I was responsible for the child's death. I was banished from the community.

People respond differently to the occurrence of their loved ones' death. *Bikpakpaam* and *Dagbamba* ethnic groups in Northern Ghana often make a spiritual inquest of deaths in their communities. This was similarly found in Burkina Faso by Barbier (2020) among the *Mossi* ethnic group and Kahn (2011) among the *Fɔn* of Benin. There is an assumption, as revealed to me by some research participants, that there is a spiritual dimension to every death. It is because of the belief in the spiritual dimension of deaths that experts are called in to make an inquest into every death in the community. Sarpong (2004) noted that the worldview of an African is anchored in the concept of duality. He indicated that there are two sides to everything, including the physical and the spiritual. Relatives of dead persons seek to identify the spiritual dimension of every death that occurs within their families. This view was also corroborated by a Catholic priest who shared the following thoughts with me:

> Basically, when misfortune befalls, for example, when somebody dies suddenly, for us Africans, Ghanaians, Konkombas, and Dagombas, nothing happens by chance. Everything has a cause, and there is a need to identify what caused the death. When a young person dies, they feel the person has died prematurely . . . somebody has experienced some frequent deaths in the family so there are a number of them. So, when these things happen to our people, they believe that it is not just by chance. Something is wrong, and that must be the act of witchery.

Similarly, a community member in Gnani told me,

> There is a belief in the Gnani that when someone dies, another person might have been responsible for the cause of the death. So, anytime death occurs, they will need to find out who has caused that death.

The Catholic priest, although a native of the Upper East Region of Ghana, was born and raised in Bimbilla in Northern Ghana. He was also schooled in the region. Since becoming a priest, he served among *Bikpakpaam* and *Dagbamba*. He is therefore conversant with the belief systems and practices of both ethnic groups.

It is important to add that although every death in the Gnani community is subject to spiritual verification, the effort people invest in finding out the causes of such deaths differs greatly. The deaths of young men and women, pregnant women before, during, and after delivery, deaths resulting from snake bites, accidents, and people with great potential and with some level of success call for immediate investigation. These types of deaths are considered unusual and invariably implicate the hand of a malicious witch. Every death is subject to verification. The verification also seeks to identify what the people could do to cleanse the community. Usually, sacrifices are made afterward.

The Notion of Illnesses and Witchcraft Accusation

Illness is present in the case studies here too; illnesses were raised as some of the reasons for accusation. In the case of Waja, he fell ill, and the illness was attributed to witchcraft by the *Unyɔkdaan*. In the second case, Pigri was sent to the hospital due to a medical emergency. When I asked other people that I interviewed, who were accused of witchcraft, why they were accused, 13 percent of people accused of witchcraft in Gnani asserted that their accusations were due to illnesses in their communities.

In particular, diseases are believed to be more deeply associated with a spiritual cause than any medical reason could provide. Often, people seek the spiritual cause of an illness before they even attempt treatment. Such was the case of Pigri as I observed from the field. In most cases, especially among people who are members of African traditional religions, there is a need to consult a *Uwadaan* or *Ubɔa* before any move can be taken regarding the treatment of a sick person. In some instances, people can die at home, or their conditions deteriorate because *Uwadaan* or *Ubɔa* proclaims that they should not be taken to the hospital. Once people in the community accept that sickness has no medical/clinical diagnosis, then it is taken for granted that there is no need to take the sick person to a clinic or hospital. Such people prefer to treat the person with traditional medicine, the preparation of which is shrouded with mysticism and spiritual influence.

In the above case of Waja, the belief in the spiritual nature of his illness by some of Waja's family members meant that the diagnosis from the medical team was irrelevant. This mentality was deeply influenced by the *Unyɔkdaan*. The children believed that their father was bewitched and that his treatment must therefore be found in the spiritual world rather than a medical facility. The children had even conjectured names of people whom they blamed for causing the illness. The people they accused were those with whom Waja had poor relationships with before he fell sick. Thus, the children believed the *Unyɔkdaan* who visited Waja at the hospital.

It is important to note that there is a distinction between spiritually induced illnesses and those that are not as participants would remind me. A participant informed me that witchcraft could be used to inflict illnesses on a person to limit their ability to work. In that line of thought, if a witch sees that another person is progressing, such a witch could inflict an illness on their target to curtail the person's ability to engage in their daily activities, leading to them becoming unsuccessful. Sickness is a common avenue for framing people as witches. Agyekum (2004) noted in her study among the Anufo of Northern Ghana that diseases were blamed on people accused of witchcraft.

The issue of illnesses being blamed on witches can be interpreted within attribution/ scapegoating theories, as applied by Sefa-Dadeh (2004), Adinkrah (2004) and Comaroff and Comaroff (1999a). In her study on witchcraft mentality in Ghana, Sefa-Dadeh (2004), a psychiatrist at the University of Ghana Medical School, explained the causes of sicknesses, accusations, and self-confessions of some individuals by applying attribution theory. Attribution theory is the internal or external explanation of individual behavior that is associated with another thing, in this case, witchcraft. She found that the people who were usually accused of witchcraft were "those who had little control or ability to assert or defend" (Sefa-Dadeh, 2004, p. 98).

Witchcraft Accusations and Dreams

Dreams also play a significant role in creating fertile ground for witchcraft accusations to grow. A few people (3 percent) accused of witchcraft in Gnani said that their accusations were due to dreams or partly influenced by people's dreams. I was informed several times of how someone can tell who his spiritual enemies are through dreams. Dreams, according to my participants, are a revelation of what the witch or enemy thinks or intends to do to you. These dreams are communicated through spiritual forces that are protective of the dreamer. Participants talked about good and bad dreams. Bad dreams are images, thoughts, and revelations that come during one's sleep. Such dreams show the witch's intentions toward either the dreamer or a third person. A quotation below from a community member in Gnani supports how dreams can be used to verify the witch trying to bewitch you:

> I saw her in my dream. She was chasing me with a cutlass. I was screaming out
> loud, but no one could hear me. I ran and fell several times. Each time I fell I

got up before she got to me. I wasn't making much effort while running. I was scared she was going to catch me.

I was curious to know what happened next. He indicated that he told his father about it the next day. The father advised him to go and warn the person he saw in the dream. Yami followed the advice and threatened to kill her if he ever dreamt of her again. It is believed that if one sees a witch in their dream and keeps silent, the witch can overcome them and will eventually lead to their death. It is believed that the only way to protect oneself is to make a direct warning to the person seen in the dreams. Using dreams as the basis of accusations can be problematic. This is because witches can un-wear their skins and mask themselves with others. In that case, one is likely to accuse the innocent person whose face is being used as a mask. In such ambiguous circumstances, the dreamer may need to consult the spiritual seer to determine who exactly was appearing in their dreams.

Failure/Success Paradox

Of the people accused of witchcraft in Gnani, a few mentioned the reason for it as due to an issue of failure experienced by someone attributed to them or that their own success leading to them becoming targets for accusation. This is also supported by the explanations offered by a Catholic priest as follows:

> Basically, when misfortune befalls, for example when somebody is doing business and the business is not going on they think . . . or somebody marries and they are not getting children, or somebody has written exams and there are repeated failures, or somebody's farm is not productive. When these things happen for our people, they believe that it is not just by chance. Something is wrong.

Witchcraft is one of the many explanations that people adopt to cope with complex situations in their lives (see Mabefam, 2017). In fact, manifestations and blaming of both fortunate and unfortunate events on witchcraft is a recurrent theme in most scholarly accounts of witchcraft (such as the classic Evans-Pritchard study of *Witchcraft, Oracles and Magic among the Azande*, 1937) as well as in local communities. Success in any aspect of a person's life opens them up to possible accusations that they employed the services of witchcraft and other spiritualties (see Adinkrah 2015). Here, the findings of Comaroff and Comaroff are also relevant. Comaroff and Comaroff (1999a) found that people in the rural setting of the Northern Province of South Africa accused others of employing the services of the zombies to improve their wealth. For example, people who had distinguished themselves in their farming, trading, schooling, and animal rearing and who had experienced few unfortunate incidents were often associated with witchcraft.

I had a conversation with a community member, and he narrated how some farmers employed occult power and other spiritual rituals to improve the quantity of their farm yields. He indicated that if you went to the farms of most of these people, you would find physical evidence of such spiritual powers:

> It's just that it is wrong to go to another person's farm without his permission. I would have taken you to the farms of some of these people. They employ the services of spiritual forces to help them in their farm work. Among Bikpakpaam, it is called kisamook. You will see the physical evidence of what I'm telling you. They are made up of clay pots which are stuffed with a mixture of herbs, roots, and stones. Various rituals are performed, and the mixture is placed under a big tree on the farm. Signs are made on the stones which are placed on the first yam mound at all four corners of the yam with cross-like signs on them.

Although there is a difference between occult power and witchcraft, sometimes some occult power can lead to witchcraft accusations as will be discussed in chapter 4.

I did not have the opportunity to observe any of the farms my informant talked about. No one would admit that he had performed such a ritual or take me to his farm to see it. The people who were thought to have employed spiritual rituals on their farms were men. I am yet to come across any female who has done this. The fact is that no one wants to come out publicly as having engaged spiritual forces to improve their farm yields. The relationship between development and witchcraft will be explored extensively in chapter 4, and thus the employment of witchcraft, and spirituality for fortunes will be examined. The purpose of noting it here is to give an insight into how witchcraft is thought to be reflected and practiced in different forms in Ghana or elsewhere in Africa. The next section will discuss different strategies that are adopted by experts to determine who a witch is. The section delves into expert approaches to assessing witchcraft accusations.

STRATEGIES: EXPERT APPROACHES TO VALIDATING WITCHCRAFT ACCUSATION

This section deals with the strategies that local experts adopt for the assessment and purification of people accused of witchcraft. Witchcraft accusations are framed as fact by the accusing parties. However, they are usually contested by the accused until there is substantiation of the claim by local experts who have the "power" and "expertise" to do so (see Goody, 1970; Green and Mesaki 2005 [Tanzania]; Igwe, 2016b; Mutaru, 2019; Riedel, 2017; Smith, 2005 [Kenya]). But, as was explained by Materi, *Uwadaan* of Gnani, not every accuser wants the verification to be done. Some accusers prefer the person accused of witchcraft simply leave the community. I argue that the manifestations of an accusation without any form of assessment by experts may pose danger to cohabitation in the community. It exposes people, who are often already vulnerable, to the whims and caprices of those who feel there is something unusual about their lives, something that can only be categorized as an act of witchcraft.

The thirty-eight people accused of witchcraft and interviewed for this study were all assessed and went through purification rituals. The methods of assessing a cause of a death discussed below include mounting the dead, consulting *Ubɔa*, gaining assessment from a Gnani shrine, or calling in a witch doctor. Below I give a detailed account of each.

The Mounting of the Dead

Regarding the mounting of the dead body, participants indicated that any-time there is a death, the family of the dead person may decide to mount the corpse by placing it on a wooden frame designed for such a purpose and usu-ally involves two relatives of the deceased carrying the wooden structure on which the dead person is laid. Not every dead person is mounted, and the pre-rogative of mounting depends on the family. If they decide to do so, the head of every household comes to invoke the spirit of the dead person as they are mounted. The family heads come in turns, starting with the eldest of the com-munity. Each family head will invoke the dead person's spirit by name with the following words as an example, as recounted by one of the participants:

> Uja. Naja, you are one of our sons in this community. We have lived and worked together as members of the same family until your untimely passing away. We do believe that your death is unnatural and might be caused by witches. If I or any member of my family is responsible for your death, this is the hall, go and show us (point their hands towards the hall they are standing in front of).

The invocation of the spirit of the dead person (corpse) through carrying was also briefly touched by Esther Goody among the Gonja in northern Ghana. She asserted

> In pre-European times the divisional chief had the power of disposal over the witch in serious cases, that is, where the woman had been accused by the victim either before he died, or during the carrying of the "corpse," that is, after his

death. Indeed, it appears that the victim's accusations were usually tested and ratified by the subsequent carrying of the "corpse." (Goody, 1970, p. 213)

Similar to the Gonja as Goody describes above, I also found that carrying the corpse is a practice among the *Bikpapkaam* or *Mossi* as found by Barbier (2020). However, unlike the Gonja, *Bikpakpaam* still practice it today. It is meant to invoke the spirit of the dead person to identify his or her killers. Thus, if the person addressing the dead person is found not guilty, an opportunity is given to other people in the community to address the corpse in order of seniority terms. In a case where a member of an addressed family is accused of having bewitched the dead person, the opportunity to address the dead person is vital for clearing their name, but often the process continues until the supposed witch is found. Women do not invoke the spirit of the dead person. It is their male family head who does so on the behalf of any female accused. However, a woman can put forward a defense if she thinks she is innocent of the accusation. Moreover, it was argued by some members of the community that witches can camouflage themselves in the skins of others during such operations. In the critical moment of verification, the innocent person whose skin masked the "real" witch will be accused and confirmed as a witch. The "real" witch will be innocent in this case.

Understanding of the mounting of the dead ritual has come about through the stories and accounts of others, and I did not personally observe such ceremonies within the span of the research period in Gnani. This might also be because this approach is employed by relatives in secret. That is, it is considered a strictly family affair and was therefore conducted when strangers or people who were not part of their kin were present. To support this observation, while I was staying in the community there were people who died.

There have been some contests among community members regarding this approach. They often accuse the carriers and not the dead person as biased and of having undue influence in pointing out the supposed witch, which as carriers is their primary role. This foreknowledge of animosity toward another in the community might be a reason for the carriers of the dead person to point out one as the bewitcher of the dead person. Nonetheless, others have refuted the potential bias of the carriers and instead emphasize that the dead person oversees the moving process and the carriers. I had the opportunity to interact with someone who had previously carried a dead person in the mounting process. This is what he had to say:

I had doubts about mounting the dead process as a way of determining the person responsible for bewitching another person. I always thought it was the carriers of the dead body who intentionally moved to point to one of the people the dead person had issues with as being responsible. However, on this fateful day, a woman in her mid-thirties died. She was too young to die as advanced by her relatives and hence someone (a witch) must be responsible. We, therefore, had to conduct the mounting ceremony. I volunteered to carry the dead body in the company of another young man. The head of the household from which the dead woman came was the first to address her. She stood still/otherwise we stood still. The second elderly in the community came into the address, and we stood still again. The next elder stepped out to address the dead woman. Before I could realize, my feet had moved. So was the other person. I must be honest, I lost control of my movements. It was controlled by a force other than me. The dead woman moved us and hit the hall three times. This confirmed that the one addressing the dead woman had bewitched her. It was clear. Everyone left the scene. Most people were angry, and bitter and had shown signs of withdrawal from the relationship with the man who had been confirmed as being responsible for her death.

The local community members believe in mounting the dead as a way of identifying people who had bewitched them. One of the persons who took part in carrying the dead person in the above scenario told me that the process is effective and transparent and has been used for decades in the community.

The Ubɔa (Diviner/soothsayer) Approach

Another popular way to determine the cause of death in northern Ghana is to consult an *Ubɔa*, as in the cases of Pigri and Waja discussed above. This approach can be private or public. *Bibɔab* perform a key role in finding fault in society and advising on how to mend the broken relationships that come with witchcraft accusations. The *Ubɔa* was used to determine the causes of death in the first and third case studies earlier in this chapter. Participants in this study also highlighted the role of the *Ubɔa* in witchcraft accusations.

So, most of them will go to *Ubɔa* or a diviner to find out what is the cause of this. So, the diviners or the Bibɔab have the authority to decide that this is what has killed the person. It's a witch or it's normal or it's out of something. Most of the time, these are the people who can look and just say this person has been killed by a witch. Sometimes they are even able to tell who. Sometimes to be on a safer side, they put it in a bracket. They don't make it so clear. But now the family members or neighbours go ahead to point accusing fingers at certain people they feel have bewitched these people or have caused those misfortunes or have brought those hardships. So, it's either the *Ubɔa* can say directly, or he gives some characteristics that the people are able to see and say that oh no it must be this person. So once that is done then everybody gets to know that it is this person who killed that person.

Uteenbɔa (Public Consultation Approach)

In the second and third case studies, Bibɔab were consulted publicly to assess the cause of the death of Pigri and Waja. However, their verdict aroused different debates. While some people agreed that the people they named witches were responsible, others disagreed. This is where the politics become obvious and seeking further assessment by Uwadaan of the Gnani witch camp community became necessary.

After the soothsaying ceremony for Pigri, people offered different interpretations. Some contended that it was not the parents who had bewitched her, but rather a witch in the community of the marital home. Some had also accused the *Ubɔa* of being told what to say. They were aware of tensions between the woman's parents and the husband, and it provided a suitable narrative. This was a story that everyone who knew about the relationship would believe. In the case of Waja, people were hoping to hear the Bibɔab talk of a particular man who had been known to have a bad relationship with Waja. This expectation was that even before his death, he had complained to people about how the accused person worried him with witchcraft. Ultimately, the bibɔab decided that it was one of the wives and her children who were the guilty parties. Insider arguments also raised some issues that matter here. Most often, there were frequent quarrels and fighting in the man's home. These often occurred between step-siblings, co-wives, and between the man and his children or husband and wives. The wives each accused the other of being responsible for their inability to progress in life. Those cases expanded after the man's death. In fact, before the soothsaying ceremony, a relative of the man had chronicled to us why the man died.

People who were fed information before it was repeated by the *Ubɔa* doubted the authenticity of his spiritual assessment. The accused wife, for instance, contended that the *Ubɔa* was told who to blame. She was not on good terms with the person who had consulted the *Ubɔa* and in fact was another suspect due to his poor relationship with the dead man. She argued that to deflect the blame from himself, he found a way to relay the in-fighting at home to the *Ubɔa* and influence his assessment. It also appears that the man had better ties with the co-wife than the one who was accused.

The Private Consultation Approach

People in the north also consult *Ubɔa* privately to determine who could be harming them or intending to harm them. Individual consultations with *Ubɔa* differ from public consultations. First, the consultation takes place at the home of the *Ubɔa*. Second, it takes place at dawn. And finally, it is conducted with one individual at a time. However, the *Ubɔa* who conduct public consultations also offer private consultations. *Bibɔab* are special people in society who are believed to possess the gift of being able to see into the spiritual realm. They can see into the lives and endeavors of all others except themselves.

Among the *Bikpakpaam* ethnic group, it is believed that every individual is born with a spiritual gift. People are classified according to their spiritual gifts at birth. After the birth of any child, the father consults spiritual seers to reveal the spiritual affiliation of the child. The spiritual affiliations include *Ubɔa*, *Kijaaŋ* (either twins, triplets, or individuals who even though they are single at birth are believed to have spiritual powers as twins) and *Biponib* (dwarf spirits). An individual cannot be affiliated with *Ubɔa* and *Kijaaŋ* spirits at the same time. During my interaction with the study population, I found that a few people were born without any spiritual affiliations. This issue arises during verification at birth. Upon determination of a person's spiritual affiliation, specific rituals are performed before the person can achieve spiritual stability. Some participants told me that if these rituals are not performed, the person is unlikely to prosper and likely to have psychological issues. People who are not successful in their economic activities—mainly farming and petty trading—are inclined to search for the cause of their problems. The outcomes of such searches usually point to the activities of witches or that they are affiliated to a spiritual sect for which they have not gone through the correct rituals. The spiritual sect they belong to could punish them through continued failure. Through divination, people come to realize what causes their failures and appropriate rituals can be performed to remedy this situation.

The Verification of Witches at Communities of Refuge in Ghana

On the surface, just as in formal state courts in Ghana, witchcraft trials conducted by spiritual experts follow well-established and reinforced codes of procedure. The experts in these trials are required to consider both sides before performing the assessment ritual. They also operate within a hierarchical system. For example, an *Ubɔa* can validate an accusation and pronounce the accused as guilty, but this decision can be appealed and referred to the Biwadam of the witch camp. Their verdict is final and not open to appeal. The crucial point however is that the assessment and adjudication by the expert has a fundamental impact on the future of the accused. That is, the power resides with the expert to dismiss or confirm an accusation that cannot be resolved in other ways.

Another important thing emerging from the trial by Uwadaan is that the people accused of witchcraft are expected to go back home after the trial.

He does not force people to stay in the camp regardless of their status as witches. We saw this in the case of the women from Tamale, who did not stay in the community. However, it is uncertain whether community members would allow the woman to stay in Tamale after she was confirmed as a witch. Considering the animosity in the community toward people accused of witchcraft, it is possible she would return to Gnani or one of the other witch camps. Again, there are some instances that the accusers make it clear that they do not want the accused back in their community regardless of the outcome. The accusers state this even before Uwadaan starts the assessment process. He states "some people just bring their person here, they just tell me, and they don't want any verification. What they want is that the accused should remain here with me. The contrast is that I cannot keep anyone in this community if they do not go through the process." The Uwadaan must take everyone through the assessment ritual, whether they choose to stay or leave is another concern. However, when I posed the question to many of the residents of the Gnani community whether they would choose to go home if the opportunity presented itself, they would usually give responses that are similar to the one below.

> Aaah to do what again? The reasons they accused me are still prevalent. People still die, diseases affect people and people dream. If I go back, I would be re-accused. I prefer to stay and die here.

A community of refuge serves three basic purposes in Northern Ghana. First, it is a place of refuge for ostracized people accused of witchcraft. Second, it is a place for the assessment and purification of people accused of witchcraft. And finally, it is a place where people go to search for spiritual protection and fortification against witches or evil persons. It is this community that has been captured by development actors as "witch camps." The structure called the "witch camp" is different from the shrine itself. In many of the communities, these settlements called "camps" have been established in close proximity to the anti-witchcraft shrine. The shrine is known for the spiritual aspect of things. This resonates with the findings of Redmayne in East Africa (Nyasaland), where Chinkanga had gained an international reputation for his ability to identify and cleanse people of witchcraft spirits, treat people who had been bewitched, and fortify the people who had come to see him (Willis, 1970). Willis (1970) found a similar situation in some parts of Africa, where he asserted that the common characteristics of witchcraft cults can be described in the following ways:

> Use of relatively simple ritual procedure intended to detect witches and neutralize them, at the same time giving protection against mystical attack to

supposedly innocent; lack of a formal organizational structure, though there may be nominal recognition of a remote, semi-mythical founderhead; hanging-on of cult secrets and ritual from initiate to acolyte as cult spreads; ability to cross ethnic boundaries, at the same time adapting ritual and ideology to the traditional ideas and institutions of each ethnic group. (129–30)

This approach has been documented in several other African countries such as Tanzania as detailed by Maia Green and Simeone Mesaki (2005) as well as Jane Parish (2003) captured the role of shrine priests in witchcraft assessments in southern Ghana. With regard to northern Ghana, several others have made mention of the role of Uwadaan in assessing and adjudicating witchcraft accusations, though weighted differently. Here, I return to the studies of Wumbla (2017), and ActionAid (2008a) although they do not consider hearing and adjudication by Biwadam as "proper" and hence their provocative and sensational prefaces to their papers. Others such as Musah (2013), Mutaru (2019), as well as Naboo (2017), just to mention a few, make reference to the witch camp assessment as a crucial part of witchcraft discussions in northern Ghana.

Unyɔkdaan Approach

The occurrence of deaths considered unusual in a community demands that action be taken to prevent future deaths. In such instances, a witchdoctor (Unyɔkdaan) is brought into the community to identify, pacify, and purify the community from the spiritual filth that has bedeviled it. Participants in this study spoke of the belief that physical beings are limited in their ability to conceptualize the spiritual dimensions of death. As a result, witchdoctors are needed to conceptualize on their behalf. An elderly participant explained to me the processes involved in bringing a witchdoctor into a community:

When there are frequent deaths that involve a lot of young people, the whole community gets alarmed. Close relatives of the deceased make a proposal to the towns' people to consider calling in a witchdoctor for general cleansing and finding those deaths. Basically, it is believed that those deaths are not usual and either something spiritual has gone wrong or there is increased bewitchment in the community. The call-in of witches is by clans. The head of the clans calls a general meeting. At the meeting, people are tasked to propose powerful witch doctors they are aware of or have heard of. Names are proposed, and they agree to go for whoever they think is most powerful. A delegation is sent to see him and tell him their intentions.

The witchdoctor is a powerful juju man. Some people believe that the witch doctor himself is a powerful witch. His spiritual powers enable him to see into the spiritual realm and diagnose the spiritual issues within a community. The witch doctor's arrival demands that the entire community gathers for such a diagnosis. This approach was utilized by the government of Benin as captured by Kahn. Kahn noted that in the quest of the government of Benin to build a modern state, it sought to sanitize the country of witchcraft (2011). Similarly, Smith found that in Kenya, the local people also employed the services of a witch doctor to sanitize them of witchcraft, to which the state was equally implicated as state institutions such as schools also relied on the services of witch doctors (Smith, 2005).

CONCLUSION

This chapter focused on local management of witchcraft accusations, assessments, and purifications. In order to do this, I divided the chapter into three parts. In part 1, I presented three cases of witchcraft accusations, detailing the assessment processes in each case. The cases are then used as a basis for analysis and discussion in the other two sections. Section 2 examined factors that lead to witchcraft accusations. These included deaths, illnesses, dreams, and the success/failure paradox. The last section delved into "experts'" knowledge and strategies of witchcraft assessment. This section outlined different experts and the methods they used to assess witchcraft accusations. There is evidence judging from the chapter that people across African countries rely on local epistemology to manage witchcraft accusations. This is despite the fact that there are state institutions where such issues could be assessed, but rarely do people make use of them. There have even been instances where the state as a whole makes use of the services of local knowledge to handle witchcraft, such as was reported by Kahn in Benin, and Smith in Kenya. The next chapter engages with the fate of a person who has undergone the assessment rituals. The chapter will examine the experiences and resilience strategies of people accused of witchcraft.

Chapter 2

After Judgment

Experiences of Navigating Life in Communities of Refuge

In this chapter, I explore how people who have sought refuge speak about themselves and their circumstances after their judgment using the Gnani-Tindang community as a case. I assert that discord exists between the over-concentration of such communities by development actors that is primarily focused on closing such communities. The debates on the closure of "witch camps" will be explored further in chapter 4. Though intervening in such communities is essential to highlight, the broader debates are fixated on the existence of, or lack o,f witchcraft. This leads to a conversation that communities of refuge should be closed with those seeking refuge returning home. In this chapter, I depart from conventional scholarship as the above and make the real experiences of persons accused of witchcraft at the various stages as a way of highlighting their voices in these debates.

In this chapter, I make three main theoretical contributions. First, I underscore individual experiences and call on scholars and development practitioners to recalibrate their attention to highlighting individual experiences and local epistemologies (see Pieterse, 2001; Rahnema and Bawtree, 1997; Matthews, 2004; Escobar, 1995, 1999). Paying attention to individual experiences and local epistemologies, especially in dealing with witchcraft accusations, is a holistic approach to theorizing, planning, and implementing interventions. Second, I assert that though attention has been focused on communities of refuge as an ultimate place of development intervention, it would be useful to analyze and view such communities as the final manifestation of the problematic nature of witchcraft accusations (Ritchter, Flowers, and Bongmba, 2017) and early development interventions would have the potential to prevent or reduce accusation and banishment in the first place. This also adds to an emerging scholarship that has become critical of development interventions in communities of refuge. For example, Riedel (2017) has challenged NGOs (nongovernmental organizations') "presence" and "effectiveness" and the government of Ghana's "witch camps" interventions. He has argued that media attention is more propaganda than real actions in such communities. And thirdly, drawing on the cases presented, I highlight witchcraft as a gendered phenomenon, a point that builds on several scholars in the region and discusses it with broader scholarship on the same subject matter.

ANTHROPOLOGICAL THEORIZING OF
WITCHCRAFT IN AFRICA AND GHANA

In endeavoring to present this chapter, it is also important to contextualize how other scholars have explored Ghanaian society and witchcraft. From a broad perspective, there are similarities between Ghana and many other sites across Africa in terms of the prevalence and increase of witchcraft, the connections to the past, the colonial and post-colonial experiences, and its articulations within modernity, as I highlighted in chapter 1. Further, some aspects are considered more unique to Ghana, especially in relation to the strategy in Ghana where some communities offer refuge to people who have been banished based on witchcraft accusations as a local development intervention. Indeed, as part of endeavors to account for the increasing prevalence of witchcraft in the case of Ghana, many scholars highlight the particular intertwining of spirituality and personal and economic advancement (such as "traditional" spirituality, conversion to Christianity, the increase and globalization of Ghanaian anti-witchcraft practices). Overall, what is clear to most scholars is that witchcraft beliefs and practices are deeply embedded in Ghanaian society.

The view that witchcraft beliefs and practices are deeply embedded in Ghanaian society is supported by the emphasis placed on witchcraft in what are now considered classic anthropological studies and ethnographies of various linguistic, religious, and ethnic groups across Ghana (see, for example, Gray, 2001). As Crampton notes in relation to the anthropology of Ghana,

> Ghana has hosted some of the discipline's most famous scholars, such as Jack Goody (1967, 1962) and Meyer Fortes (1945, 1940). This is in part because witchcraft is part of spiritual beliefs and practices that permeate much of daily life in Ghana within a multicultural region of many ethnic groups and multiple languages. (Crampton, 2013, p. 201)

Even in more recent scholarship that focuses on the intersections between modernity, development, and witchcraft, the legacies of previous scholars such as that of Fortes and his study of the Ashanti around the issue of the increasing presence of witchcraft and anti-witchcraft shrines is notable. For instance, though many recent scholars focus on modernity or contemporary societies, they often further what had previously been observed by several scholars. In particular, Fortes and Mayer (1969), (Fortes, 2017 [1969]), and Fortes (1948) noted that amid the social, economic, and political turmoil and the struggle for political power prior to the end of colonization among the Ashanti, there was an apparent rise of "new witch-finding cults."

Likewise, Ward affirms Fortes's assertion of the increase in witchcraft and new cults by quoting conversations with both young and elderly Ashanti who declared that "there never used to be so many witches in the good old days" (Ward, 1956, p. 47). Moreover, Ward argues that in the case of the Ashanti, increased European contact, rapid economic advances and political change, education, and the spread of Christianity "had been accompanied not simply by the persistence of witchcraft beliefs but by their very considerable increase, and by the emergence of new cults designed to deal with them" (ibid.).

Such observations of the increase of witchcraft and the emergence of new cults designed to deal with the changes, as Ward phrases, typically draw on functional analysis. Prominent in many twentieth-century ethnographies, there was an endeavor to account for the extent that witchcraft is embedded in social life and a mode of navigating ruptures in society. According to Wyllie, who studied the Efutu of Southern Ghana,

> at the heart of modern social anthropological theory relating to witchcraft is a form of structural-functional analysis which focuses upon witchcraft accusations and treats these as indices of social tension and vehicles of social change. (Wyllie, 1973, p. 74)

This is not an inaccurate depiction of contemporary witchcraft in Ghana and many parts of Africa, given that there is a notable increase in witchcraft beliefs and practices also noted by scholars today of contemporary societies such as Ghana that suggest it is a *reaction* to change. But it can equally be argued, such as in this chapter, that witchcraft is a mode of *enfolding* new experiences and contexts within local epistemologies, indicative often of new economies and innovative ways of incorporating change within the known and understood cosmic order. In some studies, the economy *of* witchcraft (occult economy as termed by Comaroff and Comaroff, 1999a, 1999b; Geschiere, 1997; Mabefam, 2022) is noted just as much as witchcraft being a reaction *to* capitalism, modernity, or development. A detailed discussion is contained in chapter 3.

In Ghana, the strong beliefs in witchcraft can be explained from the perspective of socialization processes. Like many other issues, Adinkrah (2015) observed that the ideation of witchcraft in Ghana is acquired at the formative stages of life and has a long-lasting impact on an individual. He notes that when children acquire ideas in their formative years, it becomes difficult to eradicate them, especially when the ideas are continuously reinforced by various modes of socialization, such as the family, peers, the media, the school curriculum, religious organizations, music, and local movie narratives (Adinkrah, 2015). This socialization process suggests that witchcraft is indeed perceived and experienced as a normal part of the everyday.

Like elsewhere, in northern Ghana witchcraft is equally pronounced. However, although both men and women can be accused of possessing and practicing witchcraft, it is predominantly women who are forced out of their communities, making the case a gendered phenomenon, a point that has been made by many other scholars in the region. In the five communities that offer refuge across northern Ghana, the only one to house some male residents as accused is the Gnani-Tindang (ActionAid, 2008a, 2012, 2014; Baba, 2013). Nonetheless, it has been particularly argued in the case of communities of refuge in Ghana that the accused are female and victims of male dominance (see Akurugu, 2019). And, in the debates relating to the closure of communities of refuge for instance, it is often argued that there is an endorsement of gender-based violence against women by allowing communities of refuge to be established and to continue to exist (Badoe, 2005; Federici, 2008; Palmer, 2010).

I argue that accusations and banishment highlight the tensions between *de jure* cultural norms and values and the *de facto* realities of prejudices, and discrimination in relation to age, gender, and poverty/wealth. Such factors shape development interventions and have received attention from NGOs, government departments, and humanitarian organizations. However, the issues continue to persist, casting doubts on the effectiveness of such interventions.

THE BEGINNING OF THE JOURNEY: INDIVIDUAL ACCOUNTS OF THEIR BANISHMENT FROM COMMUNITY

While there are similarities between Ghana and many other sites across Africa—in terms of the prevalence and increase of witchcraft, the connections to the past, the colonial and post-colonial experiences, and its articulations within modernity—some aspects are more unique to Ghana. One difference to elsewhere is the refuge offered by particular communities to people who have been banished based on witchcraft accusations. I now turn to an ethnographic examination of individual experiences of accusation and banishment. This section of the chapter provides individuals' accounts of their journeys as they are gossiped about, accused, confronted, and removed from their communities. All the individual cases presented differ from accusation to banishment, and how individuals navigated their lives in the Gnani-Tindang community is equally different.

Gossips/Rumors and Confrontation:
The Case of Upinyaan

Amid the usual merriment of preparations for New Year's Eve festivities in Gnani-Tindang, a lone woman named Upinyaan sat on a stool in front of her house with a child who appeared to be around ten years old. Upinyaan was one of the many people accused of witchcraft and banished from her original community. Upinyaan, who seemed to be in her late fifties or even older, looked somehow lost and despondent, and her child was no different. An active member of her local church, this woman's behavior seemed particularly strange. On greeting her and enquiring about her mood, she told me what had led to her feeling of fear and panic about what was to become of her and her child. She said that some members of her clan had expressed unhappiness about her being in Gnani-Tindang with an argument that members of their clan have never been known to relocate to a community based on witchcraft accusations. In short, there was reputational damage to the clan, and the clansmen tried to compel her to leave. However, where was Upinyaan to go? The clansmen were not proposing to offer her a place to live; it was simply that she should not be there because it negatively impacted on their reputation.

Upinyaan was accused of witchcraft and banished from her community by her father-in-law. Since her banishment, she has resided in Gnani-Tindang with two of her daughters and a son living in one room. No further communication had occurred between her and her immediate family. She narrated that she was accused because her two male children had died. Since the death of her first son, rumors emerged that she was a witch and had killed her children through witchcraft. At the time of her accusation, she had just given birth to a boy, and her father-in-law wanted her to live in Gnani-Tindang, where the powers of the shrine could prevent her from bewitching the child. Despite both her husband and her contesting the accusation, the father-in-law not only insisted but was also ready to forcibly evict her, saying that he could not live in the same house with a witch. Weighing the options, especially threats of potential violence and social ridicule, she left the community with her children with the promise of her husband coming to visit. However, tied to eventual inheritance, the husband remained with his belligerent father. In this case, as in others, kinship played a significant role in shaping the outcome of accusations and women's post-accusation lives.

Upinyaan told me that when she was still living with her father-in-law, the threat of violence grew, and each day, she lived in fear. She did not wait to be forcefully or violently driven out of her community but instead packed up a few things and walked for about an hour before boarding the car heading toward the Gnani-Tindang community on a market day. Market days are the only days that some areas like hers can have car transport. She said she had to leave at dawn because she could not stand the embarrassment of people waking up to see her leave. Word had gone around through gossip that she was a witch who killed her sons. She wondered at the point of leaving what life would mean for her. Initially, she took only her son with her to Gnani-Tindang. It was only later that two of her daughters joined her.

Since moving to Gnani-Tindang, Upinyaan narrated that life had not been easy. She did not take anything with her except a few cooking utensils and clothes. She is entirely responsible for taking care of her children, yet she is not engaged in any activity that can earn her money like she used to. At the time, she had just built two more rooms to accommodate their needs in the Gnani-Tindang, from minimal savings from her peasant farming. However, following a ruling from the Tindana/Utindaan who also doubles as shrine priests of Gnani-Tindang, she was not allowed to roof it with sheets.

Upinyaan reminisced about life before her accusation and wondered why anyone would accuse her of bewitching her sons. She said she carried her sons for nine months in her womb, suffered a lot during those pregnancies, and still cannot understand why anyone would think she bewitched them. As she narrated, her only support system while living in Gnani-Tindang is her daughters, the church, and occasional assistance from NGOs.

Upinyaan reported that she was a farmer and a housewife in Jounayili, her matrimonial village. She has not had any form of formal education. She is a Christian and an active member of the Gnani-Tindang chapter of the Christian Mothers Association of Ghana. She has been married for the past thirty years at the time of my study and only separated from her husband following the witchcraft accusation.

Accusations and Confrontation:
The Case of Jilma

It was my third day in the Gnani-Tindang community. Among the many people I interacted with, I highlight Jilma here to demonstrate an instance of confrontation. Upon greeting Jilma in her residence, she gave me a stool. She sat on a mat just in front of her room. Jilma recounted what had brought her to Gnani-Tindang and her experiences.

Jilma was about eighty years old and from Dipa. She has been in Gnani-Tindang for two years. She has never been to school and was a housewife and peasant farmer. Her husband passed away a decade before I met her. She then lived with her eldest son until she was accused of witchcraft. One of her brothers-in-law said that his son had gone to labor on his farm. The son set a fire, placed a yam piece, and went back to continue farming. When he went to turn the yam, he noted that it was already turned and yet he was on the farm alone. So, he came home and told his father. Jilma said the brother-in-law claimed that after an inquest into who turned the yam on fire, it came out that Jilma did it through witchcraft. The brother-in-law confronted her, but she said she did not know anything about it.

The boy died a few months later, and Jilma was summoned to the chief's palace and questioned, but she maintained her innocence. It was agreed at the chief's palace that she should be sent to Gnani-Tindang for witchcraft testing. Before leaving for Gnani-Tindang, Jilma's son worried that he would have issues with his brother-in-law if his mother were declared innocent after the testing. Upon conclusion of the testing process, there were contradictory narratives of the outcome. While Jilma indicated she was declared innocent, her brother-in-law who had gone with her said otherwise. She recounted,

> When we got home, he told the community that I was confirmed as a witch. After that, the youth in the village started insulting, backbiting, and shaming me. My son, who was the assemblyman (local or village representative of the decentralised political system) of the community, did not take it kindly with the youth. My son was preparing to visit another village when the youth threatened to kill him. By the time he entered his room to dress up for the journey, the youth had obilized themselves and surrounded him. They said they wanted to kill my son before killing me too. This was because he was very protective of me. "How can someone be in his house, and you surround the house to kill him? Will anyone in their right senses allow himself to be killed under such a circumstance?" My son thought it was a joke. But before he could realise it, they wanted to kill him. One came with a cutlass and the other with a pestle. At that time, my son took his gun and started shooting at them. He killed two of the young men and wounded the third one. My marital village was not safe for me, the reason I returned to Gnani-Tindang.

Jilma disclosed that the community got furious after the incident, destroyed all her son's property, and burned his yam harvest. Her son's wife fled the community with her children to her parents after being threatened.

> Knowing what had happened, I eavesdropped on a conversation that the youth would kill me at night. I did not doubt it because people were really angry. I fled to Gnani-Tindang to save my life. I waited, and at night when everyone was asleep, I left the community without knowledge of anyone. I walked for a long way before dawn. I reached Makayili and boarded a car from there to Yendi

and subsequently to Gnani-Tindang. I told Uwadaan that I needed to stay here to save my life. Uwadaan accepted but said I needed to drink the shrine water first—this is the purification ritual that every person accused of witchcraft goes through before they are allowed to stay. I did and stayed.

Jilma currently lives in Gnani-Tindang with another woman accused of witchcraft. Jilma shared her experience of living in Gnani-Tindang with me. She said it was challenging for her, and she wished she could go back home. But the shame, fear, and threat of violence were also lingering in her mind. Her son was in prison, and she felt she had lost everything due to the witchcraft accusation. She was old and could not do much for herself, and there was no one to help her. She said to me;

> Look at me; I'm old and weak now. I can't do much for myself. But I must fetch water, firewood and beg for food to eat. It is lonely here. I don't have anyone to chat with except this other woman I live with.

She only casually mentioned that *Tindana/Utindaan* supported her sometimes, but she did not receive any help from any other person. She had to beg for food from some of her peers who were also accused of witchcraft and much stronger and also seeking refuge in Gnani-Tindang. As a testament, while still interacting with her, another woman brought a bowl full of guinea corn to give to her. The woman greeted her and said, "I have brought food for you. You told me you didn't have anything again. In the meantime, you can have this part of what was given to me by another resident of Gnani-Tindang."

Banishment and Relocation:
The Case of Tiya

Tiya was a widow who was about eighty years old. She was originally from Krachi in the Volta region of Ghana. Prior to her accusation, she was a peasant farmer in her community. She spent the past twenty-five years in Gnani-Tindang. She did not have a carer. She currently lives in a roundhouse alone in Gnani-Tindang. Before being accused of witchcraft Tiya had a normal social life. She had children, was happily married, and engaged in social and economic activities.

Tiya described life in Gnani-Tindang as challenging because she had no one to help her. She was weak and blind due to her age. The lack of support was concerning. She had this to say when I asked her about her life in Gnani-Tindang:

> My issues are too much to be discussed. I don't have anyone to support me. If I need water, I must beg people at the borehole fetching water to fetch some for

me. If I don't get anyone merciful enough to do so, I try to do so by myself. But imagine me, I'm blind totally, sick, and old. It is tough for me.

I reproduce below a conversation we had.

Interviewer: What led to you being accused of witchcraft?

Tiya: After the death of my husband, the relatives accused me of witchcraft. My in-laws said I killed my husband, but I don't know anything about it. He fell sick and died afterwards. How can I kill my husband?

Interviewer: What happened after they accused you of bewitching your husband?

Tiya: I was lucky I wasn't killed. There were lots of chaos, and some of the people suggested that I should be killed. Others disagreed and suggested that I should be brought to Gnani-Tindang for testing. It's my husband's people who brought me here. They are no more in Krachi. They migrated to another place. I don't even know where it is.

Interviewer: Will you go home if your brother's children come for you?

Tiya: Where will I live? I have no one to care for me! I won't get a house to live in if I go. The elder whom I was living with is no more; he died, and his children are dispersed. If I am here, I like it, but the only problem is that I can't see again. I am just sitting like that. I can't fetch water; I can't do anything. It is my God who will touch someone's heart to give me a token, and I will use it to buy flour to cook. I was rearing fowls, but thieves stole everything. In Gnani-Tindang here, that is what others who can see rear to take care of themselves. I woke up one day, and all my fowls were gone.

Tiya: I'm in pain. I am suffering too much as I sit here. At least if I had someone to fetch water and cook for me to eat, it would have been better. If I manage to cook, and want to dish the food into a bowl, sometimes I put it on the ground because I can't see. Is it good for me to live this way? It is only people who are merciful who will bring me some vegetables from their farms. The Uwadaan of the Gnani and his family have been good to me. If they go to the farm, they bring me some vegetables and some even cook the soup and serve it to me. Also, my room has been leaking. It was last year that my son gave money for them to buy some thatch to roof it.

Interviewer: Are there some people apart from those you have mentioned that also support you?

Tiya: I have been told some ukalnja (government) people come here to support, but they only support the lucky ones. Not all of us. It was last year that someone like you came here and gave me something. I don't know whether he was a government worker or not.

WHAT DO WE MAKE OF THE ABOVE THREE CASES?
AN ANALYSIS OF ETHNOGRAPHIC CASES

First, let's start with Upinyaan. In analyzing this case, my attention is focused on the first stage of witchcraft accusation-*gossip/rumors*. At this stage, there is suspicion that someone might be a witch among community members through the grapevine, which quickly spreads. This is often spurred by many factors such as death or sickness befalling another member of the community, dreams, or being extremely poor or rich (as was captured in chapter 1). While the rumors are ongoing about the individual as a witch, such an individual may have no idea about it or eavesdrop on such conversations. Still, no action is made at this point to confront them. Also, at this stage, those making the accusation gather evidence that can be used to make a case against the suspected witch when they are confronted. These include spiritual consultation with local experts discussed in chapter 1 to validate or invalidate their gossip.

In the case of Upinyaan, being identified as a witch started as a rumor triggered by her sons' deaths. The accusation leveled at her was gendered. The death of two male children, in a patriarchal society, was seen as suspicious, when the girl children lived. For Upinyaan, the emotional trauma of losing her two sons was followed by rumors, confrontation, and an eventual rejection from her community. This was devastating for her. She does not even have enough time to grieve the death of her sons before rumors emerged that she was the witch. Not everyone gossiped about as a witch is confronted: rich, young males and/or those in positions of power in society are less likely to be confronted as compared to poor, elderly women. Her husband was neither accused nor banished from the community, although the children belong to both. Therefore, there is a need to highlight the important role of gender in witchcraft accusations.

Second, in analyzing Jilma's case, at this stage, the individual suspected of being a witch is confronted, and the accusation is made publicly. There are several ways by which this could be made known to the person accused of witchcraft. First, they are often invited to family, clan, or community meetings where such accusations are communicated. One of the main challenges of being accused of witchcraft is violence or the threat of it. Violence is commonly perpetrated against people accused of witchcraft, especially at the point of confrontation. The world can be cruel to a "witch," and where the state is not present, the recourse to protection is also absent. This brings forth a form of violence and conflict that exposes the witch to a harmful lifestyle, abuse, discrimination, or even death (ActionAid, 2008b; Baba, 2013; Igwe, 2016a). The journey to the Gnani-Tindang community is not a smooth removal of people accused of witchcraft but a painful transition that exposes the accused witch to different cruel treatments. Before the eviction, some of the people accused of witchcraft said they were beaten, insulted, and shamed in front of the public. For example, the case of Jilma led to violence and gun use, leading to the killing of two young men. Jilma's son had been charged with murder and was in jail for illegal gun use and murder. The community has vowed never to have Jilma and her son back. Jilma narrated to me that she only narrowly escaped the anger of the community to resettle in Gnani-Tindang, which has offered her refuge.

The threat of violence, or violence itself, is always present in witchcraft accusations. In addition to Jilma's narrative, other people accused of witchcraft recounted how their lives were threatened emotionally, physically, and psychologically. The following views espoused by some people accused of witchcraft in Gnani-Tindang capture the plight and the potential threat of violence they experienced before relocating to Gnani-Tindang.

> They finally threatened that they were going to do their juju, and if I had any knowledge about the child's sickness, I was going to die within four days. I told them they should go ahead; I was willing to die if I were the one responsible for the child's sickness. After the ritual, I didn't die. However, they said I could no longer stay with them in the community.

The above quotation sums up the emotional, psychological, and physical violence that people accused of witchcraft go through. In the first case, the woman was threatened and forced to go through a ritual she claims she knew nothing about. The reality of the life of an accused witch in northern Ghana is, therefore, a sad one. For example, people accused of witchcraft may be gruesomely murdered by angry mobs (Comaroff and Comaroff, 1999a; Mavhungu, 2012). Others may have their powers exercised by Christian pastors, Islamic imams, or fetish/shrine priests through shameful practices. While the acts of mob injustice usually take place within the community or its peripherals, exorcism as a way of neutralizing a witch's powers can take place either in the same community or at a distance, after which the person is made to return home (see Onyinah, 2002; Parish, 1999, 2003). In short, although the communities like Gnani-Tindang and the like are physical manifestations of witchcraft accusations, they serve as a refuge for evicted persons.

The stage of confrontation also has implications for development theory, policy, and practice. One difficulty is that people act in the collective, and it is thus difficult to determine who the individual culprits are when it comes to witchcraft violence. Mabefam and Appau, (2020, p. 196) assert collectives that on the one hand, the use of *they* here about the youth mob that carry out accusation and eviction reveals the necessary collectivization of individuals that motivates and legitimizes a successful contestation of power. On the other hand, it also reveals the successful de-identification and de-personalization of agency that is intended and results from collective mob actions of usurpation and subversion. Here, *they* is everyone and no one.

Third, Tiya's case gives us an example of the lived experience of eviction/ banishment. When Tiya was accused, confronted, and evicted, there was no place for her except Gnani-Tindang. Some of the people evicted could stay in Gnani-Tindang, where the testing and purification rituals are done. Others are just asked to leave the community without any community to go to, or when they eavesdrop on gossip that they are witches, they flee for safety elsewhere (see Baba, 2013). This becomes difficult for them as gossip quickly spreads that they have been accused of witchcraft. It becomes difficult to settle in new communities other than in Gnani-Tindang and the like in such a circumstance. Another participant who was accused of witchcraft, confronted, and evicted and now residing in Gnani-Tindang recounted,

> I spent several days in the bush, not knowing exactly where I was going. I nearly died of thirst and hunger. I am from Yajool and trekked to Gnani-Tindang. This should not happen to anyone under any circumstances. Can you imagine my family abandoned me after I was accused of witchcraft? Even my wives left for their various homes with their kids after I was accused of witchcraft. I have been driven away from the community.

Where there is a conscious effort by society to remove people accused of witchcraft, it is apparent that their remaining in such societies is dangerous, as it may come with many risks. However, the strategic nature of removing people, their duties, and obligations suddenly deprives them of the special positions they once occupied in society—their sense of belonging to their communities. For instance, the majority become homeless (a lack of community to identify with). The generosity of the Gnani-Tindang community in the first place was meant to host displaced people because of witchcraft accusations (see Bakoe, 2016; Truxler, 2006; Palmer, 2010; Tayo, 2010). In becoming homeless, people accused of witchcraft have no access to resources, rights of belonging, and freedom of association. They begin to wander about, some spending several days or weeks in the bush without knowing how their next day will be spent. They are also stripped of citizenship or a sense of belonging to their original communities and property ownership; for example, Tiya, and others who were accused of witchcraft, never got the opportunity to go back to vote during elections in their community of origin where they were registered, nor access any of the resources of their communities such as their farms or interact with relationships they have built over years. The loss of property affects the livelihood of people accused of witchcraft in the most significant way. With specific reference to land access, Mutaru (2022) described them as morally compromised strangers whose access to resources in the new communities including land is through *sognism* (help). That is, supporting the broader society's members on their farms and in turn are paid either in kind (food) or cash to survive.

The convention is that when people are cleansed of witchcraft, they are free to return to their original communities. However, I noted that many people accused of witchcraft and cleansed prefer to stay in the Gnani-Tindang community. This presents us with the pressing question: why do people accused of witchcraft stay in the Gnani-Tindang community after the cleansing rituals? Local accounts for this are varied. From one perspective, there is a belief that anyone who lives in Gnani-Tindang and has had their witchcraft expelled is protected by their shrine and cannot acquire witchcraft again. That is why many accusers would prefer the accused persons to stay in Gnani-Tindang. The second narrative, mainly from the persons accused of witchcraft, was based on the fact of their safety, and protection from the psychological and social shame that comes with being accused as a witch in their original communities. People accused of witchcraft asserted that they have already acquired a special label that becomes complex and difficult to erase. The acquisition of a new label, often viewed in a pejorative sense, also comes with mistreatment and abuse. That is why they choose to stay.

The above scenario and the varied reasons given as to why people stay in Gnani-Tindang have a real impact on the lives of accused persons in numerous ways. To help us unpack the impact on their lives, I will draw on the theories of "liminality" by Arnold van Gennep (1960), which was later applied in sociocultural anthropology by Victor Turner (1967) and "bare life" by Giorgio Agamben (1998). The theory of liminality is especially relevant here as the individual accused of witchcraft goes through phases of transition, that is, transitioning from their original communities to Gnani-Tindang. Furthermore, the transitioning also extends beyond physical spaces to include the personhood of the individual. That is, from an individual with inalienable rights as a Ghanaian citizen, including the right to movement, belonging, and the ability to participate in the political processes of their communities to being stripped off their citizenship/rights-both *symbolically* and *actually*. In between the various phases of the accused person's lives, they transition from being protected by their community, families, and the state to being abused, violated, and driven away from the community among many others. The individual in this process is caught up in what Turner (1967) termed as "*Betwixt and between*" or "*the liminal stage.*"

An additional layer of all of this is a "bare life" situation to draw from Agamben. Giorgio Agamben, an Italian philosopher conceptualized and popularized the theory of *bare life*. He observed that Western political thought at the time of his writing views life in a very narrow sense, deviating from the original meaning by which ancient Greeks understood it. For the ancient Greeks, life constituted two dimensions: *bios* (the form or way life is lived) and *zoē* (the biological fact of life). He then argues that the lack of distinction between the two limited life to the biological—the *zoē* aspect while neglecting the *bios* aspect. This, therefore, means that there are not any assurances about the quality of life lived, be it political, social, cultural, or economic, so to speak, if attention is not paid to the *bios*. This is so comparable to the lives lived by people accused of witchcraft and evicted from their communities. After being stripped off their citizenship or sense of belonging to their communities, they become "bare," or reach a point of "bare life," their existence only being important on the basis of *zoē*.

Communities such as Gnani-Tindang or Kukuo or Gambaga (Poagnyaankura fongu) are thus crucial points of refuge. Toeing the line of Agamben, though of a different context, I'm seeking a redefinition of communities of refuge as a place of abuse of people's rights to a place of refuge, where the victims of such eviction begin to re-collect, navigate, and build a sense of belonging for themselves after being stripped off by their original communities. Here, the evicted persons' personhood and agencies have been politicized with varied entrenched positions, some of which are ideological and others for practical reasons. Accepting their fate as people ostracized from their societies because of witchcraft accusations, they renegotiate their survival spaces within Gnani-Tindang. This is a challenging task given the loneliness and social exclusion of having lost touch with their kith and kin and other social relations back home (See Mabefam and Appau, 2020).

Except for individual tensions, people accused of witchcraft, prior to their accusations, generally had good relationships with their kin and the community. This is manifested in their participation in communal activities and their interaction with other members of society. They ate, drank, danced, and sang together with other members of society during funerals and other festive occasions. However, the good rapport that existed between the accused and society suddenly disappeared. On this basis, it is important to highlight that when one is accused of witchcraft, confronted, and evicted, one loses his or her right to exist within their communities, a very problematic aspect of local epistemology. This results from a local understanding of the role of witches in society. The immediate reaction of the non-accused toward the accused is withdrawal. Members of the larger society do not want anything to do with the accused. The best friends all withdraw, and parents warn their children not to go near them. People avoid eating or taking any gifts from them. There is labeling and discrimination against the accused.

Almost everyone I spoke to in Gnani-Tindang agreed that they did not retain any good relationships with their communities after the accusations, including close family members and, in some instances, their children.

There is, however, a gendered dynamic to this treatment. Most men who moved to Gnani-Tindang moved with their families (that is, their wives and children), except for one man who told me his wives and kids deserted him. They might, however, still be disconnected from their extended family members and the community. However, women who move to Gnani-Tindang rarely move with their husbands. Their husbands have often passed away, which often leads to accusations. They move alone or possibly with a grand-child, usually a girl, to fetch water and collect firewood. Such children could, on the one hand, be a source of support, such as in the case of Upinyaan and others, and on the other, they could also be a source of burden as the accused is tasked to take care of them, amid limited resources. This is especially so when they are still young and need to be cared for.

Living in the Gnani-Tindang has its challenges, including shelter. The houses and rooms of the accused looked dilapidated, with many rooms leaking during the rainy season. The houses are built with mud and roofed with thatch. However, some males who were accused of witchcraft had their houses roofed with zinc. This is probably because they have some of their sons, daughters, and wives moving in with them and thus assist them in rebuilding or engaging in other activities that brought them a regular income. I was also told that the ban on roofing houses with zinc did not apply to men. For example, one of the grinding mills in the Gnani-Tindang community is owned by a man accused of witchcraft. It is the central grinding mill in the community, and people from both far and near patronize it. It is operated by one of his sons. Even though accused of witchcraft, this man is wealthy and receives a regular income from this business.

For most of the residents in Gnani-Tindang, especially the elderly, accom-modation becomes a huge problem. As is usual, Upinyaan's daughters moved with her. Although they were not accused of witchcraft, they were not per-ceived as useful to society and were not accommodated in their original com-munity. However, they support their aged parents by offering care. Upinyaan was building two more bedrooms in the community to house them. However, she explained that she could not roof her house with iron sheets because people accused of witchcraft were not allowed to. In response to my question about why she could not roof her house with zinc, she explained that a cer-tain woman invested in her house, roofing it with iron sheets, and when she was leaving Gnani-Tindang for another community of her choice, she sold it. She did not inform Utindaan. He got angry after hearing about it and ordered that no woman be allowed to roof her house with iron sheets ever again. No male however told me about the restrictions regarding house roofing. This specific directive to only women is yet another level of gender inequality to be replicated in the Gnani-Tindang community. It is also possible that a man could sell his house when leaving the community. The rest of the women had to pay for the behavior of one woman whom the community members felt had betrayed their trust by selling her house. This suggests that gender discrimination continues to exist after people relocate, even in Gnani-Tindang. This speaks to the broader gender issues in Ghana.

Health conditions were also identified as a key condition of people living in Gnani-Tindang. Because people accused of witchcraft are often of advanced ages and lack access to health facilities, they are prone to illnesses. Tiya had complained of bad health. She has lost her sight and does not have any carer to help her. She cooks and does everything on her own. I found out that others had knee problems where they could not walk.

Considering the above challenges of people living in Gnani-Tindang, there is a need for development interventions such as social security and a safety support system, improved facilities such as health and housing, secure source of economic livelihood, among many other things. These could be useful for persons who choose to stay in Gnani-Tindang and other communities alike, which offer refuge. On the other hand, for those who want to go back to their various homes, if the conditions are suitable after attention is paid to the two previous levels, development actors should support them. This could happen when such actors work in partnership with the local people with their input and the involvement of persons accused of witchcraft. This approach is more likely to succeed than if the actors insist that such communities that offer refuge stop offering such support.

Based on the above, aid and development agencies come in at the end point of a process by which individuals are stripped of social citizenship ad reduced to what Agamben might call *bare life*—by which point, from a local cosmological point of view, it is very hard to "return" people to a life not-as-a-witch. As a result, the intervention becomes one of supporting people in communities of refuge. Again, my illustrative case also shows that this development/ aid paradigm is starting at the wrong end. I am suggesting that the time to stop people becoming accused of being witches is before, not after—so if development and governmental interventions could happen then through better healthcare, work against patriarchy, and so forth, work against modernity as coloniality—then we might see a real shift in witchcraft accusations. In sum, the theory of liminality, and bare life that have been drawn upon here are a useful lens to explain theoretical insights on witchcraft accusations and eviction as well as offer a practical implication for development practice. This adds value to a larger argument that this article makes regarding development intervention. That is; by the point that NGOs intervene, people are already stripped of citizenship/rights—*symbolically* and *actually*. I, therefore, argue that before people reach a stage of bare life, interventions need to occur. Or else interventions need to be locally formulated to find ways to return individuals from bare life to active social citizenship—that is bringing back bios to the equation.

GENDER AND THE ISSUE OF
WITCHCRAFT ACCUSATIONS

Of the wealth of scholarship on witchcraft, the issue of gender, particularly the positionality of women and their engagement with witchcraft, is especially important to consider here. As Ally (2013) argues, scholars need to examine witchcraft issues through a gendered lens. In his study conducted in South Africa, Ally argued that most incidents of witchcraft concerned women and pointed to witchcraft accusations as a strategy employed by men to dominate women (Ally, 2014, p. 140). Though this view might be radical, there are many ways in which gender norms and identities are implicated in issues of witchcraft accusations. Indeed, this points to the broader observation that in the literature on witchcraft in Africa, accusations are disproportionately leveled at women (Akurugu, 2019; Badoe, 2005; Federici, 2008, 2010; Goody, 1970; Mutaru, 2018, 2019; Palmer, 2010).

Furthermore, in the case of Ghana, as in many other places, the gendered aspects of witchcraft accusations also intersect with age and poverty. This is because by and large, many women who are accused of witchcraft are also elderly and poor (see Baba, 2013; Igwe, 2016a; Wumbla, 2017; Mutaru, 2019; Riedel, 2017). In their comparative study of Ghana and Nepal, Adinkrah and Adhikari found that:

> In both countries, physical characteristics of persons vulnerable to witchcraft accusation include emaciated bodies, wrinkled faces, stooping posture, toothless, gray hair, reddish and yellowish eyes and "ugly" appearance. Women who have little to no head hair are also susceptible to witchcraft accusation and subsequent physical mistreatment. Women who have facial hair are also susceptible to witchcraft accusation. (Adinkrah and Adhikari, 2014, p. 317; also see Adinkrah, 2015; Nyabwari and Kagema, 2014)

Further, the economic advancement of women has been found to make them vulnerable to accusations of witchcraft. To give an example, Palmer (2010) reports the case of Ayishetu, one of the alleged witches in northern Ghana. According to Palmer, the evidence tended by relatives after the accusations of Ayishetu were connected to the anomaly of her nuclear family being prosperous in comparison with the general standards in the village. That is, Ayishetu's accusers presented the case against her by citing the "evidence" that her family's success must be due to witchcraft and the diversion of her spiritually external family members' fortunes to her own nuclear family (Palmer, 2010, p. 5).

In the case of the *Dagbamba* in northern Ghana, Bierlich similarly notes that women's economic advancement is considered suspect:

> Women's opportunity via the commodity market to acquire an independent economic status outside the male-dominated, domestic farming circuit, results in a fear of female witchcraft and of individualization and money rupturing the local non-commoditized moral economy—so fiercely guarded by the elders. (Bierlich, 2007, p. 24)

Bierlich further adds,

> The image of the immoral (female) witch seems to have been strengthened by recent trends relating to macro-economic changes and changes in the image of the traditional division of labour between the sexes in northern Ghana. (2007, p. 28)

Furthermore, Palmer also determined that women who were relatively rich and commanded some level of power in their communities were easily framed as witches (as in the case mentioned above of Ayishetu) and often chased out of the community (Palmer, 2010, p. 5). What stands out in Palmer's analysis, however, is that she makes a link between such occurrences and strategic deployment by men who were unable to fathom why Ayeshetu and her family were relatively rich (2010, p. 5). This suggests that the motivations for accusations against women and their subsequent banishment from the community form part of men's strategy, but it also points to the fact that men can more easily draw upon the predominantly male construct of economics as being a male domain.

According to Apter, accusations against women in Nigeria among the Yoruba related to their economic engagement and apparent success relative to men (Apter, 1993, p. 118). Apter notes that the accusations of women in the 1950s occurred alongside the significant shift in economic arrangements, particularly in relation to agriculture, in Yorubaland. This was a time when cocoa prices were booming in the world market. Most of the women were engaged in trading activities and had gained economic independence, especially as the market managers of their husbands' cocoa (Apter, 1993, p. 118). Within the local imagination, "the Yoruba cannibal-witch profited at the expense of her family, lineage, and community by taking without returning.

She profited in the marketplace by acquiring more than she spent and hoarding capital to block the flow of productive resources" (Apter, 1993, p. 118). The Yoruba businesswomen, unlike the South African zombie case, were visibly engaged in trading and making money. In what may be a product of the patriarchal society, it seems the problem was that they had gained economic independence and power and had thus displaced their men's social authority. This prompted elite men to fund the Atinga cult group that finally labeled some of the women as witches. As recounted by Apter (1993), the "new elite men" needed to reassert their own power, as they were entering a terrain already occupied by women. They financed the Atinga cult. By so doing they (a) bypassed the traditional authority of elders to forge an alliance with the "traditional" chiefs, who became indebted to them for anti-witchcraft protection; and (b) persecuted the women traders, either directly as witches, or indirectly through general intimidation, into whose traditional sphere of commercial activity the "new men" were intruding. To add further, Comaroff and Comaroff observed that in rural parts of the Northern Province in South Africa, men and women were accused, but it was mostly women who were confronted (1999a, p. 788).

From a different perspective, alongside issues of the social and economic position of the individual women accused, many studies also highlight that a common feature of accusations relates to the tensions within kinship relationships (Richter, Flowers, and Bongmba, 2017; Parish, 2010; Wumbla, 2017; Palmer, 2010; Mabefam, 2020). The witch is often imagined as a female jealous of her kin (Parish, 2010, p. 83). In addition, in times of disasters and hardships, elderly women have been accused as witches. This was the case in Tanzania as Miguel (2005, pp. 16–21) found. During famine, flood, drought, and disease, among others, women are always blamed for such calamities. In moments of hardship, witchcraft often provides a convenient explanation just as much as a potential solution to hardship, and elderly women can be accused as they are seen as a burden to their families.

CONCLUSION

In this chapter, I have argued that witchcraft accusations and banishment fundamentally disempower people as they are removed from their communities to live in Gnani-Tindang. Individuals are exposed to many risks, such as being evicted from their communities, including violence, discrimination, and the inability to sustain even the most basic livelihood. Evictions have a tremendous impact on the well-being and livelihood of the people accused and those who depend on them, especially their children. They lose their social citizenship and reach a point of bare life. Thus, though some might criticize communities like Gnani due to real or perceived exploitative tendencies, they also provide much-needed support such as refuge that is not offered elsewhere. People accused of witchcraft are accepted and provided with essentials such as land, accommodation, and a community to live in. That is, even though life is challenging, as people accused of witchcraft lack several basic amenities, they are nonetheless provided with a home, without which they would remain wanderers/homeless. Some of the challenges are also specifically related to the characteristics of individuals. For instance, it becomes difficult for many to work on their land for several hours due to their advanced ages. Here, some of the people accused of witchcraft have their children or grandchildren stay with them to give a helping hand.

In short, the challenges and needs of the accused individuals are also related to broader social processes of a shift in family and kinship structures, ageing populations and broader socioeconomic development, and the services provided by the state in the care of marginalized discriminated sectors of the society. In sum, as development scholars and practitioners engage with these complex issues, there is the need to focus on the experiences of persons accused of witchcraft at the center of their work. At the moment, there is a fixation on debates such as the closure of communities of refuge, the reality of witchcraft, and modernity, and in all of these, the experiences of persons accused only become a footnote.

Chapter 3

Limitless Opportunities for Wealth?

Witchcraft/Occult as a Strategy for (In)Equality and Economic (Dis)Empowerment

The persistence of witchcraft beliefs and practices in Africa contradicts earlier scholarly work that suggested it would disappear with modernization. In addition, theorizing witchcraft as a local discourse that only exists between people in an intimate relationship in anthropology has also long been challenged. In this chapter, I contribute to the ongoing discourse on witchcraft by exploring the linkage between witchcraft and neoliberalism in Africa. I argue that witchcraft beliefs and perceptions of their practices are a double-edged sword that can be used both as a destructive tool and a strategy for wealth creation, accumulation, and the protection of such wealth. This is important as the positioning of individuals who use witchcraft as a strategy and those who feel threatened and impacted by such strategies juggle to live in a world bridled by the sale and consumption of witchcraft in a neoliberal world.

With neoliberal values shaping the world, both in theory and in practice, the individual becomes an epicenter for measuring progress, accomplishment, and failure. The onus lies with the individual to be proactive by being innovative and adopting different strategies to participate and thrive in the neoliberal capitalist world. This expectation obviously expands opportunities and yet, at the same time, limits the extent to which people can be accomplished through the mechanisms laid by the global market forces. In this, people employ other strategies to survive the competition, some of which lie within or outside the market's laid down strategies. Here, witchcraft/occult becomes a strategy leveraged by some Africans including Ghanaians to compete in the neoliberal market space.

However, by employing witchcraft/occult as a strategy, the African is caught up in a web of paradoxes. That is, the African/Ghanaian has embraced some elements of the neoliberal world, and yet there is a desire to keep to the values of communal lifestyle. The neoliberal African struggles to navigate between often incompatible expectations placed on the individual vis-a-vis the community, both of which seek to gain attention simultaneously, the coexistence of which leads to a life of "*betwixt and between*," to borrow from Victor Turner (1967). "Betwixt and between" is a phrase that grounds Turner's theory of "liminality," which was developed to explain the rights of passage and the complex web of discursive innuendos characterized by tribal and sociocultural systems (Turner, 1981). The liminal phase, as he would argue, is one of separation from a previous status or social state (Turner, 1981, p. 154). The space in which the transition occurs is an "in-between" place that bridges "what is" and "what can or will be" (1981, p. 159). In short, the individuals caught up in the liminal stage are neither what they were, nor what they will become; they are somewhere in between.

Turner's assertion, as seen above, still holds true today and can be likened to the African discourses on witchcraft/occult, neoliberalism, and their positioning. The African struggles between being African of communal values and being a neoliberal individual. He can be considered both and none at the same time. The neoliberal African exhibits elements of both, none of which make the other complete or part of being the other-communal nor neoliberal individual. In this chapter, I draw on the "labeling" and "accumulative" forces of the occult to guide discussions. Niehaus (2005) and Geschiere (1997) in their respective works talk about both the "leveling" and "accumulative" forces of the occult. As a leveling force, it is a weapon for the weak to bring down people who are perceived to be powerful/wealthy or have the potential to be so. As an accumulative force, it is a tool for the "powerful" class in society whose power/wealth is said to be facilitated by the occult force (see Moore and Sanders, 2001). The interplay among social actors and how witchcraft is directed at others whilst the concern with protecting one's wealth compels some social actors to draw on witchcraft or the occult. Although I use witchcraft and occult interchangeably in this chapter, it is important to state that not all occult-related events are accused of witchcraft.

THEORETICAL REVIEW OF
ANTHROPOLOGICAL SCHOLARSHIP

Since the colonial encounter, anthropologists and missionaries have projected that "African" witchcraft beliefs and practices would disappear with modernity (see Tylor, 1871; Morgan, 1877; Levy-Bruhl, 1952; Parrinder,

1958). However, this assumption proved challenging as witchcraft did not automatically disappear with the supposed enlightenment, and thus interventions have been instigated in different parts of Africa to stamp out witchcraft. One such intervention was the enactment of laws to outlaw the belief and practice of witchcraft. Such legal frameworks suggested that witchcraft did not even exist, and its practice was an illusion or pretentious (see Mesaki, 2009; Ludsin, 2003).

Some governments followed the pursuits of the colonial administrations post-independent Africa and embarked on a state-wide intervention to eradicate witchcraft. However, this invokes a conversation of contradictions, especially if witch doctors are always invited to identify those who were purported to be witches (see Geschiere, 1997; Smith, 2005; Kahn, 2011). Unlike the colonial regime, some post-independent regimes acknowledged witchcraft's existence (for example, Cameroon, Gambia, Benin) except that it was perceived as inimical to development. In this regard, their quest to eradicate witchcraft was mainly to pave the way for development. In the 1970s, 1980s, and 1990s, countries such as Benin, Cameroon, and South Africa were among many that embarked on nationwide or community-wide programs to eradicate witchcraft (Kahn, 2011; Smith, 2005; Smith, 2008; Dolan 2002). However, neither automatic disappearance nor instigated stamping out of witchcraft has not yet happened. Some authors argue that people in Africa believe that witchcraft is more prevalent. Kyriakakis states,

> Within all accounts about witchcraft that I read during preparation for this paper, there was a common confession: "In the old day's witchcraft was much less than it is now." Although the variety of the "old days" is rather long and vague in each case, the truth is that almost everyone in West Africa today believes that witchcraft activity is at its peak. Of course, it can be far away from "us," the educated urban citizens, or it can be thriving among the neighbor people, not among us here, but this does not make it less active. (Kyriakakis, n.d., p. 5)

The increase in witchcraft activities has led to a renewed scholarship in witchcraft, examining why it exists alongside modernity—leading to novel contributions to witchcraft studies. Some authors have argued that the prevalence of witchcraft in African countries can be attributed to how people struggle to adjust to "modernities" as they navigate between the local and global (Ciekawy and Geschiere, 1998; Comaroff and Comaroff, 1999a, 2001, 2002; Geschiere, 1997; Parish, 2003, 2005, 2011; Stenberg, 2010). The argument here is that witchcraft is part of modernity and does not lie outside of it. However, the modernity of witchcraft scholarship has been criticized for being vague (Kroesbergen-Kamps, 2020). Kroesbergen-Kamps (2020) has therefore, for the sake of clarity, categorized modernity and witchcraft scholarship into two. That is, witchcraft is *in* modernity, and witchcraft is *of* modernity. She contends that the institutions of society that can be considered modern are not devoid of witchcraft discourses. It is indicative that Peter Geschiere's work, *The Modernity of Witchcraft: Politics and the Occult in Postcolonial Africa* (Geschiere, 1997), would fall under this category. Witchcraft is *of* modernity in her view; it is the scholarship that speaks to global forces that govern economic and political conditions that create inequalities and exploitations and instill fear and anxieties (see Ashforth, 2005; Comaroff and Comaroff, 1999). One important criticism of the modernity thesis is that the so-called "modernity" does not exist as a singular phenomenon. On the contrary, there are "multiple modernities" (read Moore and Sanders, 2001).

Comaroff and Comaroff argued that the reason for the occult rise in Africa, and South Africa in particular, is

> on the other hand, the dawning sense of chill desperation is left out of the promise of prosperity, of the telos of liberation. After all, in South Africa, the end of apartheid held out the prospect that everyone would be set free to speculate, accumulate, consume, and indulge repressed desires. But, for many, the millennial moment has passed without palpable payback. (Comaroff and Comaroff, 1999, p. 284)

The disappointment of being left out of the promise of a better post-apartheid South Africa was deeply felt as wealth remained in the hands of a few while the majority struggled to cope or survive. The pervasiveness of occult practices in economic activities led Comaroff and Comaroff to coin the term "occult economy" in South Africa. They suggested that apart from the visible capital economy, which people navigate by engaging in production, distribution, and consumption of goods to make money, others covertly employ occult means to make themselves rich to the detriment of the general society (Comaroff and Comaroff, 1993, 1999, 2000). The wealth obtained from occult means, as argued by Comaroff and Comaroff, is covertly navigated. Yet, it is dispensed overtly in the physical capital economy. The irony, however, is that for a long time, witchcraft was often taken for granted or viewed as a local issue and presumed to be part of the belief systems of people who are yet to develop. This view is deeply rooted in colonial and missionary thinking but continues to influence development thinking until today. This marks a shift and makes a novel contribution to witchcraft scholarship. The ideas of witchcraft are no longer consigned to a particular locality or localities, but something concerned with connections and relationships—relationships between individuals, societies, and continents (see Dolan, 2002; Rowlands and Warnier, 1988).

Let us briefly take a look at Ghana's economic development. The table below shows development inequality estimates in Ghana.

Table 3.1 above presents a decomposition of inequality in Ghana, as measured by the Theil measure into two components, inequality which is due to

Table 3. 1: Inequality Estimates (1992–2013)

	1992		1998		2006		2013	
	Gini	Theil	Gini	Theil	Gini	Theil	Gini	Theil
National	0.373	0.249	0.388	0.259	0.406	0.301	0.409	0.296
Decomposition by Region								
Western	0.326	0.190	0.324	0.198	0.355	0.227	0.368	0.233
Central	0.338	0.200	0.332	0.188	0.388	0.278	0.370	0.254
Greater Accra	0.354	0.223	0.300	0.158	0.410	0.323	0.356	0.220
Eastern	0.327	0.192	0.346	0.198	0.319	0.186	0.365	0.243
Volta	0.339	0.197	0.304	0.160	0.346	0.206	0.402	0.318
Ashanti	0.376	0.256	0.380	0.240	0.377	0.253	0.371	0.240
Brong Ahafo	0.349	0.224	0.333	0.190	0.357	0.217	0.369	0.244
Northern	0.400	0.285	0.389	0.291	0.400	0.272	0.413	0.322
Upper West	0.326	0.203	0.316	0.161	0.413	0.360	0.477	0.440
Upper East	0.346	0.195	0.316	0.176	0.399	0.274	0.395	0.276
Within regions	.	0.221	.	0.198	.	0.255	.	0.250
Between regions	.	0.028	.	0.061	.	0.046	.	0.046
Share of "between regions" inequality in total inequality		0.112		0.236		0.153		0.155
Decomposition by Urban/Rural								
Urban	0.347	0.213	0.349	0.206	0.373	0.257	0.373	0.242
Rural	0.342	0.212	0.369	0.239	0.366	0.238	0.389	0.277
Within urban/rural	.	0.212	.	0.224	.	0.248	.	0.254
Between Urban and rural	.	0.037	.	0.035	.	0.053	.	0.041
Share of "between urban/rural" inequality in total inequality	0.149	0.160	0.135	0.155	0.176	0.192	0.139	0.176
Decomposition by North/South								
North	0.382	0.255	0.375	0.269	0.424	0.312	0.423	0.330
South	0.363	0.237	0.362	0.226	0.378	0.265	0.391	0.270
Within North/South	.	0.240	.	0.230	.	0.270	.	0.276
Between North and South	.	0.009	.	0.029	.	0.031	.	0.020
Share of "between north/south" inequality in total inequality	0.036	0.057	0.112	0.151	0.103	0.163	0.068	0.101

Source: Author created with information from Cooke, Hague, and McKay calculation based on GLSS datasets (2016)

differences between the regions (in their average consumption levels) and that which is due to inequality within the regions (collectively). The authors found that "inequality is higher within each area (regions, urban–rural and North–South divide) than across areas, implying that much of the inequality observed is due to wide differences in welfare within each area" (Cooke, Hague, and McKay, 2016, p. 15). The data in the table suggest that northern Ghana as a whole (northern region, upper east and upper west) is the most unequal place in Ghana. Again, the figures in the table show that regional inequality contributes to national inequality as well, which has been demonstrated to be huge. For example, 15.5 percent of national inequality in 2013 according to the Theil index is due to differences in average living conditions between regions. In addition, the difference between the north and south is also large as a further 10 percent of national inequality in 2013 was due to that. Finally, inequalities between the rural and urban areas now account for 17.6 percent of Ghana's inequality. Taking into the totality of the foregoing discussion, it is obvious that the north and, for that matter, northern region of Ghana is unequal at all levels—that is a regional, north–south divide, and rural–urban divide. This inequality among the population might account for the high level of witchcraft beliefs and accusations. In short, various aspects of navigating the neoliberal capitalist world and social and economic development coalesce with issues of gender disparity, discrimination, and the inability of some to access the advances that have been made in society.

In this chapter, I take into consideration the different dimensions of the issues discussed above and extend the scholarship on witchcraft and modernity themes by focusing on Ghana and some other examples with Benin. Different strands of literature are drawn from other countries in Africa to support my argument. Ghana is an interesting illustration because the nature of witchcraft discourse is unique; there exist communities of refuge where people are accused of witchcraft and resettled. The existence of communities of refuge against the government's wish and yet its inability to disband them suggests that the issue of witchcraft is complex in Ghana. Studies on communities of refuge thus far have focused on gender dynamics (Badoe, 2005; Musah, 2013, 2020), development organizations/human rights (Mutaru, 2018, 2019; Roxburgh, 2018; Mabefam, 2019), old age (Mabefam and Appau, 2020; Crampton, 2013). Building on existing scholarship, in this chapter, I present a current ethnographic account of how occult forces are utilized by individuals as a strategy for wealth gain and protection and serve as a narrative for the challenges individuals are experiencing when having to navigate between often incompatible expectations placed on the individual vis-a-vis the community. This is further exemplified through the ethnographic account of how occult forces are employed against individuals who are pursuing success in a neoliberal socioeconomic context.

ETHNOGRAPHY OF INDIVIDUAL
ENTREPRENEURSHIP AND COLLECTIVE GOOD

Kachi (pseudonym) and I stood under a tree in front of the University of Ghana African Studies Library. The place is usually busy with the influx of other students in and out of the library. When I told Kachi I was studying the relationship between witchcraft and development, he immediately told me that he had some interesting cases about witchcraft, which he hoped could help me delve deeper into the dynamics of the relationship between witchcraft and development. Kachi mentioned the case of a young man who completed a high national diploma (typically referred to by the acronym, HND) program. This man returned to his village to start a business enterprise. This enterprise became highly successful, and virtually every person in the village was a customer. Typical of a business run by a community member, there was also an expectation, according to Kachi, to sometimes give out things for free. One day, the entrepreneur's aunt (father's sister) asked him for money. The entrepreneur did not refuse to give money to his aunt but told her that he did not have it that day. The aunt, however, became angry and, according to Kachi, bewitched her nephew.

Kachi explained to me that the man fell sick with an unusual sickness. He was rushed to the hospital in Tamale, but the doctors could not find anything medically wrong after all the laboratory tests; yet, he was slowly dying. Since biomedical means could not diagnose what was wrong with him, the family decided to consult *ubɔa* (a spiritualist) to offer a spiritual diagnosis, a common practice in the area. At the end of the consultation, *ubɔa* revealed that his aunt bewitched the man. *Ubɔa* explained that the aunt bewitched him because she had asked for money, which she knew he could provide, and was angry when he denied her. The aunt was confronted; she confirmed she did bewitch him and was too late to save his life. A few days later, the man died.

This story, shared by Kachi, shows that there is a link between witchcraft and economic development. For example, the fact that the business was flourishing points to the issue of wealth being made, an aspect of the neoliberal system that allows market forces to operate. He was selling products, and those who had money purchased them to meet their needs. However, the aunt and others, with the expectation that he needed to give them things for free, felt that his wealth did not benefit them as he refused to share it with them. In this case, it would appear witchcraft is the antithesis of development, or the dark side of development, as the entrepreneur was bewitched, which subsequently led to his death. The death of the entrepreneur led to the collapse of the business too, the way Kachi told the story, and the form that the explanations of bewitchment were given framed it as having something to do with a lack of generosity or sharing. This is the crucial point that opens a more critical view of individual/ collective development conceptualizations.

Individual wealth and collective identity present a society dependent on navigating between personal development and the inherent generosity or sharing that makes for a socially constituted person. Nevertheless, instead, it is the balancing/ negotiation between individual and collective. This raises arguably more interesting issues around the introduction and appropriation of neoliberal market rules, their applications, and local impacts. This assertion is not neglecting other factors that also contribute to witchcraft cases. The neoliberal approach is one lens through which I have explored this chapter. Within a neoliberal philosophy, the man's reluctance to share with his aunt seems legitimate. Adopting the current focus on individual improvement, his efforts had led him to where he was, the gains of which were his to enjoy alone. This is in stark contrast to collective interests, the communal concept, that is prevalent in his community.

The communal concept has no bounds concerning everything that people in a community do, primarily when such people are related (see Dogbe, 1980). The case of the aunt and entrepreneur demonstrates this. As Kachi would reveal, there was community support during the shop's building where some people were responsible for digging soil and others fetching water. Others carried the mortar, and yet others were responsible for the mason work. This brings into focus how different strengths of people in the community are drawn upon to help one another. Contributions from different individuals to making others' lives better also mean that those who have contributed have a stake in the venture, probably not in ways people own shares in financial sectors or make investment portfolios that can be measured or valued, but arguably labor, and emotional and spiritual stakes. Here, it is not often spoken about but taken for granted that the community members are all part of the corporate entity. This communal relationship has been well documented in the literature for some communities in Africa. For example, Dogbe (1980) noted that among the Asante of Ghana, it is called *Nnoboa*; in Tanzania, it is called *Ujamaa*, while among the Macha of Galla in Ethiopia, it is referred to as *Dabo* (see Bartels, 1975), and in South Africa, it is called *Ubuntu*.

What then unfolds from a communal entity is a sense of community owner-ship of whatever it is: "we-ism." The "we-ism" philosophy, embedded in the aunt's thought, is common in Ghana and other parts of Africa (Dogbe, 1980). It translates into collective ownership of property, problems, and successes. In such communities, people consider direct contributions such as money and in-kind gifts and prayers and wishing others well as part of their contribution. The aunt did not contribute money to the man's schooling or establishing his business but argued that they had all prayed and wished him well, as Kachi told me. Even having good thoughts or *lipobipiln* (a good heart) contributes to a kinship member's success. In return, she expected distribution and a share of the success to anyone who needed help in the family, including herself. A community member vividly revealed the concept of contributing to others' success with expectations who asserted that a relative who never contributed any money toward his education asked for money, claiming it was his time to pay back. When he asked what the payback was for, the relative said,

> We all contributed for you to go to school. I prayed for you and wished you the best of luck anytime you were going to school. All these prayers and well wishes made you successful. I didn't have money to give you, and money should not be the only contribution to having helped someone. Our prayers protected you from the evil ones.

We see here that *we-ism* inherent in the aunt's thought is not an isolated case. This is also supported by Hord and Lee (1995). They note that the philosophy of "I am because we are" is a central element of most African communities, making it difficult for an individual to claim something entirely theirs. This implies that individuals, regardless of what they achieve, cannot claim total ownership of it. It will always be perceived as "ours." However, this does not suggest that individuals do not aim for self-realization; what it means is that such individual successes must be able to meet the collective need of the community when the need arises. There must be a balance. In the absence of balance, here the problem arises. This is well encapsulated by Dogbe when he asserts,

> The emphasis is not simply on social development but rather social self-development. There must be self-realisation and social-self-actualisation. The norm that this connotes is the maximum satisfaction of the wants and needs of both individuals and groups, not either of individuals or groups. (Dogbe, 1980, pp. 788–78)

The complicated discussion of the concept of communalism and we-ism and how they have been implicated in witchcraft in the case of the man and his aunt suggests that witchcraft is used as a reprimand for neglecting the balance between individual and group success. This was a cautionary tale that presented witchcraft as an opposing force. However, witchcraft narratives can also be framed positively, where individuals consult occult forces to advance their business activities to create more wealth. Though people who consult occult forces are typically not accused of witchcraft, when such occult forces demand other rituals that lead to the death of people to make wealth-making potent, then they can be implicated in witchcraft accusations.

Due to the above analysis showcasing the bigger picture of development in Ghana, local communities have always strived to improve their condition, and at least meet the necessities as a collective, and, also, as individuals. The term *"m-mumuun"* became a common theme across many communities I visited. Though captured by different terminologies due to linguistic differences, "m-mumuun" a term of *likapkpaaln* origin is used to vaguely describe "development." For example, during my initial visit to *Utindaan* in Gnani, he stated that *"M-mi le ye utindaan Gnani ating ke pu. Ni ye matuln le ke n-lik maga gna pu kiting ke muun muen na* (I am the landowner of the Gnani community. It is my responsibility to devise strategies to make this community develop)." I wondered what he meant when he said it was his responsibility to devise strategies to develop the community. I asked Utindaan in what ways he was going to help the development of the community and how he planned to achieve these goals. In his response, he said he was going to adopt communal labor, which would bring all members of the community to work for collective interest, collaborate with government and nonprofit organizations that show interest in his community as well as proactively pursue all stakeholders who could support his community. He also mentioned that as part of his role and strategies, he performed spiritual rituals and served as intermediaries between the dead, the living and other important spirits. In short, any development that was benefiting the few was not desired. Selective benefits for individuals, to the neglect of communal interests, were not acceptable to the Gnani community.

During my fieldwork, I asked people whether they thought witchcraft could be a strategy for wealth creation and accumulation. One of my participants—for the purpose of this chapter, let's name him Alhaji—gave his thoughts. Alhaji is about fifty-eight years old, married, and with kids. He revealed that although witchcraft has been perceived as unfavorable, some people use it for good purposes, except that such people would not be accused of witchcraft and rarely do people even consider that as witchcraft. He cited the case of how there is a perception that local businesspeople from southern Ghana rely on witchcraft as a way of navigating business innuendos. With specific reference to economic activities, he said,

> Of late, we've been seeing people come from down south to get spiritual support to help them travel or engage in business activities. For example, it is believed that a witch in the night can travel to Accra and come back. So, people now come to women who have that juju and use it to do business between Africa and Europe. You see, so that's the positive aspect. (Alhaji, fifty-eight years old, 2016)

Alhaji does not view witchcraft in a negative sense here. Instead, he sees witchcraft as being employed by people to help them in their business activities (see Smith, 2005, p. 147). According to Smith, "some witches are also said to be more concerned these days with making money than with destroying the wealth of others" (Smith, 2005, p. 147). This illustrates that witchcraft is not always perceived as unfavorable; it is also used for positive things. However, there is a need for some conceptual clarification here. What Alhaji might be referring to is what constitutes occult power or magical power. For example, as can be seen in the quote, people are believed to go up north where there is the perception that powerful witches can help them travel abroad for business transactions and return to Ghana without any difficulties. Similarly, Smith (2010) reported a woman in Kenya who argued that if they brought in a witch doctor to cleanse the village of all the witchcraft, entrepreneurial activities would stall, as some people employ it for their businesses.

Contemporary witchcraft beliefs and practices shape how people engage with development in neoliberal Ghana. There has been an increase in witchcraft accusations in Ghana, as people adapt to more individualized lifestyles than before, acting against the communal spirit that has always guided the communities. This distinguishes between the neoliberal approach to development and other forms of development. Moving further, the conceptual understanding of neoliberalism is necessary for a nuanced discussion on the relationship between witchcraft and development.

In this case, I draw on Harvey's (2005) definition of neoliberalism to support the ongoing discussion. Neoliberalism is both an economic and a political ideology, where state intervention is minimal except to provide a conducive environment where the private sector drives the economy. In this case, individuals are interested in amassing wealth, which then seems selfish and acts against communal interests. The assumption, in this case, is that individuals who are navigating their entrepreneurial agenda may ignore the contribution of their kin toward their success and are likely to assume that it was all due to their effort, and hence their own work ethic. That is the case of the entrepreneur who was said to be bewitched by his aunt. I, therefore, argue that the abrupt changes that have accompanied the neoliberal economy, where people are realigned to the pursuance of self-interests vis-a-vis collective interests, have led to conflicts and many standing apart (inequitable development), something unusual that seems to be acting against the ethos of communal life or interests, and thus affecting relationships and wealth making. To further this discussion, let's explore how witchcraft is employed as a strategy for wealth-making (accumulative occult forces).

LOCAL-GLOBAL NEXUS

Theorizing witchcraft as a local discourse that only exists between people in an intimate relationship in anthropology has been challenged. Comaroff and

Comaroff (1999) argue it needs to be embedded in the local–global nexus, as a strategy for leveling (see Moore and Sanders, 2001) as well as protecting wealth. In this section, I argue that witchcraft as a strategy of wealth lies outside the prescribed rules of the market and yet it competes within the market rules that are set within the global market system. One way to talk about global market rules is the application of neoliberal policies. For example, the current set of global market rules is in such a way that individuals become the center of focus for survivability, and thus, the individual must adopt different strategies to survive. However, focusing on the individual brings up issues of collective well-being. In this instance, the Ghanaian is not against collective well-being or individual accumulation, but the two struggle to coexist and that is where issues of jealousy lead to issues of collective beings, equity, and their struggle to coexist.

There is undoubtedly a connection between the local and global, enabled through technologies and globalization that has penetrated the aspirations of individuals. In its current form, identities and cultures have intertwined and led to a taste for things that were hitherto unknown to people in some locations. The promise and application of neoliberal principles have localized the global and globalized the local (Comaroff and Comaroff, 1999; Ferguson, 1999; Smith, 2008) in an intertwining interface of everyday interaction, either in physical or virtual spaces. Pragmatically, the promise of neoliberal market principles comes from everywhere—media outlets (both international and local), interactions with foreigners, and locals in the diaspora who are returning home to show off their achievements.

The impact of neoliberal market ideals on society emerges in several ways. The first is that people receive benefits unequally. This is driven by the fact that people are exposed to different opportunities and environments that empower or disempower their competitiveness in wealth accumulation. For example, an individual seeking to advance their well-being by acquiring wealth is one significant way of describing micro-level development. However, individual taste and being perceived as neoliberal individual at the local level is linked with global tastes, influencing each other. Neoliberalism is therefore a relational affair (Smith, 2008) that compares one unit with another at an individual, family, village, town, regional, and national level, even across continents. Relational, interactional positioning has much to say about a distinction of self-relative to others; what or who is perceived as developed and modern relates to what happens elsewhere or within the local community, where people who stick to the traditional way of doing things are somehow considered poor, backward, and archaic, people who have simply refused to evolve with time and hence are *un*-modern.

The idea of an egalitarian society is no longer possible under the neoliberal epoch motif. This is because capitalism, and by extension neoliberalism, which are part of the modern frameworks, create power differentials and serve as prisms that recategorize people into class systems: classes of moderns and non-moderns, poor and rich, and so forth. The application of neoliberalism and capitalism is used as a barometer for development, adopted by mainstream development institutions such as the International Monetary Fund (IMF), the World Bank, and the United Nations. Neoliberalism, a key feature of modernity, was initially supported and enforced by mainstream development institutions. Such institutions "forced" developing nations to adopt free-market approaches as qualifying conditions for aid and grants (ISSER, 1991; Loxley, 1990). It has been suggested that development interventions by mainstream development organizations in Africa, and probably elsewhere, were stopped until governments adopted structural adjustment reforms, a model driven by neoliberal thought (Green and Mesaki, 2005; Smith, 2008). This policy only served to deepen the differences that already existed in such societies.

The neoliberal approach to development assumes that once governments have created a suitable environment, individuals can compete in the free-market economy to meet their needs, leading to limited involvement of governments in the economy (see Tarp and Aryeetey, 2000). The fact is that this assumption is problematic and has led to many people losing their jobs, with others seeking greener pastures elsewhere. Leaving behind their families and their social networks for unknown geographies has had its problems. Several criticisms have already been offered against neoliberalism in scholarship and development practice, and it is not my intention to do the same here but instead to give a snapshot of how it is linked to inequality in northern parts of Ghana, and how it has interacted with the deepening of views on the mechanization of witchcraft in the local development discourse, in comparison with the global.

My observations from the field have led me to argue that the taste for modern things is not necessarily disliked and entirely frowned upon by local people, but the changes and struggles to adapt to the new order in a culturally sensitive way are problematic. It is challenging to reconcile neoliberal individuals, a paradigm that values individuality, with cultures where standing out is unvalued if that standing out only satisfies individuals' interests and not that of the community. Within this complex landscape, witchcraft becomes reinforced as a means of making sense of a new order. It is plausible the reason for the large-scale incidence of accusations and confrontations in Ghana at present. In this sense, Ferguson is relevant as he talks about "the whole terrain of an urban Africa that continues to be haunted by the ideas of modernity that are harder and harder to make sense of concerning the existing present" (Ferguson, 1999, p. 21).

This chapter also speaks to the broader power discourses that are ingrained in witchcraft debates. As it would appear in the ensuing case below, as the local people are pitted against each other, it is not farfetched to argue that witchcraft functions as a way of detracting attention away from the "real" power structures that are connected and interact with the global. As accusations and counteraccusations emerge, those who are in the actual position of power and the structures that enable them to benefit from the insecurities and competition on a local level are represented by witchcraft strategies. Witchcraft divides society, prevents the coming together and thwarts real calls for a more equal distribution of wealth and power in Ghanaian society. This can be deduced from the ethnographic account of all cases presented as attention is shifted from state authorities to the individuals in the community who are all victims struggling to compete in a space that has so many limitations and thus trying to improvise for wealth creation. It is also important to note that as capital and access to capital are often only available for the few, and people struggle to get their piece from it, the strategies of witchcraft (occult force) become more drawn upon to have access to the global economy, thereby connecting local to the global.

WITCHCRAFT AS A STRATEGY/TACTIC FOR WEALTH-MAKING (OCCULT FORCES AND ECONOMY)

This section argues that increased interest in personal accumulation has led many people to adopt different strategies/tactics to advance their wealth. Here, I draw from de Certeau's theory of strategy and tactics (1984). De Certeau defines "strategies" as the hidden means by which institutions and structures of power, or "producers," circumscribe a place as *proper* and generate relations with targeted individuals, or "consumers," who consequently enact "tactics" to unsettle or diverge from the prescribed conventions of such environments. It is here that occult forces are deployed both as a strategy and tactic depending on the positioning of individuals who are perceived to use it within the neoliberal market environment. That is, those who are powerful and draw on occult power to make more wealth as well as protect it are considered "strategists," whilst, on the other hand, those who are feared, usually the poor, with the assumption that they will use witchcraft to destroy wealth acquired by the powerful can be described being *tactical*.

From the field, I observed that witchcraft has emerged as a strategy to make wealth (*ilik aa nyɔk*, for example, among the Konkombas of Ghana—money rituals), and protect it as well. The "new" form of witchcraft for wealth-making (occult power/forces) can be employed between kin and non-kin. As narrated to me in the field, there is the assumption that the only limitation is that the first person purported to be sacrificed in the ritual must be a family member (not just any member but the most loved) to be highly potent. After this initial family member, any other person can be sacrificed to subsequently aid in wealth accumulation and the protection of what has already been accumulated.

As an illustration, while in the field, I was told of a story concerning four men who had consulted a spiritualist to help them attain wealth quickly. When the spiritualist came, they met him in a room in one of their houses. Having laid their complaint before the spiritualist, he agreed he could help them meet their demand, but each had to present the name of one person from their family who was most loved. They inquired whether it was possible to name another member of the community. When the spiritualist maintained that it must be family, they exited one after the other to reflect on such a task. They never returned to continue the ritual.

When I questioned the facts of the story, the narrators disclosed the names of the four men. In typical witchcraft discourse, accusations and confrontations start with rumors such as this. At this stage, the four men did not know that other community members were making this allegation behind their backs. When I questioned my narrators why they did not continue with the ritual for money-making, they revealed to me that they were not ready to sacrifice their family members. They had thought they could sacrifice other members of the community. If that were the case, my informants felt they would have gone ahead with the ritual. They told me that the spiritualist was a nice person, and that was why he agreed to let them reconsider their participation in the ritual. Other spiritualists would have led people on until they could not turn back. Then they ask one to present the name of their most-loved family member. If the person refuses this, they are threatened with death or mental illness (Mabefam, 2017). In such a case, the person may feel that they have no option but to follow the dictates of the spiritualist.

Although the notion of employing witchcraft as a strategy to improve economic well-being is not new in African societies, more comprehensive scholarship is required. The works of Ardener (1970), Geschiere (1997), and Comaroff and Comaroff (1999) allude to some connections between witchcraft and economic development in Cameroon and South Africa. For example, Ardener found that emerging wealthy elites among the Bakweri ethnic group who engaged in banana cultivation were accused of killing people, resurrecting them, and converting them into zombies to work on the invisible plantations on Mt Kupe. In the view of their accusers, the employment of zombies on the plantations was behind the newly acquired wealth (see Comaroff and Comaroff, 1999; Parish, 2003, 2005, 2011). Geschiere similarly found that among the Maka of Cameroon, the newly rich were accused of employing witchcraft to acquire and protect their wealth. They argued that if they were not witches themselves, their wealth would have been destroyed by the malicious witches in their communities. The malicious witches being referred to here per de Certeau's theory would have deployed a *tactic* in this instance to destroy the wealth. But because the rich have used witchcraft as a *strategy*, they are more powerful and hence have been able to protect their wealth with it.

The narratives of people engaging in witchcraft (occult power) to make wealth and protect were familiar in Ghana. It was seen to be prevalent among people engaged in farming and trading activities. Besides eavesdropping on conversations in that regard, I also followed up with some who were willing to open up with me. I asked participants whether they thought occult power/ force was employed by people engaged in economic activities. Most of the time, they responded in the affirmative and shared either personal experiences or other people's experiences that they were aware of. For example, one of the elders, during an interview, shared the following with me:

> Business activities are full of competition. People would engage in anything that would make them get more customers than others, even if that means crippling the other. Around here, they will always go for what they call "*Liyimɔɔln*" (good luck medicine). *Liyimɔɔln* technically is witchcraft. This is because it seeks to spiritually manipulate customers to patronise their goods to the neglect of the other competitors. In some circumstances, they could even eliminate the competitor by killing them through bewitchment. I can tell you for the fact that most alleged witches in the camps, especially women, may not have gone for the spirit of witchcraft intentionally but sought for this *Liyimɔɔln* for their petty trading purposes.

It is becoming clear that witchcraft can be used either to harm others or improve the fortunes of the individuals practicing it, the latter often described as occult power, as the above case has demonstrated. In this case, witchcraft can be theorized as a strategy and tactic depending on who is viewing it. That is, the two can be located even in the same person. In addition, during fieldwork, another participant told me that a man of advanced age was brutally beaten after he was accused of being a witch. On his part, the man confessed to the people gathered that he had not gone for witchcraft to harm others, but rather, for *Liyimɔɔln* to improve his farming yield. Among *Bikpakpaam,* the particular type of *Liyimɔɔln* is called *nagbatoo*, a type of occult force used to protect the owner's property but destroy the property of others. In the view of the local people, they explained that anything he praised amounted to nothing after the man went for the *nagbatoo*. For instance, if he saw a yam farm blooming and praised it, the yam farm owner would not have a good harvest that year. It is believed that by using *nagbatoo*, he was stealing harvests for himself. As a result, his farm was going to blossom, leading to a bumper harvest. To illustrate further, at Gnani, one of the communities I stayed while conducting my research, a neighbor called me one day and said,

> Njor (my friend), I'm confused. I don't know what is happening. My yam farm has almost dried off at the time it is supposed to have green leaves. The leaves are gone. It is like the dry season. Other people's yam farms still have fresh leaves and are still growing.

While growing up, I occasionally engaged in yam farming on my father's farm and a small plot of my own. I am, therefore, familiar with the dynamics of yam cultivation. Relying on my experience, I tried to explain to him that it could be because of a plant locally known as *ujal* that is not compatible with yam cultivation or that his yam farm was in a waterlogged area. Either case could explain the early falling off the green yam leaves. My neighbor disagreed with me. In reaction to my opinion, he said,

> I have been a farmer here in Gnani for a long time. I know the nature of the land, and which one is suitable for crop cultivation. I think you are getting it wrong. I think there is a hand of an evil one (witch) on my farm.

He implied that witches, especially the *nagbatoo* spirits that I discussed in the previous paragraph, were responsible. This is closer to what Shaw (1997) found in her study in Sierra Leone. Shaw (1997) found that witches could steal growing rice invisibly through the *ka-hɔfi* spirit, a type of witchcraft that either transported the growing rice to the witch's farm or to the witch's place, where the witch ended up harvesting more at the expense of the bewitched farmer.

It is difficult to know precisely when this new form of witchcraft for wealth accumulation emerged as a strategy. Despite this, inhabitants of different communities I visited while in Ghana made guesses, suggesting that the new form of witchcraft was noticed first in the 1990s through to the current era. Reference was made to *kisamookwambiik*, which emerged in the middle 1990s, and a comparatively less harmful type of witchcraft called *kisamook*. *Kisamook*, according to local cosmology, is normal, and most yam farmers in the northern part of Ghana who follow the traditional African religion regularly engage in it. It is a spiritual ritual derived from a powerful spiritualist to aid the receiver in his yam cultivation. It comes in different forms. Most farms would usually have a pot stuffed with herbs and different roots and adorned with animal bloodstains. This is thought to help make the yams grow big, leading to a bountiful harvest. There is also a ritual where stones adorned with crosses are placed on the first mound at every corner of the yam farm.

This is meant to prevent the stealing of farm produce by a witch, as found in my example of *kisamook* in Gnani and that of *ka-hɔfi* spirit by Shaw (1997) in Sierra Leone.

Kisamookwambiik emerged when people's quest for money and property acquisition intensified. The economic hardships in Ghana and people's quest to become rich have always been blamed for this emergence. World Bank conditions on accessing aid and grants from the Bretton Woods institutions resulted in many people losing their public and civil service jobs in the 1980s through to the 1990s. Unemployment rates, as I write today, are high, especially among university graduates. Farm supplies such as fertilizers, hoes, and other implements have always been expensive, and are now almost out of the reach of farmers. As a way of adapting to a harsh new economic life, some farmers sought out *kisamookwambiik*. *Kisamookwambiik*, unlike the older *kisamook*, involves the use of human blood rather than animal blood for ritual purposes. An allegation that has also emerged among the youth in Ghana regarding the strategies of economic innovation is *sakawa*—a form of occult forces that are purported to use human blood and body parts for ritual purposes usually employed by the youth in Ghana (Oduro-Frimpong, 2014; Riedel, 2017; Mabefam and Alexeyeff, 2023). It is believed that the youth combine such occult forces with technology to outwit their victims (see Armstrong, 2011) have been reported in recent times. Here we can see the connections between witchcraft and wealth acquisition as Ghana adopts a neoliberal economy.

Like *Sakawa*, I was told by people that there was the perception of people being bewitched and their blood was offered for the ritual to make the *kisamookwambiik* effective. Others also explained that laborers from elsewhere who worked on the yam farms would lose a colleague after returning home. At the peak of such rumors, specific communities in the northern part of Ghana gained notoriety for using human beings to boost their yam production. The rumors were so widespread that laborers refused to work there. Once, when I was engaged in a conversation with a person from one of those communities, he told me that it was an embarrassment to his community because people no longer trusted the achievements that came out of it. He cited the assumption that all wealth (cars, money, etc.) in the community was obtained through *kisamookwambiik*.

Not only was there the belief that people were killed, and their blood used for the ritual, but there were also rumors suggesting that during the planting season, some farmers, especially those along the roadside, used people who passed by for the ritual too. It was explained that they held a yam seed that they would quickly put into the mound after the passer greeted them. In this way, that person was used for the ritual. The person would die after a few weeks or months, after which the yams would develop well, especially for economic purposes. Children and relatives were often cautioned not to greet people while they were working on their farms. There were rumors of people who forced farmers to remove yam seeds from their mounds after they had greeted them.

It was also believed, as revealed by my research participants, that *kisamook-wambiik* was more potent when loved ones were sacrificed. With this kind of *kisamookwambiik*, the farmer is asked to give the name of a loved one for the ritual. After the name is given, the person would be used for the ritual. After the death of the person, the yam farmer would have a good harvest that year. In one of the examples that I was given, a man named his brother for the ritual. He received a good harvest, but the spirit of the brother haunted him. I was told he went mad after leading a yam buyer to his yam hut to sell the yams but instead saw his dead brother in the hut. He never recovered and left the community. The above discussions are further supplemented with the following two case studies.

Case One: The Shop Owner and Money Rituals: Strategist

During my fieldwork, I frequented a shop close to my house for convenience. My first encounter with the shop owner was within the first week of my stay in Gnani. I was looking for an extension cord to connect my laptop charger. I did not know the local name, and the shop owner, an older woman of about fifty-five years named Naju, did not know the English name either. She gave me the chance to enter her shop to identify what I was looking for. The shops are usually so small that it is only the owner who is allowed inside. You stand outside and tell her what you want. I finally found it, and we had a good laugh about the encounter.

Naju's shop stocked a wide variety of products, including assorted drinks, electrical gadgets, and toiletries. I found it convenient to shop there for things I needed for my daily living in the community. While in the community, I met a group of local university students studying in the community too. I became a close friend to one of them. He visited me at my house, and on one of the visits, I decided to buy him a drink at the shop. I noticed he seemed unhappy about going to the shop, but he did not resist either. After we left the shop, he said he had a story to tell me. I was eager to hear what he had to say, especially considering his mood at the time:

> I know you are still a stranger in this community and might not be privy to much information. I have stopped buying from this shop, and so have my friends too. We were told by some community members that she was involved in money

rituals that manipulated people to always come to her shop to buy things. That is why people are always crowded at her place while other shops are empty.

I was very attentive to my friend. He went further to mention a few names I could consult to verify what he was telling me. I thanked him for the information and promised I was going to follow up. Following up on issues like this is very challenging. From conversations in the community, people were still skeptical about me and were unwilling to open up. They still saw me as a stranger and were careful regarding what information they could tell me and what to keep secret. However, I was not going to rush this matter. As long as I was in the community, I would eventually find out about such rumors, at least from the friends I would make and from everyday interactions.

After some time in the community, I was finally informed about how Naju engaged in occult forces to manipulate people to purchase things from her shop in my eighth month. This resonated with what my friend had told me about Naju. *Uja,* (referring to a man as I was usually called in the community), there is something I wanted to tell you, someone said to me:

> You see, in the shop from which you usually buy things, the owner is wealthy, but her riches are not expected. She inherited the money from her husband, who passed away, a former staff of a government department.

In providing his version of the situation, the man told me that the husband of Naju had gone for money rituals that would only be potent when he sacrificed people and used their blood. The rule was that on the day of his return from the journey where the ritual was made, any person who helped in carrying his bag would die. After the death of the person, he would become rich overnight. But, on the other hand, he would die if no one came to assist in carrying the bag and carrying it home by himself. After his death, the money would still come, but he would not live to enjoy it, but his family would. He agreed to the terms of the rituals and entered into a contract with the ritualist.

Unfortunately, for Naju's husband, at the time he got home from that trip, there was no one around. They had all traveled to another village for a funeral. He, therefore, carried the bag home all by himself. He died mysteriously, after which the money came. His wife, the shop owner, inherited everything. She moved back to Gnani and started her shop business.

In Ghana, generally, assisting people with their bags on their return from a journey is a sign of respect, hospitality, and a way of building relationships and bonding together as members of a community. It is unusual for one to carry their bag to the house all by themselves on returning from a journey. Children are usually in competition to help with the bag. I enjoyed this kindness several times while in the community and my home village. Elders would call on children to assist if the children did not see you themselves. The woman's husband was undoubtedly sure that someone would help him carry his bag home. Based on that surety, he accepted the terms of the ritualist. From the other stories I heard in northern Ghana, some people were willing to die to liberate their families from the perpetual poverty that had plagued them. I do not know whether this was sincere or if it was a sign of the frustration they had been experiencing due to poverty. "If I die, I die as a rich person, and I am going to be given a befitting burial. My family would, after all, enjoy the riches." This was uncommon, though, and I am doubtful that this man had taken that path.

Ordinarily, the assumption would have been that working with a government department would be an average earner and would not be one who would struggle to survive. This assumption could be untrue, too, depending on his role in the department, extended family members' responsibilities, as well as his consumption patterns. I am aware that people's aspirations are unique, and the aspiration of one might be to live a lifestyle that is incongruent with his take-home salary. To gain more respect, power and control in the community, such people are willing to engage in other ventures to make more money. In this instance, the man seems to have chosen the occult as his strategy.

This narrative fits with many local narratives of the modern-day occult economy. It is clear from the narrative above that people's lives were sacrificed in the pursuit of self-interest. He was willing to sacrifice a life to make money, but in the moral of the story, it was his own life that was sacrificed.

Case Two: Transnational Witchery and Money Rituals, a Journey to Benin: Strategist/Tactic

I met up with a middle-aged businessman named Naja, who was once very rich in Accra, the capital city of Ghana. We had met countless times and conversed about several topics, including education, social life, family, and life abroad. However, the content of our conversation on one occasion was unusual. He narrated to me how he was a rich man in the past and had fame for it. Songs and appellations had even been made about him. Only the young might be oblivious to who he was. However, the sources of his riches were a point of debate. Some believed that he was involved in money rituals, while others argued that he was hardworking and that his riches reflected this work ethic. From my observation, he was hardworking. He left for work very early, at 4 a.m. and came back at 7 p.m. every day except Sundays. He also hated to see his children sit idle and would often find something for them to do.

However, in the conversation, he revealed how he traveled to Benin, a neighboring West African country, to participate in money rituals. In Ghana, it is not uncommon to hear stories of this kind. It is often rumored that politicians, magicians, people of authority, businesspeople, and sometimes pastors visit Benin to acquire power from the spiritual world to aid them in their respective endeavors and capital accumulation. On another occasion, at the bus station waiting to travel to the northern part of Ghana, a group of people, one woman and four other men, engaged in a conversation that I eavesdropped on with eagerness. It was an issue that attracted my attention, possibly due to its relatedness to spirituality and money rituals in Ghana, a significant portion of my study. They were engaged in a heated argument about where one could access the most potent ritual/spiritual support to get rich and protect what they had already acquired. A consensus suggested that Benin was the best destination for anything spiritual at the end of the debate.

The man continued with the story about his journey to Benin. He told me he had several properties, including cargo trucks and houses. He was engaged in petty trading in northern Ghana. After that, it developed into a big store, and finally, he moved into the cargo truck business, where he used his cars to cart goods between the south and north of Ghana. He suggested that when you have property, it is inevitable that people will become jealous of you and will want to destroy you. Therefore, you need to protect yourself in such instances:

> You don't just leave yourself flat with these properties. You have enemies who would want to bring you down. You must protect yourself. I have been to many earth deities to seek help and protection, some in the Upper East, Brong Ahafo, and Volta regions. That was when things started going wrong for me. My enemies found a way out to pull me down. I heard about Benin from a friend, and I decided to go.
>
> On that fateful day, I got to Benin and asked for directions to the place my friend told me. I was well received, and my intentions were made known to them. They said they could be of help to help me protect my property, wealth, and my family from witches. It got to a point where they needed to explain "the rules of the game," referring to the terms of reference. The ritualist said: "I can help you make more money and all the other things you have asked for. But you must always come back to pay some fee every year to us." He also told me that any person who collected my bag while I was returning from the journey was going to die, and after the person's death, I would gain the money and other things I had asked for. At this point, I was scared. He was yet to perform the rituals. So, I told him I was going out and would be back. I went out and never returned. I came back to Ghana.

When I asked him why he was scared, he cited the gravity of engaging in ritual. It was dangerous for him, leaving him vulnerable to accusations of witchcraft. Second, anyone who assisted in carrying his bag from the journey would die before the money would come. He would be responsible for their death, and this would most likely be repeated every year he had to revisit Benin to pay the annual fee: "I would have become rich by engaging in such a ritual, but people dying would have made me be accused as a witch too."

In short, in the two cases discussed above, that of the man who journeyed to Benin and the woman entrepreneur in Gnani, the individuals were wealthy and considered "developed" as they were both considered relatively wealthy and could afford to meet their needs. The implications of these cases are two-fold; first, they highlight the fear, panic, mistrust, jealousy and even hatred that surround witchcraft and ideas of how wealth is accumulated. People who knew about these rumors of the two people employing occult forces to make their riches avoided buying from them, feared them, and would even warn others, including me, to stay away from buying from the shop. Interestingly, I am unsure if both alleged occultists knew about these allegations against them. People accused them of using occult forces to attract customers; in the first case, and then in the second case, people gossiped that he was a witch that manipulated the fortunes of others from the community for himself. The irony, though, is that none of them was confronted, talk less of being evicted. This leads us to the second implication; it leads us to understand that rich or developed people who are alleged as witches are not often confronted or banished from their communities. Instead, it is poor and vulnerable. Witchcraft is therefore relational, taking into consideration people's economic statuses and positions in society.

Again, what is exciting but unsurprising is that both Naju and Naja feared being attacked by witches as well. In the second case, the Naja had gone to seek the protection of many anti-witchcraft shrines spotted across the country (Lentz, 2000; Martin, 2014; Parish, 2003). He was afraid that if he did not do that, witches, whom he called "enemies," would destroy his riches and thus serve as a limitation to his entrepreneurship. Even, as would appear, he was not as rich as before at the time of my meeting with him. In those instances, he started seeking support of deities and anti-witchcraft shrines to help him out. It was also in the same light, and his eagerness to acquire more riches led him to go to Benin.

THEORIZING *(IN)*EQUALITY

Neoliberalism, with its deepening of inequalities, has come to stay (see Comaroff and Comaroff, 1999; Smith, 2005, 2008; Geschiere, 1997, 2013). Focusing on self-realization without thought to collaborative development is becoming a norm, leading to the projection of some members of Ghanaian society above others. Thus, other community members have adopted mechanisms to protect what they have acquired. One of these mechanisms is witchcraft, seeking the help of supernatural powers to gain and maintain wealth, as was found in the field. One of these is how people visit shrines to help them become rich (Lentz, 2000). In addition, people are engaging occult forces so as not to be left behind. This belief in witchcraft is embedded in many activities and is assumed to be the bedrock of success and failure. The question, however, remains as to how and in what ways people employ occult means in their wealth-making practices.

It does appear that the conceptual categories made by Kroesbergen-Kamps (2020), that witchcraft is *in* modernity and witchcraft is *of* modernity exist in Ghana. Thus, this section uses the two conceptual categories to theorize *(in)*equality in Ghana. The engagement of occult forces as a strategy by people to enrich themselves and protect their wealth, property, and families is not necessarily perceived as evil. This idea resonates with the Ghanaian religious discourse, where almost everyone belongs to one form of religion or another. The various religions encourage their adherents to seek spiritual understanding in all aspects of their daily lives, including their economic and development initiatives. It is not uncommon to find traditionalists seeking help to become wealthy in shrines or Christians and Muslims praying for financial breakthroughs (see Mabefam and Appau, 2020). In this case, it can be said that witchcraft or such occult means are *of* modernity. It is also important to note that not all occult-related issues are equated to witchcraft. There is a blurred line where witchcraft is often seen as negative, but the occult could be both positive and negative. This is because it involves individuals using such means to leverage their economic disadvantage and turn the situation to their advantage. That is equalizing their inequality in the modern capitalist world.

Development at the micro- and macro-levels is pitched against what happens at the individual and community levels. The neoliberal individuals who perceive themselves to be developed or on the track toward development have an extreme taste for foreign goods and lifestyles. Neoliberal discourse has affected the perception of people about what development means. Some community members recounted that development referred to large family sizes, having several wives, and children, a large farm, and many animals in the past. They never thought of converting the animals and the produce of their farms into monetary terms as is done today. A wealthy man could feed his family and had many hands on on his farm, mainly with his children and immediate family members. In addition, one was considered developed to get immediate help from kinship members in times of need. Today, the neoliberal agenda has swept across Africa without sparing even the remotest village in Ghana. Though complex to define, the strong equation of wealth and people's worth in terms of development is no longer the size of their families. Instead, the critical measure is the monetary value of their possessions.

The monetization of property due to the neoliberal agenda has led to the individualization of people in communities that traditionally valued collective success. Individuals in those communities are now more concerned about their wealth accumulation than the communal good. People who once saw one another as family, and farmed together, are now drifting toward individual farming and personal wealth accumulation. A man of eighty years old told me that while growing up, all his siblings and cousins farmed together, harvested together, and the food was collectively stored. During every farm season, they started work on his father's farm as he was the eldest and moved to the next in terms of seniority until everyone's farm was completed. The father was, therefore, in charge of all the food produced. He, however, served everyone who needed food at regular intervals. Again, since agriculture was the only activity they engaged in, anyone who needed anything, they came together and decided what to sell to offset whatever cost was demanded. Jealousy and competition were less of an issue in the family. But of late, he explained that his children do not even go to his farm or work together. They are all interested in what they make for themselves. This has compounded the problem of jealousy and competition (key triggers of witchcraft in communal societies) in the family and has reduced the level of trust among kinship members (see Gershman, 2016; Geschiere, 1997, 2013). This finding supports what Gershman's study (2016) outlines of the beliefs in witchcraft among nineteen sub-Saharan African countries. Gershman found that witchcraft beliefs and practices eroded social capital among community members.

As seen from the ethnographic account, witchcraft strategies in Ghana also touch upon the concept of the "occult economy"—the term coined by Comaroff and Comaroff (1999). It could be seen that people buy and sell witchcraft products. Within this view, witchcraft is also a commodity that is traded—and perhaps to a certain extent only accessible to people who have the means to procure such services, illustrating how power structures and relations also engage with witchcraft as a strategy for wealth and power accumulation and protection.

CONCLUSION

As discussed in this chapter, there are many ways in which there are interactions between witchcraft and both personal and societal development. The values espoused and interactions brought forth by the processes adopted at individual and collective levels in the pursuit of socioeconomic development are often at odds with the cultural framing of social relations and identities. Nonetheless, witchcraft is essential to consider as part of these processes and is a response to modernity rather than its antithesis. I sought to explore the problematic nature of the introduction of neoliberalism in Ghana and its various implications in how identities and relations unfold. The focus on the individual, for instance, creates tensions between the pursuit of personal socioeconomic development and the need for individuals to live among others of their families, communities, and the broader society. Thus, there are tensions between individuals who stand out as having achieved relatively higher standards of socioeconomic development than others. It can often lead to mistrust, jealousy, and accusations of witchcraft as the reason for their advancement. These findings are essential to incorporate into the broader understandings and conceptualizations of development and the approaches taken in the interventions taken regarding development in Ghana and elsewhere. This chapter has advanced the theory of de Certeau as being deployed both as a strategy and tactic, as well as Kroesbergen-Kamps (2020) theory of witchcraft *in (of)* modernity.

Chapter 4

Intervening in "Witch Camps"

A Contestation and Controversy

In the previous chapters, I drew on several case studies to discuss how witchcraft is implicated in economic development in many parts of Africa. This discussion drew on development theories such as capitalism, modernization, and neoliberalism, and argued that the localization of these theories has led to tensions between capitalist modern ideals of self-realization and the traditional values of the community. I argued that there is nothing inherently problematic about pursuing self-realization, but in the African worldview, there must be a balance between personal and community achievement. In chapter 2, I dealt with different groups of people who were accused of witchcraft, confronted, and ejected into the Gnani-Tindang community, for example. Although they were resilient, many of their needs were left unmet. Against this backdrop, chapter 4 explores how the welfare needs of people accused of witchcraft are being met in Ghana and elsewhere in Africa. I also highlight a conversation around the controversies surrounding some of the interventions employed by different actors in communities of refuge.

By way of illustration of the point above, in some of the tensions in intervening in communities of refuge, I draw attention to the case of ninety-year-old Madam Akua Denteh who was murdered on Thursday, July 23, 2020, in broad daylight at Kafaba in the East Gonja Municipality of the newly created Savannah Region in Ghana. As reported across various media houses, her only perceived crime was that a soothsayer declared her to be a witch who was responsible for the mysterious burning of the New Patriotic Party (NPP) youth shed in the community. In addition, the soothsayer accused her of being responsible for sporadic rainfall in the community and recommended that she be lynched. Unlike others, Akua's lynching was streamed on social media. It was a public event with many people watching while she was subjected to inhuman treatment until she died. Hysteria and public outcry demanded that the Ghanaian authorities act swiftly and bring the perpetrators to book. Politicians, human rights organizations, and other stakeholders have made many speeches and pledges condemning the act. Many have called for draconian punitive actions against the perpetrators of the despicable act, but concerns remain that this is yet another addition to the many such incidents that have caused the death of many people and yet without any punishment for their perpetrators.

In Africa, incidences such as the killing of Madam Akua Denteh are not uncommon. There are many people who are accused of witchcraft and murdered or banished from their communities. Unlike Madam Akua, those who are "fortunate" to escape death by lynching must seek refuge elsewhere. In Ghana, some villages have become known as places that provide refuge to people banished from their communities. It is important to emphasize that these villages were not created for this purpose but, rather, are already existing communities that have chosen to provide such refuge as a local protection mechanism to people who would otherwise have been lynched. These villages offer temporary accommodation (sometimes permanent), food, and a sense of community and belonging while efforts are made to help them transition to making such places their homes.

This local approach to providing refuge, however, has come into tension with the approach of development actors to deal with the issue of witchcraft accusations and banishment in Africa. Drawing from different ontologies and epistemes, in much development discourse such places of refuge are reconfigured and constructed as "camps," with the prefix "camp" added to the names of the communities involved. With those communities now designated as "camps," their very existence has been questioned and has generated intense debates. They are framed as places of human rights violations and abuse and calls are issued for their closure by development actors. In 2014, around the vicinity where Akua Denteh was lynched, the Bonyasi community that provided refuge for people accused of witchcraft was compelled by the Ghanaian state in collaboration with some NGOs (nongovernmental organizations) to stop receiving these people. Had this directive not been given, it is possible that Akua Denteh would have ended up there rather than being killed.

Similar communities exist in some other countries such as Burkina Faso, Benin, and Cameroon among others. The difference though is that in the case of these countries, other than communities, development actors such as government and NGOs are involved in creating these communities to host people who have been accused of witchcraft and driven out of their communities to protect them (e.g., Burkina Faso) or punish them (Cameroon and Benin). In the case of Cameroon or Benin, the states are actively involved in criminalizing people accused of witchcraft and sentencing them to a prison term. In this case, the intentions are to protect the communities from the supposed "wicked" actions of people accused of witchcraft. However, it seems commendable and acceptable that governments and NGOs in these countries offer these structures either to protect people accused of witchcraft or to punish them for their supposed criminality in society. The difference between the acceptability of these structures in these countries and in Ghana is, in the case of Ghana, local communities provide refuge through these villages. That is where I would suggest the controversy lies, which speaks to a broader issue of how development actors perceive and treat local development interventions. If the Ghanaian state or NGOs in Ghana had equally instituted these villages to offer refuge elsewhere, the conversation I argue would have been different.

Overall, the chapter contributes to ongoing debates about the controversies of intervening in witchcraft issues and communities of refuge in Africa. I explicate the role of the state, NGOs, and FBOs (faith-based organizations) and how they engage with witchcraft and communities of refuge arguing that although they have played key roles in meeting some of the immediate needs of people accused of witchcraft, their actions could exacerbate the plight of the people accused of witchcraft (see Riedel, 2017), especially in the case of Ghana. In making this assertion, I will tease-out the particular differences in providing witch shelters in Burkina Faso and witch prisons in Cameroon or Benin. The chapter highlights that the actions of these actors might be well-intentioned, but their applications can be challenging due to the dissonance between local realities and the various philosophical underpinnings guiding the way their projects are designed, implemented, and their ways of measuring successes (Mutaru, 2018, 2019; Riedel, 2017). This points to the need for government and development workers to pay attention to local epistemologies.

CONTAINING WITCHCRAFT ACCUSATIONS AND ITS LIMITATIONS

Governments across many societies in Africa have responded in various ways to witchcraft beliefs, accusations, and practices, often as a response to public outcries for something to be done about them. Witchcraft issues are a "minefield of ambiguities" as Geschiere (1997) says and thus, the positions, roles, responses, and approaches of states are also different and need to be examined within particular contexts. In this case, when I talk about "state" or "government" I do not assume a monolithic, essentialist, or homogenous actor. There are different positions, personalities and variations across political, public service, public institutions, and regional dimensions that show heterogeneity in terms of approach to witchcraft issues. Moreover, the "state" and "government" comprise human actors with different and complex understandings and engagements with witchcraft issues. Further, responses by "the state" or "the government" to public outcries invariably start with the political leaders who pursue and frame witchcraft issues through policy. These responses could be in the favor of the accusers or the community considering the nature of public outcries (as in the cases of Cameroon or Benin, for example) or in favor of the accused who are considered victims and subjected to human rights abuses as we shall find about in Ghana. This section engages with some of the ways various actors have approached the ongoing existence of witchcraft beliefs, practices, and accusations, and their limitations.

Many authors focusing on the African region have explored the varying positions and approaches taken by states in witchcraft containment. In post-apartheid South Africa, for example, the rise of witchcraft accusations and ensuing violence in the early 1990s compelled the state to set up the *Commission of Inquiry into Witchcraft Violence and Ritual Murders* in 1995 leading to interventions that continue to be debated (see Comaroff and Comaroff, 1999a; Joseph, 2014). As Natasha Joseph notes, "the commission recommended police-led interventions to teach communities about the dangers of false allegations and witch hunts" (2014, p. 47) and thus making public education and awareness creation an epicenter to witchcraft responses in South Africa. Comaroff and Comaroff also referred to the South African case and make the point that due to conversations about the widespread witchcraft accusations not "even the state has remained aloof" (Comaroff and Comaroff 1999a, p. 465; 2000, p. 787).

In contrast, Kahn (2011) notes in the case of Benin that as of the 1970s the state's agenda to "modernise" meant policing and criminalizing people accused of witchcraft and as a result, there was a nationwide witch-hunting exercise, with the people identified as witches imprisoned. The irony, however, is that the Benin government's approach to identifying witches before imprisoning individuals was to confirm their status by engaging "local experts" (i.e., "witch-doctors"), which are often employed by communities as well (see Green and Mesaki, 2005 for Tanzania; Smith, 2005, 2008 for Kenya).

In the context of Cameroon, Geschiere (1997, 2005) notes that both local and national politicians in Cameroon have drawn on witchcraft to champion their cause. Paradoxically, some of the people who are accused of witchcraft are reprimanded while others are not. As one accused witch is standing trial, others are called on as experts to assess their guilt of a person accused of witchcraft (Fisiy and Geschiere, 1990, p. 135). Geschiere notes that witchcraft issues are "a minefield of ambiguities and shifting meanings," highlighting the lack of clarity, certainty, or consistency (Geschiere 2005, p. 94). In post-independent Cameroon, the state acknowledged the existence of witchcraft and thus was determined to punish those found guilty of the crime of practicing it, including imprisonment of no less than ten years. Fisiy and Geschiere captured it more succinctly:

> Since the end of the seventies, the State Courts in the East Province of Cameroon have regularly convicted "witches." This is a novelty. Until then, conviction by the State Courts was only possible when there was concrete proof of a physical attack. . . . But recently, people accused of witchcraft are convicted without such concrete proof and often without having confessed. The Courts then impose heavy sentences—fines and nearly always imprisonment, even up to ten years. (1990, p. 135)

The range of positions and responses by states, in other words, varies across different contexts as well as different societies. And there are varying degrees of complicity between state and community understandings and approaches to witchcraft issues. In the case of Benin, or Cameroon where the states are implicated especially in the imprisonment of people accused of witchcraft when found guilty, the case of Ghana is different. The relationship between witchcraft and other entities such as NGOs, faith-based organizations (FBOs), and civil societies is not as apparent as in communities of refuge in Ghana.

One of the unique features of the Ghanaian case is the presence of communities of refuge and the fact that this has drawn in different conversations with different actors such as government and nongovernment actors; NGOs, FBOs, and local authorities have taken entrenched positions. There are some similarities among the various actors in that the main lens through which the Ghanaian government and NGOs intervene in communities of refuge is through a human rights approach (ActionAid, 2008b, 2008b, 2014; Government of Ghana, 1998; Issah, 2017; NCCE, 2010). It is often argued that the witchcraft accusations and communities of refuge are an abuse of human rights, threatening the dignity of the people living there (ActionAid, 2008b, 2008b, 2014; NCCE, 2010). Unlike in the case of Benin or Cameroon, where the states were implicated in the imprisonment of people accused of witchcraft, in the case of Ghana the state and other actors' campaigns revolved around the abolishment of locally constituted communities of refuge that were accused of "imprisoning" people. The human rights approach to intervening in communities of refuge in Ghana, I would argue, has merits but needs to be contextual. The application of human rights to the abolition of communities of refuge sometimes has the potential to endanger the lives of the very people it seeks to protect (see Mutaru, 2018, 2019; Riedel, 2017). For example, in 2010, National Commission on Civic Education (NCCE) strongly recommended the closure of communities of refuge across northern Ghana even though 89.6 percent of people accused of witchcraft in them said that they did not want them closed (2010, p. 99). NCCE argues that the communities of refuge ignore their human rights and the constitution of Ghana, which guarantees everyone the right to live with their families (2010, p. 99). The preoccupation with the human rights of the people from this perspective needs to be contextualized with the realities, as presented throughout this book, of the fact that it is normally family problems that lead to accusations by family members. That is, attempts to reintegrate people back into their families and communities come with their own risks, and the resulting rejections may also constitute abuse. This is especially true within a society that is likely to disengage, discriminate, and even commit violent acts toward people accused of witchcraft (see Igwe, 2016a; Riedel, 2017).

What is even more telling is that similar actions by the government in the past have failed miserably in managing the complex and sensitive issues surrounding witchcraft accusations. According to Naboo (2017, p. 99), in 1998, two government delegations, one by CHRAJ, and the other by a caucus of Parliament visited Gambaga and ordered the chief to release the people accused of witchcraft. In the aftermath of the CHRAJ (Commission on Human Rights and Administrative Justice) commissioner's visit in 1998 to the Gambaga and his subsequent order that the alleged witches be released to go back home, the response from the alleged witches was rather surprising because of their refusal to go home. Even when the *Gambarana* gave them permission to leave, they refused to do so. Similarly, in 1998, after the Women Parliamentary Caucus had visited the Gambaga, and presented clothes, food items, and utensils, the fervent pleas from the alleged witches to the female parliamentarians were for the government to allow them to live in the communities of refuge for the rest of their lives since they would die or be killed as soon as they return to their communities (see Naboo, 2017). They argued that the stigma attached to them makes it impossible to return to live in the society that has traumatized and banished them.

Although the debate about the closure of the so-called "witch camps" is not new, the incessant call to close them is problematic. The government and its partners could further expose people accused of witchcraft to danger if such communities are disbanded (see Igwe, 2016a; Mutaru, 2019; Riedel, 2017). One thing that becomes clear is the decision by the government and its partners to close down communities of refuge have not worked. It is a top-down approach that has the potential of ignoring local realities and the voices of the very people that it seeks to protect.

THE GHANAIAN STATE AND THE
"PROBLEM" OF "WITCH CAMPS"

The Ghanaian state continues to play key roles in the containment of witchcraft accusations. As a result, while in the field, I identified certain state institutions and held conversations with them regarding witchcraft and "witch camps." The National Commission on Civic Education (NCCE), Commission on Human Rights and Administrative Justice (CHRAJ), and Domestic Violence and Victims Support Unit (DOVVSU) of the Ghana Police Service were identified as being particularly relevant. They are institutions charged with the responsibility of educating people about their rights and the abolition of cultural practices that may hinder human development. They have the responsibility of seeking redress in the case of abuse of people's rights and overseeing providing security to all Ghanaians. Previous scholarship has taken these organizations to represent government policy on witchcraft and communities of refuge issues in Ghana. I take it, therefore, that the views expressed by people occupying portfolios in the state institutions represent the stands of the state, however, where they express their individual views, they make it clear.

The two case studies below highlight some tensions, and disjuncture between the individual officers relative to their positions and the approaches of the state that they represent. That is the police officer case that highlights the issue of criminality, notions of intent, and whether it is manslaughter or murder. The director of CHRAJ highlights the issue of human rights and "relational dynamics" between the state and the individual occupying the position as well. Both cases highlight the tensions not only between the state and the different instruments it has (police, CHRAJ) but also between the different individuals in such positions who often have to navigate between their official roles in reflecting the state's regulatory frameworks and their being "cultural" beings, needing and sometimes personally agreeing or accepting the ways that communities view, approach, and adjudicate on issues of witchcraft and communities of refuge in Ghana. See table 4.1 for the government departments and demographics of position holders in those departments who participated in my study.

The heads of the various institutions were interviewed, except that of DOVVSU who preferred to interact with me in a group interview. The directors of the various institutions were all men. Thirty-three percent of government officials had a high school leaving certificate while 67 percent had a tertiary degree certificate (diploma and first degrees).

Table 4.1 Socio-Demographic Characteristics of Government and NGO Officials

Variable *Government/state*		*Frequencies*	*Percentages*
Agencies	Police	1	17
	CHRAJ	1	17
	NCCE	1	17
	DOVVSU	3	50
Position	District director	4	67
	Other staff	2	33
Gender	Women	0	0
	Men	6	100
Married?	Yes	6	100
	No	0	0
Educational status	No formal education	0	0
	Basic education	0	0
	SHS	2	33
	Tertiary	4	67
NGOs			
Name	ActionAid Ghana	4	44
	Songtaba	1	11
	Humanist Service Corps	4	44
Position	Head of the various NGOS in the Region	3	33
	Other staff	6	67
Gender	Women	6	67
	Men	3	33
Married?	Yes	3	33
	No	6	67
Educational status	No formal education	0	0
	Basic education	0	0
	SHS	0	0
	Tertiary	9	100

Author created

Case One: District Crime Officer and the Discretionary Power to Intervening in Witchcraft Accusations

The police as a state institution is charged with the responsibility of maintaining law and order and has the discretionary power to make a choice of what, when, and how to intervene. This discretionary power gives the police the room to navigate different cases of witchcraft accusations and what they choose to handle when such issues are brought before them. This also depends greatly on various aspects of the personality, and character of the individual, how they see their role, as well as their relationship with others in the community. Here, I detail my interaction with a police officer in one of the witchcraft accusations that led to murder and how the police intervened.

Mr. Joe is a fifty-three-year-old man and crime officer of the Ghana police service. He holds a diploma in public administration and is married with three kids. During fieldwork, I spoke with Mr. Joe because he handled a case that involved a witchcraft accusation that ended in murder. Mr. Joe stated.

> The case started as the State vs Ndo. That's the name of the suspect. It so happened that on the 1st January 2015 at 2: 30 PM, Mr. Ndo came to our station to report himself for shooting community members as a way of defending his mother who was accused of witchcraft. Two people were killed in the process including one Mr. B who accused the suspect's mother of being a witch, and this degenerated into a scuffle. Things intensified leading to the suspect running into his room, brought a gun and shot at the three persons. Mr. M, aged 18, died on the spot while Mr. B and Mr. N were rushed to Bimbilla and Tamale Government Hospitals respectively for treatment. However, Mr. N 28 years passed away on the 3rd January 2015. The third victim Mr. B was discharged on 3rd January 2015, and the suspect is currently on remand in Prison. However, in the Ghanaian setting, witchcraft accusation is a human right issue. Such issues are usually taken to the Commission on Human Rights and Administrative Justice. So, we as police can only deal with the murder aspect and hence took it as murder which is a criminal offence in our criminal code. Section 46 of the Criminal Offences Act 1960 is murder. There is no current Ghanaian law that deals with witchcraft specifically, and the more reasons why we cannot look at it as a witchcraft case.
>
> We arrested Mr. Ndo and remanded him at Bimbilla magistrate court, pending further investigation. Because in our settings here, there are certain cases you cannot try at the lower court. Post-mortem of the dead persons needed to be done first. Then after everything, if it is confirmed that this is the court of the case, then we prepare a duplicate docket to the Attorney General's office in Tamale. Then Attorney General Office will also study and analyse the docket and prefer the charge: whether it was manslaughter, that is the unintentional act or an intentional act, that is murder. That is when you form the intention to kill, it is murder. But if you accidentally kill, they don't consider it to be intentional so that one can get manslaughter. So, now, his case has gone to the Attorney General's office. They have studied the docket and have reported that he: should be charged with murder. So, they have taken him to district court again and he has been committed to stand trial at the high court of Tamale.

Judging from the case, there are two things that come up: a witchcraft accusation as a criminal case and a civil case. Through the crime officer's report, it is clear that Mr. Ndo's trial was criminal and thus, it was the State vs. Mr. Ndo for the intentional act of killing and wounding people who accused the mother of witchcraft through gun use. While the trial of Mr. Ndo was criminal and handled by these state institutions, what is interesting is that Mr. Ndo was not even the subject of a witchcraft accusation. It was his mother. It would appear in this case that the government apparatus did not intervene in the witchcraft accusation itself as no attention was paid to Mr. Ndo's mother, and the potential threat to her life in her community. What then happened was that Mr. Ndo's mother relocated to Gnani to seek refuge as I detailed in chapter 2.

Case Two: CHRAJ Director, and Witchcraft Adjudication in Ghana

CHRAJ is an independent organization for the safeguarding of human rights in Ghana. It was established in 1993 by Act 456 of the Parliament of Ghana as directed by Article 216 of the 1992 Ghana constitution. Below I detail my interaction with an officer of CHRAJ and how it has adjudicated witchcraft accusations in northern Ghana.

Mr. Mahama is a thirty-seven-year-old man and director of CHRAJ. He holds a university degree and is married with four kids. During fieldwork, I spoke with Mr. Mahama because I was told by the police officer in case 1 above that the police usually refer issues of witchcraft to his office. I wanted to find out how CHRAJ, as a state institution, adjudicates witchcraft and its related issues. Mr. Mahama has held the position of CHRAJ director for the past seven years and therefore has witnessed enough cases to be able to speak for the institution he heads. For seven years, cases of witchcraft accusations have been brought to his office for redress. Mahama stated that

> in my capacity as a CHRAJ director, I have witnessed and adjudicated on some witchcraft accusations issues. Witchcraft accusations are prevalent here but not many of them are brought to my office. People in the local communities prefer to take such issues to community systems for adjudication. No accuser will prefer to bring an accused to my office for arbitration. Because accusers will be at fault as it is difficult to prove witchcraft accusations with facts to be appreciated by our office. It is people accused of witchcraft who sometimes report to us that they have been accused wrongfully.
>
> We don't even use the word witch. We prefer to use alleged or suspected witch. Within the legal framework used by the state drawing from the constitution, if you say something exists, then you should be able to prove beyond reasonable doubt that it exists. In the case of witchcraft, no one can do it within the law court. The evidence should be factual and convincing and not based on rumours or speculations. Witchcraft issues cannot be proven in the law court as a matter of evidence or facts.
>
> However, from the traditional perspective, by this, I am now moving away from my human rights capacity as an officer of CHRAJ to that of a cultural being and an indigene of northern Ghana. As for the traditionalists, they have a

way of proving that somebody is a witch or a wizard. Although I'm not a part of the people who conduct that ceremony, I come from here and have knowledge of the tradition and can speak to it. People who are suspected as people accused of witchcraft are sent to witch camps and shrines to prove their innocence. Shrines such as the ones at Gnani, Kukuo and Gambaga are crucial for such purposes. Over there, they are given concoctions and a sacrifice of chicken is used to determine people's fate. A lot of people who go to the shrines to have their accusations assessed remain there afterwards. They rarely go back home. It is challenging to ask them to go back home if they don't want to.

From the legal perspective, a mere calling of somebody as a witch is considered an act of defamation. This is because one is unable to provide the evidence needed by the court. You have no evidence to support your claim that is admissible by law. If you can prove that Mr. A or Mr. B is a witch, then you exonerate yourself of the crime, otherwise, you will be penalised.

In short, the conversation with the director of CHRAJ highlights some key points including the fact that although his office does handle issues of witchcraft, people in the communities preferred to handle those issues at the local level. This is because of the different understandings of handling witchcraft that are uniquely different, as will be discussed in the next section.

Analysis and Discussion of the Two Cases

The analyses of the two cases demonstrate that different government institutions such as the police, court, prison service, and the health services department are implicated in the issue of witchcraft accusations in Ghana. The roles of these institutions differ based on their experiences and expertise and what they are mandated to do by law or special acts that established them. The first case was seen as a criminal case and as a result post-mortem of those who were shot needed to be done to determine the charge to make against Mr. Ndo (see Forsyth, 2016). While such an assessment was ongoing in the Bimbilla Hospital, the police had to detain Mr. Ndo. Of course, the courts were also implicated as a docket was prepared for their assessment after it was determined by the medical experts in the hospital that Mr. M and Mr. N were indeed dead. At this point, the Ghana prison service also became a part of it, the government officials implicated in the witchcraft issues as they were responsible for keeping Mr. Ndo while his trial kicked off in the Tamale High Court.

What has emerged so far is that there are different engagements of "government" personnel with people who are accused of witchcraft and others implicated by such accusations. Government personnel and their roles regarding witchcraft are limited judging from their engagement with witchcraft itself and accusation. Drawing from the examples above, the two government institutions were clearly concerned with the defamation or criminal aspects of the cases (Adinkrah, 2015; Igwe, 2016b), and not with witchcraft itself, which had led to such criminality or defamations. Little attention or no action was even given to Mr. Ndo's mother whose life was equally at risk, and she had to relocate to the Gnani community for fear that she might be killed for being accused of witchcraft (see chapter 2). This is because such institutions have jurisdiction over criminal cases but not witchcraft. The level of competency, knowledge, and expertise of court, police, and government officials to assess or adjudicate accusations is questioned as they are not perceived as having the expertise to do so by local people as I gathered from the field—the locals prefer to go to the local experts who were discussed in chapter 1. Despite the concern by the local people that the state modern institutions do not have the expertise to preside over issues of witchcraft, Igwe asserted that such institutions do actually preside over witchcraft accusations (Igwe, 2016b). However, if witchcraft accusations are sent to the state institutions, then it highlights the disjuncture between formal state apparatus that lends itself toward rational, human rights notions of law with that notion of justice and adjudication that is more culturally emergent (see Mutaru, 2018, 2019). That is why the CHRAJ director would mention in his interview that the locals rarely come to his office with witchcraft issues.

From the two cases, it also emerged that the staff of government agencies hold dual positions regarding witchcraft; this was more pronounced with the CHRAJ officer who was of northern descent. This was something that the director of CHRAJ was open about, contrasting his human rights-based approach as a director with his traditional beliefs. The CHRAJ director revealed to me that it was illegal to even accuse someone of being a witch while also admitting that as an individual he believes in witchcraft. The contrasting positions of individuals on matters of witchcraft are intriguing, especially when government policy formulations and implementations are influenced by individual dispositions of the staff working with such agencies. It does seem there will always be a conflict between the dual positions contained in one person. This is because individual actors working in state institutions are cultural beings who often believe in witchcraft themselves, as was suggested by some participants of my study.

Unlike the state, which is silent on whether witchcraft exists or not, as individuals, all the state officials I interacted with admitted that they believed in the existence of witchcraft. Within these interactions, a distinction was made between their role as individuals and as representatives of state agencies. This distinction was necessary as I noted that their responses depended on which of their positions I was engaging with. From the perspective of the state, they did not only report their bias toward accusers; they also asserted that communities of refuge were illegal within the state, and thus efforts should be channeled toward disbanding them (Government of Ghana, 1998; Wumbla, 2017; NCCE, 2010). The government of Ghana started to deal with the issue of communities of refuge in 1998 when its attention was drawn to the fact that there were scores of women whose rights were abused through witchcraft accusations (see Mutaru, 2019; Naboo, 2017).

The backdrop to this call was that in 1997, there was an outbreak of a deadly Cerebro-Spinal Meningitis (CSM) epidemic that killed about 542 people in the north of the country (see Mutaru, 2019). The outbreak of the CSM epidemic was attributed to the work of witches and thus some, many suspected of doing so, were aggressively hunted, violently abused, and banished from their communities (see Adinkrah, 2004). The government has since viewed such banishments as abuse and infringements of the people accused of witchcraft rights adopted different strategies to deal with the problem of witchcraft, but faced difficulties, as the discussions below show.

The ongoing discussions reflect the findings of Fisiy and Geschiere in Cameroon, where they suggest that court judges preside over witchcraft issues because they believe in witchcraft, with some having consulted witch-finders for protection prior (1990). But unlike the case of Cameroon, the Ghanaian state is silent on whether witchcraft exists or not. The various state institutions mandated to deal with witchcraft issues are more interested in the consequences of witchcraft accusations than in witchcraft itself, and the case of Mr. Ndo is a clear example. Thus, ill-treatment of people who are accused of witchcraft could be prosecuted in the law court if such cases are reported to the appropriate institution (Igwe, 2016b). It is one of the reasons why Igwe argued that people accused of witchcraft contest their accusation within the modern state apparatus such as the law court, the police, CHRAJ and others. As suggested by the CHRAJ director, accusers always end up being the losers when state institutors investigate and arbitrate on witchcraft accusation issues. The challenge, however, is that the accusers do not feel that justice has been done in such instances, and that is why accusers prefer to take witchcraft accusations to local systems. These local arbitrations provide accusers with justice that fits in with their worldview.

As highlighted in the interaction with the CHRAJ director, it is not only the conflict between government structures and agencies of individuals working within them but there is also inter-structural conflict, which makes the issue of witchcraft more complicated. Acknowledging the bifurcation of the Ghanaian state in terms of rulership, traditional authorities occupy significant space in the sociocultural and political landscape of Ghana. I explored how the matrix of such relationships plays out in witchcraft matters. On the one hand, the traditional authority acknowledges and presides over witchcraft matters, while on the other, the state is silent on whether witchcraft exists or not and yet acknowledges the traditional authority as a structure. The issue is that the traditional authority can, through their mode of verification, unravel evidence that can be used against the prosecution of persons accused of witchcraft as was detailed in chapter 1. Their mode of seeking evidence is quite different from what the Ghanaian nation-state requires. The division between the Ghanaian state and the traditional state is made clear through codified rules and regulations where the legal jurisprudence of the nation serves as an overarching framework through which the constitution takes precedence over the customary law.

The challenge with these two parallel systems, however, is that the evidence of the traditional legal system cannot be used as evidence in the formal courtroom. As part of jurisprudence, no one is considered a criminal until proven guilty. It is just as difficult, if not impossible, to prove in the legal court system that another person is guilty of witchcraft. In this case, the accusers become vulnerable to charges of defamation. As was discussed in chapter 1, the people accused of witchcraft would have gone through "expert" local verification where there are doubts, but these expert verifications are not considered proper by the court system in Ghana (see ActionAid, 2008a, 2014; Wumbla, 2017)

The silence of state agencies regarding the existence of witchcraft is not limited to CHRAJ. Others, such as the Ghana Police service, and NCCE hold similar views, as we saw in the interaction with the crime officer of Ghana police in Bimbilla. The existence of communities of refuge is indicative of a backward state, which the state is bent on closing down (Igwe, 2016a; Riedel, 2017). Thus, I assert that in the eyes of the state, communities of refuge should not exist, because people accused of witchcraft are forced out of their communities, which is against their fundamental human rights, hence such people should be reintegrated (see ActionAid, 2008a; Wumbla, 2017; Mutaru, 2018, 2019; NCCE, 2010). Riedel (2017) in his provocative work titled *Failing State-Interventions and Witch-Hunts in Ghana*, further accuses the state of further traumatizing an already traumatized population through its actions. He says "a recent resettlement-campaign led by MOWAC and the NGO ActionAid Ghana has aggravated the problem and exploited victims emotionally in a staged mass-resettlement" (2017, p. 1). According to the Minister of Gender, Children and Social Protection at the national conference on witchcraft accusation, "Ghana's constitution endorses the human rights of all persons; we have a legal framework that criminalises such accusations" (ActionAid, 2014, p. 3). At the same conference, the keynote speaker, Prof. Kenneth Agyemang Attafuah noted that a similar conference was held in 1998, and yet sixteen years on, Ghana is still grappling with the issue of "witch camps" in northern Ghana. He further espoused that Ghana has specific provisions in the constitution that can deal with issues of abuse in relation to people accused of witchcraft. "There are specific provisions in the Ghanaian constitution that protect the dignity of all persons: Article 15, subsections 1 and 2. Despite a strong legal and institutional regime, people (especially women and girls) continue to suffer "colossal indignities" (ActionAid, 2014, p. 4). It, therefore, appears that all these interventions and legal frameworks that are designed to deal with the abuse of human rights are ineffective and, hence, need a rethink. However, these are general legal frameworks; they are not specific to witchcraft. Such general legal frameworks are limited when dealing with issues of witchcraft.

From another perspective, communities of refuge are considered illegal, and their existence affects the reputation of Ghana globally. For example, Dr. Hussein Zakaria, a lecturer at the University for Development Studies who presented at the witchcraft conference noted that "the camps put a dent on Ghana's human rights credibility" (ActionAid, 2014, p. 7). Judging from my discussions with key government officials and reading government documents, conference reports and news articles, there are many people calling for the closure of communities of refuge, and on a number of occasions, the government has been active in that. Here, I refer to the statement the government made to Gambarana to close the community of refuge (Poagnyaankura fongu) under his control and allow the women to go home, and the parliamentary caucus visit to Gambaga (see Mutaru, 2019; Naboo, 2017; Riedel, 2017). Both actions did not lead to the closure of the community of refuge and several other efforts at closing such communities have failed miserably.

While efforts are underway to close the communities of refuge, the state is making intermittent donations to residents of the communities. For example, the Ministry of Gender, Children and Social Protection occasionally donates food items and other packages to people accused of witchcraft who are residing in communities of refuge. On August 25, 2017, the minister visited Gambaga *Poagnyaankura fongu* and was reported to have donated "bags of rice, canned fish, detergents and a cash amount of GH¢800.00 for people accused of witchcraft upkeep." In her speech, she asserted,

It still remains in the plans of the Ministry of Gender, Children and Social Protection to disband the remaining five alleged people accused of witchcraft camps in Northern Ghana. The laws would deal with anyone or group of persons found culpable of lynching or causing harm to suspected people accused of witchcraft or wizards. President Akufo-Addo has been adjudged a gender champion in Africa. He is also co-chair of the UN Sustainable Development Goals. It is not right for him to be leading Ghana in the fight against poverty and dehumanisation against children and women whilst, in his backyard, there are people accused of witchcraft. (Naatogmah, 2017)

Previous governments have registered some community members for free National Health Insurance, which gives members free medical care. They have also registered members in the Livelihood Empowerment Against Poverty (LEAP), which gives them access to a monthly stipend (see Mutaru, 2019). These stipends at least offer people accused of witchcraft and ejected from their communities money to enable them to buy food and other basic necessities, in principle. However, as Mutaru found in his study, receiving such stipends is fraught with challenges including inconsistent payments, and access issues as they have to travel to the nearest district capital, which is sometimes far off as well as being limited to a few in communities of refuge (2019). My findings align with that of Mutaru as some residents of the Gnani community revealed they were not registered and did not benefit in any way from the government. For example, one of the people accused of witchcraft told me, "They only come to select a few and register. A lot of us are not registered for any services. We are at the mercy of nature and generous individuals."

Again, I observed in the field that LEAP had a broader focus, and multiple beneficiaries and people accused of witchcraft and residing are one of the categories. People accused of witchcraft and residing in the various communities of refuge who meet the selection criteria may benefit from such government intervention. Such interventions are not unique to people accused of witchcraft, and during the fieldwork, about 50 percent of my research participants reported that they were not even registered. Taking into account the unique precarity and vulnerability of people accused of witchcraft, it would have been great for the state to extend support to everyone. In short, the government's intervention in the communities of refuge is severely limited.

I overheard a conversation among some government officials, which suggested that if the conditions of the communities of refuge were improved by government interventions, more people would be likely to move there. In their view, the government would appear to be supporting the institutionalization of such communities. This would, however, contradict its intentions to close such communities. Nonetheless, an official from the CHRAJ office in Yendi disagreed with such arguments and makes a point that food, shelter, water, and health are basic human needs, and people have the right to enjoy them regardless of their status in society.

Witchcraft accusation in and of itself is not criminal, the mishandling of people accused of witchcraft leading to severe abuses can, however, be criminal. As found by Igwe (2016b) people who were accused of witchcraft in his study contested their accusations in state institutions, did so on their own and sought that those institutions pronounce them as not guilty of the accusation. Such contestations were between the accusers and the accused. In the case of criminal cases, the legal battle was always between the state and the individual who committed the crime. In case 1, presented earlier in this chapter, one of the sons of the woman accused of witchcraft was in prison for murder (Mr. Ndo), and this, rather than the accusation of witchcraft, was the focus of official proceedings. In short, if there is any state-level engagement at all with the issue of witchcraft, it focuses on the problems that emerge from witchcraft accusations and not from witchcraft itself. The cases discussed above frame witchcraft and the accusation of witchcraft as a criminal issue. The criminality comes from factors other than witchcraft itself. However, in many cases, where no violence erupts from the accusation, the accusations are usually treated as civil cases, and the state is relatively silent.

To summarize, it is clear that there are many facets to the way that the government (through its various instruments) approaches witchcraft and witchcraft accusations. As highlighted, there are tensions, controversies, and disjuncture. Overall, it is clear that how the government approaches witchcraft and witchcraft accusations is limited and does not satisfy some people in society. In the following section, the significant gap is filled by traditional authorities in communities of refuge as a way of highlighting both the limits of government intervention and also of the nuances, challenges, and critiques associated with the roles played by traditional authorities in the communities of refuge.

AN INTERVENTION FROM BELOW: THE ROLE OF TRADITIONAL AUTHORITIES IN COMMUNITIES OF REFUGE

In contrast to the approach by the Ghanaian government to close communities of refuge, the roles of traditional authorities in such communities are quite different. Different actors from the local communities such as to Bibɔrib (Ubɔr-sing), Biwadam (Uwadaan-sing), Bitindam (Utindaan-sing), Binyɔkdam (Unyɔkdaan-sing), argue that the resettlement of people within their communities is a social welfare or care provision mechanism and protection of people who would otherwise be killed or abused in their original communities as I gathered from the field (see also Igwe, 2016a; Riedel, 2017).

To draw back on the role of local experts on witchcraft, I refer to chapters 1 and 2. In these two chapters, I detailed the specific roles different local actors play to manage witchcraft accusations assessment, purification, adjudication, and many others. For example, based on the outcome of various local experts' assessments (see chapter 1), people accused of witchcraft may never return to their original home communities or may return temporarily but when tensions arise, they will be back in the communities of refuge and become the last resort for people seeking safety and fleeing persecution. This is true in the case of Mr. Ndo's mother (see chapter 2), who after initial assessment at Gnani was declared innocent. However, when she returned to her village, tensions began to rise as the brother-in-law presented a different narrative that suggested that she was guilty after the verification ritual. In the midst of the tensions, there were casualties as a result of gun use by her son (Mr. Ndo). His mother (Jilma) no longer felt safe as there were threats to her life in their village. Note that her son's property was already destroyed, and his wife and children fled for their safety. Mr. Jilma had nowhere to go, except to return to the Gnani as a way of saving her life. Equally, Upinyaan, and Tiya suffered a similar fate when their communities ejected them. What happens to people like Jilma, Unpinyaan, and Tiya and a host of others who are no longer wanted by their communities? Who will provide protection and safety for them amid violence or potential threat of violence, discrimination, and destruction of their properties? It is also important to highlight that Madam Denteh was killed in the presence of the public and streamed online, and yet there was no state security to protect her. This is where the role of traditional authorities becomes crucial. But this also presents a complex dynamic, in that the local authorities in the community supervised and directed her to be lynched. What do we make of these complexities?

As discussed in chapter 1, during fieldwork I interacted with various local leaders, to understand their perceptions or views on witchcraft and communities of refuge. Traditional authorities here refer to both local religious and political leaders that work together in dealing with witchcraft and other issues at the local level. In those conversations, it emerged that traditional authorities in synergy with one another play four main key roles, which are discussed as follows.

First, traditional authorities assess and adjudicate issues of witchcraft accusations. The institutions of chieftaincy, family, and lineage headships particularly, preside over issues of witchcraft in the communities (see Baba, 2013; Igwe, 2016b; Wumbla, 2017). They convene sittings and hearings on witchcraft matters in various jurisdictions. For example, if there is ever a case of a witchcraft accusation case brought against a family member, the family head is most likely to convene a family meeting to discuss the issue or report to the clan head or the chief of the community for further deliberation (see Baba, 2013; Wumbla, 2017). Initial deliberations are held here at this level; however, if no resolution is found, the case is escalated to the next level. Here, it is not much about the spiritual investigation of whether the accused is a witch or not, rather it is about asking them some basic questions about their knowledge of the accusation. This offers the accused and accusers the opportunity to be able to take the next level of action if the accused confesses to the accusation or otherwise.

The next level of assessment is the spiritual diagnosis of an accusation, which lies in the domain of local experts discussed in chapter 1. Here, the local experts are either invited to the community where the accusation took place such as the cases 2 and 3, where Bibɔab were brought in to do a spiritual inquest or diagnosis of deaths that were implicated in witchcraft, and that of Pigri, who died immediately after given birth and Waja—a local businessman who died after a short illness. Or take the accused to the communities of refuge for assessment and adjudication and here, again, I refer to the Uwadaan's (Materi's) assessment of the three women who were accused of witchcraft and brought to Gnani captured as case 1. It is at this level that the case of an accused is determined, that is, whether she or he is guilty and should stay or return home. Those who are ejected from their communities, such as those described in chapter 2, have nowhere to go either and head to the various communities of refuge.

Third, after people accused of witchcraft are ejected from their communities and seek refuge in the various communities, the traditional authorities here again lay the onus on them to provide land and resettle people as was o in chapter 2. Here, Bibɔrib work in synergy with the others in the communities to resettle people accused of witchcraft and become the main actors who are also responsible for providing them with food, water, shelter, and social security, among other things. During an interaction with the Bibɔrib of both *Bikpakkpaam* and *Dagbamba,* ethnic groups in Gnani, they asserted that they had given their approval for the people accused of witchcraft to be resettled in Gnani. In addition, *Bibɔrib* said that when issues of witchcraft are brought to them for deliberation, they refer to the way the issue was handled at the family and lineage levels. Their judgment was therefore a review of the previous judgment at those levels and the decisions reached. At the *Bikpakpaam* chief palace, a member of the council of elders asserted the following:

> There are two chiefs, the *Bikpakpaam* and *Bidagbam*. They collaborate to rule the town. This is because the town is now large and needs to have sub-chiefs to assist in the ruling of the community. Even the people accused of witchcraft have their own sub-chief who reports to the main chief in his palace. The sub-chief is responsible for witchcraft matters and is contacted if a person accused of witchcraft is brought into the community to be re-settled.

According to *Utindaan*, who also doubles as the *Uwadaan* of Gnani,

> The gods of the land welcome everyone. So, if anyone is brought in here as a witch, we can't drive them away. As Utindaan I receive them but before I give them a place to settle, I must notify the chief of Gnani for approval through his representative at our sittings.

It could be inferred that traditional authorities are committed to establishing and recognizing communities of refuge within their jurisdictions. They do not see the resettlement of people accused of witchcraft into their communities as an abuse of their rights. They see their actions as a welfare package and a system of providing care, where people accused of witchcraft are given land to settle on, houses to live in, people to interact with, and a community where they can continue their lives. In Gnani, it was reported that a woman who was banished from her community roamed for some time in the bush (Tayo, 2010). She finally arrived in Gnani and told *Utindaan* about her circumstances. She was accepted in the community after *Utindaan* consulted the shrine of the community. She went through a spiritual cleansing afterward. In Kukuo and Gambaga, the stories were similar. A woman each went to seek help from the imam (Islamic cleric) in the two communities after they were accused of witchcraft and were to be banished from their communities (Baba, 2013; Bekoe, 2016; Mutaru, 2019; Palmer, 2010). The Imams accepted them, asked for forgiveness on their behalf and performed spiritual cleansing. The Imams asked the people accused of witchcraft to stay if their communities did not want them anymore. After news spread of this kind gesture, other people accused of witchcraft also sought refuge in these communities. Such communities are what is termed today as "witch camps." The locals, however, do not refer to these communities as camps. This position by the traditional authorities is contested by the government, and other non-state actors, and has attracted some controversies that will be discussed in more detail below in relation to FBOs and NGOs (see Forsyth, 2016). Some of these other actors have accused them of exploiting the vulnerability of the people accused of witchcraft through manual labor, and the benefits they receive through NGO work.

FAITH-BASED ORGANIZATIONS

In examining the roles of religion and faith-based organizations (FBOs), the issue of similar tensions, controversies, and contestations as noted above are equally present in Ghana. Alongside the role of traditional authorities in communities of refuge, there are various faith-based organizations that are also engaged in offering services to individuals in such communities. The faith-based organizations also point to the overall positions of different religions and the ways such religions engage with witchcraft and people accused of witchcraft.

There exists a body of scholarship that explores the relationship between witchcraft and religion or Christian churches (see Adu-Gyamfi, 2016; Meyer, 1998; Onyinah, 2002). Religion arguably contributes to the deepening of witchcraft beliefs. Over the decades, various religions have believed in the existence of witches and their malevolent intentions. Belief in the existence of witchcraft, with support from the Bible and Quran, as well as traditional oral histories, has placed people accused of witchcraft in a vulnerable position where their lives are constantly at risk. However, Adu-Gyamfi (2016) studied witchcraft among the Ashanti Christians in Ghana and argues that the understanding of witchcraft from the Christian point of view is a misinterpretation of the term, and hence has been inappropriately applied to witchcraft in Ghana.

While in Gnani, it did not take me long to realize that the Catholic Church was one of the religious bodies that supported residents accused of witchcraft. During a conversation with the Catholic priest in charge of the parish, he revealed that although he personally believed in witchcraft, the Catholic Church has the power to exorcise people who have been accused of witchcraft. In his view, instead of creating communities of refuge where people accused of witchcraft reside, the ideal thing would have been to bring the accused to the church for the evil power to be exorcised so they could return home. However, he did admit that this view was limited in practical terms, as many people would not want to have supposedly cleansed people accused of witchcraft back in their communities, whether they had had their powers exorcised or not. This is intriguing because according to local narratives, people who have been accused of witchcraft and have gone through the cleaning rituals are no longer harmful, at least in principle (see Palmer, 2010). This is a view mostly held by people in the various communities of refuge. However, people outside of communities of refuge are cynical about whether people accused of witchcraft are harmless after going through the ritual of cleansing. Some of the people told me that the reason they prefer people accused of witchcraft to stay in the Gnani is that they are never sure, such as in the case of Upinyaan in chapter 2. But if they settle in Gnani, the powers of the shrine would be able to contain them rendering them harmless.

The role of religion in relation to witchcraft and communities of refuge is multiple. While the various religious organizations contribute to the belief in witchcraft and have put in place some mechanisms to pacify those accused of it and contributed to the creation of communities of refuge as a safe space for displaced people on the basis of witchcraft accusations, they have also been implicated in the controversial closure and reintegration discussions in Ghana (Baba, 2013; Government of Ghana, 1998; Palmer, 2010). The very first initiative to reintegrate people accused of witchcraft was started in 1994 by the Presbyterian Church in Gambaga under the project titled Gambaga Outcast (GO) Home project (see Wumbla, 2017; Mutaru, 2019; Naboo, 2017). Here the church supports meeting the basic needs of the people accused of witchcraft as well as working hard to reintegrate them back into their home communities.

In Gnani, the Presbyterian Church was not present. It was the Catholic Church that supported people in Gnani. There was also a new church established by the brother of the shrine priest, who doubles as the secretary of the Gnani community. Despite such kind gestures, the role of religious organizations in witchcraft and communities of refuge is also controversial. While on the one hand, they have contributed to the creation of the communities of refuge in the first place, on the other, they are also offering an alternative to reintegrate people accused of witchcraft as can be seen from the GO-Home project.

In spite of the controversies, my observation in Gnani and speaking to different religious persons, I analyzed and present the role of the church in meeting the welfare needs of people accused of witchcraft into the following: *physiological*, *spiritual and social*, *shelter and security*, and *emotional and psychological* support after interacting with the Catholic priest, and the pastor of the new church as well as others.

PHYSIOLOGICAL SUPPORT

First, one of the biggest challenges of people accused of witchcraft in Gnani is the availability of and access to potable water. There is often a water crisis in Gnani, especially in the dry season. There are no taps in homes. There are limited boreholes in the community and the few available do not have enough water to serve the whole community. The only source of water that is reliable all year round is the distant river Oti. However, it is far from the community. It takes about thirty minutes to walk there and back. People accused of witchcraft who are usually advanced in age, with health needs, struggle daily to get water for cooking, drinking, and for laundry. The Catholic Church, realizing this need, drilled a borehole with a water collection reservoir in the parish that pumps water through the taps into the Gnani refuge community (Tindang). This brought relief to the residents of the community for a short while. However, at the time of my research, the reservoir had broken down and was unable to pump water to the community. The people accused of witchcraft could, however, go to the parish to fetch water for free. The rest of the community members are expected to pay a fee to fetch water from the parish borehole as they are considered capable. The parish priest explained that this token fee is a way of raising money for maintenance purposes.

Second, food is also another physical need of people accused of witchcraft. Although a basic need, most of the people accused of witchcraft are unable to get a year-round supply of food. In the northern part of Ghana, there is a food shortage in the months of June and July. This period is referred to as *Likpasiil* (lean season). Although some peasant farmers are affected by the food shortage, the situation of the people accused of witchcraft is worse as they are unable to engage in economic activities due to inadequate land, labor, or the capacity to farm. In a conversation with the parish priest, the catechist, and other church members, the Catholic Church encouraged its members to contribute food once a year, as a donation to residents of Gnani-Tindang. This information was corroborated by three main sources: members of the Catholic Church in Gnani, the shrine priest of the Gnani community, and people accused of witchcraft residing in Gnani. Thus, assorted foodstuffs such as yam, maize, pepper, okra, cassava, and sorghum are contributed and given to people accused of witchcraft to share. Besides the collective intervention by the Catholic Church, individual church members offer some form of support to the people residing in the community when they are asked. A woman accused of witchcraft told me that anytime she lacked food, she asked the catechist for some, and he has always given her. The shrine priest is also asked for food on a regular basis. In most instances, he offered them something temporarily to prevent them from starving. According to the Government of Ghana (1998), the Catholic Church has for a long time provided food items through the Catholic Relief Services food program to the residents of the Gambaga *Poagnyaankura fongu* in the 1970s. At present, the Catholic church is present in other places and occasionally donates food to people across the various witch camps, as I found from my interviews. For example, a community member told me that the Bimbilla Catholic Church collected food items and donated them to the Kukuo a month before my arrival.

However, the support of the Catholic Church and other churches is not sustainable as they are contingent on external and internal resources mobilization, which can be affected due to the economic situation at any given point. According to Riedel,

> After a decade of improvement through the GO-Home-Project (Simon Ngota and Gladis Lariba) at least in Gambaga, situations deteriorated again when the Catholic Relief Service stopped food-donation programs in 2005/6 and when the GO-Home-Project ran out of funding. Gushiegu and Tindang experienced serious malnutrition and water-born diseases in 2009. Individuals starved. (2017, p. 2)

The church also occasionally organizes clothes and sends these as a donation to the people in the camp. Although this is not frequent, it can provide some form of clothing for residents.

Spiritual and Social Belonging

The church also plays a key role in the spiritual and social needs of people accused of witchcraft. Apart from the Muslim residents, others attach themselves to a Christian church in Gnani. The majority of the people accused of witchcraft attend the Catholic Church in Gnani and the Tindang Worship Center. Both churches support the residents with spiritual needs as they are often seen praying together. This brings out a form of dual religious affiliation by people accused of witchcraft, by submitting themselves to the shrine priest for rituals and simultaneously attending the church or the mosque. This was evident as I attended mass with the Catholic Church and noted that every Sunday, a group of women who sat in front of the church on the left-hand side were people accused of witchcraft. This revelation was made during an announcement in which the parish priest wanted to meet elderly women in the church. The term "elderly" as used in the church, I got to know later, referred to only women accused of witchcraft. They are active members of the church and belong to the Christian Mothers' Association of the Catholic Church in Gnani.

The significance of attending church is by no means limited to its spiritual support. In addition, residents are also supported socially as they have a community of people to relate to in the absence of their kinship members. The Catholic Church in particular plays this role, as it organizes an annual get-together where all people accused of witchcraft socialize with other members of the community. During this event, people eat, drink, and dance while socializing. The argument the church promotes is that they care about the accused and their part of the community. They are all part of God's creation and Jesus Christ has admonished every Christian to love their neighbor. This is particularly important as they feel accepted by people in the church and can make friends with other members and fellow people accused of witchcraft in common social and religious spaces.

Shelter and Security

The communities of refuge provide residents with shelter and security. The shrine priest is responsible for providing immediate accommodation for any people accused of witchcraft until their relatives put up a house. However, because it is often relatives who have banished the accused into the community, it is rare for them to build this accommodation. In that regard, people accused of witchcraft are left to their fate. The church community has supported some of these people by assisting with communal labor in building their houses.

Emotional and Psychological Needs

Another need of the residents of Gnani is to be emotionally and psychologically stable or balanced. Most are unhappy due to the situation they have found themselves in, as I observed. Their self-esteem and egos are affected negatively. Witchcraft accusations make some of them feel worthless. One resident told me that it would have been better if they were dead. While living in Gnani, I noticed that they were often lonely as well, as they are rejected by their families and friends. Rarely do they have friends or family members visiting them, except for fellow Gnani residents. The church provides a space for them to socialize and bond with other church members, providing access to emotional and psychological support. They have members of the church visit them and vice versa. The church's annual get-together is also another way of promoting community bonds and boosting the emotional stability and psychological well-being of those accused of witchcraft.

In sum, through the above interventions, it can be said that the church in Gnani is pivotal in meeting the needs of people accused of witchcraft. However, examining the broader role of church in the Ghanaian society, church, especially the Pentecostals and emerging charismatic churches are as well implicated in deepening the belief in and accusation of people as witches (see Adu-Gyamfi, 2016; Meyer, 1998; Onyinah, 2002). Like the state and traditional authorities, the role of the church with regard to witchcraft in Ghana is equally complicated. Although the church has some commonalities with regard to meeting the needs of people accused of witchcraft, it does not focus on others such as human rights. The next section examines the role of NGOs in Gnani and like the state, human rights become central to their work, in addition to other interventions.

NGOS AND THEIR INTERVENTIONS IN COMMUNITIES OF REFUGE

The leadership of three NGOs were interviewed. The selection of the three NGOs was because they were active and worked with people accused of witchcraft in northern Ghana. These NGOs are ActionAid Ghana, Songtaba, and Humanist Service Corps. Unlike government institutions, the NGO sector was dominated by women. The heads of the various NGOs were all women. They were all highly educated with tertiary degrees (diploma, bachelor's, and master's degrees). The next section discusses the socio-demographic characteristics of people accused of witchcraft alongside other scholarly literature.

Notwithstanding the state, traditional authorities, and faith-based organizations as discussed above, there are also some other organizations, both local and international, that are also engaged in witchcraft accusations in Africa. This section engages with the activities of these organizations in relation to witchcraft and communities of refuge in Africa and argues that non-state actors provide crucial basic needs to people accused of witchcraft and residing in Gnani or elsewhere.

While in the field, I asked some of the participants if they have ever heard of or knew any non-state actors who were present in Gnani and if yes what were some of them. One of the members of the community said,

> NGOs come here in groups. They don't stay permanently in the community; they come and go. The Catholic Church came, ActionAid Ghana also came, Tuma kavi came and Management Aid also came . . . the USA ambassador also came and several others. They all offered some level of support to the people accused of witchcraft and as well condemned the act of accusing people of witchcraft and banishing them from their communities.

At the start of this chapter, I referred to the fact that people accused of witchcraft, though resilient, they struggle to meet all their needs. The problem is that because their accusations were initiated by their kinship members, some of them are not being visited or supported in any way by their relations while they live in Gnani community (see Mutaru, 2019). Again, the support of the government in meeting the needs of people accused of witchcraft is inadequate and limited, and the idea of closure of witch such communities as a way of protecting the rights of people accused of witchcraft is controversial. To fill their unmet welfare needs, NGO workers also do offer some level of support. In this context, NGOs provide resources and build the capacities of people accused of witchcraft in Gnani and other similar communities (see Mutaru, 2019; Riedel, 2017).

International development organizations such as the World Bank, or those who support a bilateral relationship between Ghana and other developed countries, such as UKAID, DANIDA, and USAID, are some examples of these bodies that have partnered with Ghana or NGOs working in communities of refuge. For example, the 1998 conference on witchcraft in Tamale was supported by USAID aiming at dealing with the issue of communities of refuge (Government of Ghana, 1998; Mutaru, 2019). Also, the U.S. ambassador's visit to the Gnani told by the participant above is a typical example of such relationships in Ghana. These different non-state actors offer some form of relief to the residents of the communities. This has been captured by one of the participants:

> When the NGOs come, they ask for the challenges of people accused of witchcraft. Mostly, their needs include but are not limited to health issues, water,

clothes, food and shelter. Based on the above, different non-state actors assist residents with what they can afford. For example, some NGOs have provided them with food, others have assisted them to acquire health insurance and helped them to renew their health insurance membership while the Catholic Church has provided them with pipe water.

The non-state actors sometimes employ partnership and participatory approaches. As will be discussed below, ActionAid Ghana has over the years partnered with Songtaba, a local NGO, to intervene in the case of people accused of witchcraft in northern Ghana. The closure of one of the Bonyasi refuge community in the Central Gonja district was also reported to result from a partnership between the Ghanaian state, ActionAid Ghana, and local community leaders. The next section details some of the specific issues and the lens through which NGOs look at the issues of witch camps and their mode of intervention. Essentially, their interventions can be categorized into *human rights awareness creation and protection*, *meeting the immediate needs of people accused of witchcraft*, *economic empowerment*, and *closure of communities of refuge and reintegration*.

Human Rights Awareness Creation and Protection

NGOs see the issue of communities of refuge and people accused of witch-craft as a human rights issue, and thus, their interventions are enmeshed in the human rights framework. The quotation below encapsulates the roles NGOs play in the various communities of refuge. The quote is culled from a focus group discussion (FGD) held with staff of ActionAid Ghana in Northern Ghana.

> The interventions we offer range from supporting them to meet their immediate needs. We support them with food, clothes and roofing of their houses. But over time, we realised such direct support was not sustainable. We started mobilising them to assist in advocating for their rights. We brought all the communities of refuge together. We believe there is strength in numbers. If it is only the Kukuo or Gnani community often speaking out, they might be ignored but when they (duty bearers) know that you are mobilising some women to also advocate for their rights on a large scale, they are likely to pay attention. We have therefore mobilised all the people accused of witchcraft at the various communities of refuge into one network with an executive who leads them in doing all the advocacy work. (staff of AAG at a Focus Group Discussion)

While in the field, I also interacted with another NGO, Songtaba, which is a partner organization to ActionAid, and their coordinator, had this to say:

You know people accused of witchcraft come from different places and are seen as individuals. Because of their vulnerable situations, they are not able to fight for their rights as individuals. We there organised them into a group, so that they can have one voice that is loud enough to express their concerns for the government and others to help them out. We organise and train them on leadership skills, public speaking skills, and group management.

From the above, it can be seen that human rights underpin some of the works of NGOs, to the extent that everything depends on it. For example, while speaking to the staff of ActionAid, regarding the kind of interventions they do in the various communities, one of them said,

For us as an organisation, we are not looking at whether there is witchcraft or not. That is not our focus. We are looking at how people's rights are violated, abused and discriminated against. For example, if you ask someone not to come to her community because of witchcraft accusations, you have exiled the person and it constitutes a violation of the person's rights. (staff of AAG at a Focus Group Discussion)

The abuse and non-recognition of human rights within the limits of the Ghanaian legal framework is one of the key areas in which NGOs are fighting to ensure that the rights of people accused of witchcraft are protected. While it is a fact that there is a conflict between culture and legal rights in Ghana regarding how people accused of witchcraft are treated, it is argued that banishing people from their own societies is an abuse of their rights (ActionAid, 2008b, 2008a, 2014; NCCE, 2010). Global development organizations such as the UN and others have sought to protect the rights of the vulnerable by developing legal frameworks. Beyond being signatories to these international legal frameworks, member countries are encouraged to develop local laws that ensure people's rights are protected. It is acknowledged though that although some member countries sign or rectify the laws, they lack the will to implement them to the letter (ActionAid, 2008b, 2008a, 2014; NCCE, 2010). This creates a gap where people's rights are being denied or abused and they suffer. It is in this landscape NGOs, both local and international, fill the gap by advocating for and on behalf of people accused of witchcraft. The above quotation from a staff member of ActionAid Ghana focuses on the rights of people accused of witchcraft. ActionAid Ghana does this by collaborating with other NGOs to champion the rights of people accused of witchcraft. They work with government departments, those accused, and community leaders to ensure that people accused of witchcraft enjoy their rights too. These development organizations argue that it is the right of every individual to decent accommodation, health, food, and clothing. Banishing people to unknown destinations deprives them of these basic rights. However, while development organizations and NGOs are fighting to create an awareness that it is the right of everyone to enjoy basic human rights, they are also working to provide for the most pressing needs of people in witch camps. Such needs are referred to as immediate needs as seen in the billboard of ActionAid in Gnani and other themes they focus on.

Immediate needs include food, water, accommodation, and clothes. Some of the people living in communities of refuge lack these basic needs. Some do not have decent sleeping places and, especially during the rainy season, their rooms leak. ActionAid Ghana through its local partnership supports the roofing of people accused of witchcraft, allowing them to sleep comfortably at night. They identify the houses that need to be reroofed and send money to community members to support this. They buy thatch from individuals, which is then used to roof the rooms or houses that leak.

Food is another immediate need in the camps. At the start of their work in Gnani and other communities, ActionAid Ghana provided food for distribution among the residents. They have moved away from providing food directly, and toward empowering people accused of witchcraft to engage in agriculture. To do this, they have organized skills empowerment workshops on farming practices. Other NGOs, such as the Humanist Service Corps and Louis Dreyfus Fondation d'entreprise are active in both Gnani and Kukuo and provide agricultural support systems. For example, Louis Dreyfus Fondation d'entreprise provides farmers with animals and ploughs their land for the cultivation of soya beans or maize.

At the time of the study (2016), Louis Dreyfus Fondation d'entreprise did not plough the land for farming. Participants in this study told me that Louis Dreyfus Fondation d'entreprise had ploughed the land for some years and had asked them to plough it by themselves that year. It was thought that this would instill some level of empowerment in the farmers to plough their land in case the assistance is withdrawn one day. Most of the NGOs do not operate in communities of refuge for long. They operate for a period after which they withdraw. It was unclear whether Louis Dreyfus Fondation d'entreprise would return to assist the farmers with their farm work.

Economic Empowerment of People Accused of Witchcraft

Another area that most NGOs support is economic empowerment. Beyond supporting those accused of witchcraft to meet their most immediate needs, they also support them in ways that make them economically strong. Their support for farming activities not only provides residents with food but also a stable income. They assist them with the establishment of small businesses, as well as building their capacity to run such businesses. For instance, the

Humanist Service Corps has an agricultural program where people accused of witchcraft are taught how to manage their farms. An ActionAid and Songtaba collaboration has led to the training of women in trades. However, the key issue is that the elderly people who are most often accused of witchcraft are not able to work on the farms, and hence there are lingering questions as to whether such an intervention is sustainable.

"LIBERATING PEOPLE HELD IN BONDAGE DUE TO WITCHCRAFT": CLOSURE OF COMMUNITIES OF REFUGE AND REINTEGRATION

According to interviews with some of the staff of the NGOs, people accused of witchcraft are both physically and mentally enslaved, and thus the reason they are unable to leave the communities of refuge. There is a discourse around the fact that being enslaved is one enmeshed in the cultural understanding of the position of people accused of witchcraft when sent to such communities. First, as I was told, people accused of witchcraft and sent to seek refuge are considered slaves to the shrines and hence are supposed to live and serve shrine priests. This was highlighted to me by the staff of ActionAid during my interactions with them.

> First of all, the person who owns the camp has an interest in it because like she said earlier on when you are taken to the camp you are seen as a slave and I mean in this era of economic whatever that we find ourselves in people are looking for the cheapest way to get things. So, if people come in and the family members don't take them back, they stay there, and the person uses them as labour and tries to mentally enslave them. The shrine priests keep telling them that when the accused go back to their communities, the community members will kill them. I'm (referring to shrine priests) the only person who can protect you and provide for you as well.

The key point that stands out in the above quote is that people accused of witchcraft are made to understand that they cannot leave the communities of refuge because they are slaves to the shrine and secondly, their lives are at risk when they leave. But through the interventions by NGOs, the people accused of witchcraft are now aware they can leave, and nothing will happen to them. NGOs and other institutions then partnered to initiate processes to liberate people accused of witchcraft from slavery and allow them to return to their homes.

It was at that conference that the stakeholders agreed to set up a committee to aid the reintegration of these women into their families. And the ministry of gender was very instrumental in the conference and also supported us.

The second part of the problem is that the communities do not want the people they have banished on the basis of witchcraft back in their midst. This was captured, for example, in an introduction to the witchcraft conference in 2014 which states,

> In northern Ghana, people suspected to be witches seek refuge in witch camps to escape family and community anger. Over the years, ActionAid Ghana, local partners and some public institutions have campaigned about the systemic human rights abuses at the camps, where residents live in terrible circumstances. While the campaign for the reintegration of the alleged witches has been well received by the public, particularly traditional authorities and government, there has never been a national forum to discuss the plight of victims of witchcraft accusations.

ActionAid staff told me that they formed a committee that was tasked to delve into the closure and reintegration of communities of refuge, whose work yielded some fruits.

> The committee started working to see how it can reintegrate all these women into their home communities. A road map was drawn for this. By the end of 2014, we had integrated over 200 women into their home communities. By the end of 2014, we closed one of the camps and everybody was reintegrated now the camp is no more in existence but the shrine is there, the fetish priest is there, and people can go there to consult or validate whether someone is a witch or not but nobody will be allowed to stay there.

One of the things that is also apparent in ActionAid's and its partners' interventions is the issue of gender. It appears that although organizations work to better the lives of the people accused of witchcraft and reintegrate them, such efforts exclude men who are accused of witchcraft and also banished from their communities. For example, one of ActionAid's staff noted that

> the men in the camps claiming they are wizards are lazy. It is even difficult to say they are accused of witchcraft. They are not. They follow their wives to the witch camps or because of the benefits they relocate to the camps [laughs]. They are lazy men who don't want to work. Their numbers continue to increase every day.

This perspective from ActionAid is interesting, especially in Gnani where there is a significant number of men who are also banished from their communities. Jagri, a man accused of witchcraft and residing in Gnani, showed me scars on his face, which he said were a result of the beatings he received during the accusation and confrontation. He was severely beaten and ejected from his community, and he was not told where exactly to go. After several days of wandering in the bush, he eventually found himself in the Gnani-Tindang community. I wonder why men will leave their communities to settle in communities of refuge in the name of being accused of witchcraft taking into consideration the discrimination against people accused of witchcraft and the deplorable state of such communities. It is possible that ActionAid and their partner organization, which have a strong feminist focus, are not interested in the issues of men, and the reason why they are dismissive about their plights. Also, the point that some of the men had followed their wives to Gnani-Tindang did not apply to the case of my participants. I did not find any single woman who admitted their husbands came along with them. It was rather the case that their husbands abandoned them after banishment or were dead and hence why many of the women were widows (see chapter 2). The cases of Upinyaan and other cases presented in chapter 2 are clear examples. Again, men who were accused of witchcraft and banished to live in Ghana, some of them came with their entire families, children, and wives. The case of the man who owned the grinding mill was an example. That man was not poor anyways and did not depend on support from NGOs and the government. He owned the grinding mill in the community, which was well-patronized both within and outside Gnani. He equally had a large farm with his entire family serving as labor.

Rather than keeping people in the communities of refuge, an NGO official recounted to me that

> it was only the traditional chiefs who had the power to confront a person who was alleged of an act of witchery. He revealed that in the past, anytime one was sick, or death occurred, and there was a suspicion of witchcraft, you spoke to an elderly person who in turn went to speak to the chief on your behalf. The elderly person would tell the chief that this had happened, and people were suspecting this person to be the responsible witch. An accuser could not confront the suspect as an individual. An accuser did not have that power. The suspect would be summoned to the chief's palace. After this, a spiritualist (Unyɔkdaan) would be called to verify whether she or he was or not a witch. A concoction was prepared for the accused to take after which, she was purified and allowed to go back home. At that time, there were no communities of refuge as we have today.

In sum, issues of vulnerabilities, insecurities, and threats of violence become even more heightened where communities of refuge become unavailable. As some kind of haven and support for people ejected from their communities on the basis of witchcraft. And this becomes more evident in the debates around the closure of such communities.

I must also add that it was not all cases that went through community cleansing, and the accused were allowed to stay. Some of the accused were also killed and their bodies were left to rot or eaten by vultures as noted by Riedel (2018). In this study, "in the past" refers to the earlier part of the nineteenth century and prior. In this period, there were several mechanisms through which people accused of witchcraft were addressed. These mechanisms included killing them, making them slaves, cleansing them and allowing them to stay in the community, and finally banishing them. Due to modern laws, individuals who kill people accused of witchcraft can face a jail term. As a result, killing people accused of witchcraft now rarely happens. It is also now rare to make an accused person of witchcraft a slave by the chief of their communities as captured by Esther Goody in 1970 among the Gonja. Due to a high level of intolerance among community members and family crises from which these accusations fester, cleansing and allowing them to stay in their original community is also not much favored. Therefore, in current times, the majority of people accused of witchcraft end up being evicted from their communities to live in one of the various communities of refuge.

Closure of "Witch Camps" and Reintegration Debates

One theme that stood out through all the actors intervening in communities of refuge in northern Ghana is the issue of closing down such communities and reintegrating the accused back into the communities. Different opinions abound as to whether it is appropriate to shut down such communities and reintegrate people accused of witchcraft and residing in such communities back into their original communities. This section focuses on such debates by providing different views drawing from the findings above. Written texts in the media, government documents and conference reports on such issues are also discussed. The general thesis inherent in such debates, especially of government and NGOs, is that communities of refuge should be closed as it is against human rights (ActionAid, 2008b, 2008a, 2014; Government of Ghana, 1998; Wumbla, 2018; NCCE, 2010).

Judging from the findings in this chapter, it is evident that a plethora of actors is on board regarding the closure and reintegration of people accused of witchcraft and residing in the various communities of refuge in northern Ghana. The conference introduction indicated that NGOs, government, and traditional leaders as well as the public were all up for the reintegration of people accused of witchcraft. This is questionable, especially taking into consideration that chiefs of Gnani considered communities of refuge as a welfare package and their moral responsibility to protect vulnerable people in society (see Igwe, 2016a; Mutaru, 2019; Riedel, 2017). Mutaru noted,

> During my fieldwork, traditional community leaders were not happy with ActionAid's reintegration campaigns. The *tindana* for Tindaanzhee (Kpatinga) had initially tried to avoid me when my local assistant told him about my intention to speak with him. He said that he was not free to receive me but on my assistant's pleading, agreed to accept my greetings. However, after I had introduced myself as a researcher who wanted to know more about his work, he was happy to talk. The *tindana* explained that when my assistant told him that a visitor was coming to see him, "I thought it was those people who always talk about returning the women to their communities. That is why I asked him to inform you that I was not free." (2019, p. 115)

Riedel (2017) considers such efforts by the government and its partners as staged for public media and the public and does not reflect the reality on the ground. According to Riedel,

> smaller NGOs and people who are on the ground know the staged nature of the closure of witch camps but are afraid to talk because they fear revenge from government-denying or stalling the renewal of their registrations as charity, slander and persecution by high officials. (2017, p. 1)

To some extent, the allegation that the issue of the closure of communities of refuge is a top-down approach rather than community generated is augmented through the findings of NCCE in 2010. NCCE, a state institution, asked people accused of witchcraft if they wanted communities of refuge closed and reintegrated. The findings of the report by NCCE indicated that 89.6 percent of the people did not want communities of refuge closed. The concerns of people residing in such communities bothered on safety, abuse, discrimination, and violence which could not be guaranteed if they went back home. When I asked the question "Will you want to go back home if you get the opportunity?" 90 percent of the accused people I interviewed in Gnani said that they wouldn't. This allies with the findings of the NCCE 2010 report. As highlighted in the earlier part of this chapter, two government delegations had been to Gambaga to ask the chief, Gambarrana to allow the people accused of witchcraft to go home. And even when he did, they refused and pleaded with the delegation to allow them to stay in *Poagnyaankura fungu* (Naboo, 2017).

In spite of the glaring evidence that people accused of witchcraft are unwilling to return home, the state and NGOs are burned on closing down the communities of refuge. The long-term goal of most NGOs is to have all the communities of refuge closed and the people accused of witchcraft reintegrated into their original communities or any other community of their choice.

In that regard, ActionAid Ghana, in collaboration with the Ministry of Gender and Social Protection, and local community leaders closed the Bonyase[1] refuge community in the Central Gonja district of Northern Ghana in 2014. The second one, Nabuli has also just been closed on December 24, 2019 (Mbugri, 2019). Humanist Service Corps, an American-based organization, has also been working with local community leaders and other partners in the Kukuo to reintegrate people accused of witchcraft into their communities.

But what has been the outcome of the closure of the two communities so far? It has emerged that after the closure of the Bonyase, some of the people were rejected by their families (Igwe, 2016a; Mutaru, 2019; Riedel, 2017). When people accused of witchcraft are reintegrated, and some possibly rejected, they have no other alternative than to return to another community of refuge, otherwise, they are vulnerable to repeat violence and lynching or other forms of discrimination. For example, Igwe (2016a) reported that within the first week of the forced closure of the Bonyase community, two of the people accused of witchcraft had relocated to Gnani, the primary site for this research (See Riedel, 2017; Mutaru, 2019; Naboo, 2017). This is because their families did not accept them back. Needless to say, there were only five people in Bonyase at the time of its closure. That means three people got accepted in their communities, at least by assumption. Igwe, therefore, calls on the various stakeholders responsible for shutting these communities to rethink their actions as he perceived such actions as a step in the wrong direction (Igwe, 2016a).

Riedel is even more radical by accusing the state and its partners of further abuse and victimization of an already vulnerable population by closing down communities of refuge (2017). Riedel criticizes both the Ghanaian state and NGOs and the limits of their interventions, which was discussed in detail in the earlier part of this chapter. For example, it was advertised by the media that fifty people were reintegrated after the closure of Bonyase. However, the total number of people who had sought refuge there was just five (see Igwe, 2016a; Riedel, 2017). Riedel reports that the two people who relocated to Gnani from Bonyase revealed that they were given money and sent off to the Gnani by ActionAid staff. Upon hearing this, Riedel reported that he contacted ActionAid as well, but they declined to comment on the issue.

In Tindang, we also found two of the five original inhabitants of Banyasi ([*sic*], Bonyase). In an interview, they confirmed that they were transported out of Banyasi to be resettled. At their homes, no proper preparation has ensured the support of the relatives. They were rejected, so the two workers of ActionAid (or Songtaba) brought them back to Tamale, and after some nights decided to bring them to the camp in Tindang. They were given some money, a comparably good adobe compound. (Riedel, 2017, p. 5)

Igwe (2016a) argued that communities of refuge are not the problem in northern Ghana but witchcraft accusation, which is prevalent in society.

> Most people living in these shelters did not just take up residency there without any reason. People in these camps are accused persons, who were convicted at shrines or banished by families and would have been killed if they had stayed back in their communities and not taken refuge at these shelters.
>
> So why shut them down? Why disband these sanctuaries? Why destroy the safety nets when death and danger still loom for alleged witches in Ghana? How does shutting down witch camps erase the stain of witchcraft accusation?

Igwe raises interesting questions, which beg for answers, but who will respond? The state and NGOs are fixated on the human rights bit and think that closing such communities exonerates Ghana from the "dent" of an image on its human rights records and modern society.

A staff of a local NGO, called Songtaba responded to Igwe's publication cautioning the state and its partners to exercise patience in shutting the communities of refuge down. The staff asserted that Igwe did not have a deeper understanding of the issues on the ground and made his conclusion based on inadequate information. In his response, he said,

> Mr. Leo Igwe, thanks for your educating piece but I want to respectfully disagree with you on some grounds especially your understanding on the campaign to close down the witch camps and witchcraft accusation in Ghana. . . .
>
> The fact that these places call[ed] witch camps exist people will continue to perpetuate this injustice by accusing and forcefully sending the women there to suffer. Since the "shrines" are place[s] that the people believe to possess the power to clean off the women of their witchcraft power, then after the cleansing exercise the women should be allowed back to the communities. Instead, they are still left at the camps. Another question to be answered is do the people really believe in the powers of these "shrines"? [I]f yes then where from the fear of accepting these women back? Apparently, the accusers don't have any justification for their accusation. They may just be hiding under guise of witch camps to get back at women they have issues with or are seeing as threats to them in the communities. The issue of witchcraft accusation is a widespread phenomenon for which educating people to stop accusation alone cannot solve the issue, but rather need a more robots'([*sic*], robust) approach like closing down the camps out to people who want to come and keep women suspected to be witches for years and laws passed to enforce that. so far as these camps are still open to the public to forcefully send women there and keep them, then I'm not sure accusation of women on witchcraft will end.

Although the staff above had different opinions as enumerated in the quote, after interacting with people accused of witchcraft and resident in Gnani myself, I am inclined towards Igwe's position. The basis of my position was complemented by a conversation I had with two staff members of an NGO in Bimbilla (Humanist Service Corps). They seemed worried and sad. Although I noticed their mood, I was reluctant to ask about it, as I feared they might not want to tell me, or it could be something personal. While our conversations were ongoing, one of them asked the other whether she could let me know what was happening. She started by saying that one of the people accused of witchcraft they had been trying to reintegrate was missing. They feared she might have been killed secretly, as no one was willing to talk about her or knew her whereabouts. They had been to both her community and Kukuo, where she was based, and yet there was no information about her. After a few weeks, she was reported to have been back in Kukuo because the family had rejected her. She was not comfortable living in a community where no one wanted to interact with her (Mutaru, 2019).

Another controversy that comes up when it comes to intervening in communities of refuge is the issue of gender. As seen in the discussion with the staff of ActionAid, the issues of witchcraft have been reduced to women's issues, to the extent that they are skeptical about the eviction of men on the basis of witchcraft in northern Ghana. This is challenging and suggests that the needs of men who are affected by witchcraft accusations are ignored.

Furthermore, there is also a controversy surrounding the real intent of the NGOs and government institutions working in the communities regarding issues of communities of refuge (Riedel, 2017). According to Riedel, both the government and some NGOs are there because of their interests and their actions further affect the well-being of people accused of witchcraft (Riedel, 2017, p. 1). The idea of cleansing the image of Ghana in the international community has been present in the presentations at the 2014 witchcraft conference and the various presenters from the University for Development Studies, Keynote speaker and Minister of Gender, and Child Protection as highlighted in this chapter (see ActionAid, 2014; Riedel, 2017). One staff of ActionAid in commenting on the issues of NGO exploitation said,

> These are women who are sometimes exploited by NGOs as well as certain individuals who are taking advantage of these camps. Dubious organisations and some individuals write proposals and raise funds, and nobody knows what they are doing at those camps. Such dubious entities just show up and erect signposts or billboards and yet are not actually present and working with people accused of witchcraft. They just exploit the vulnerability of the people accused of witchcraft. Again, they are actually not doing anything over there, but if you check their profiles, they present themselves to be doing a lot.

There is probably some truth to the accusations of the ActionAid staff in that during the period of fieldwork in Gnani, I did not observe or hear from members of the community about visits by NGOs despite the presence of giant billboards being scattered across different vantage points that suggested they were present and active. With regards to the ongoing discussions, the key question is what do locals, people impacted by the various interventions, think of such interventions? The next section addresses that.

LOCAL VIEWS ON THE IMPACT OF NGOS IN COMMUNITIES OF REFUGE IN GHANA

A variety of views exist regarding the impact of NGO activities in Gnani. While some believe the activities of non-state actors such as NGOs brought some relief to the people accused of witchcraft, some think otherwise. Some locals feel that NGOs do not understand the local discourse of belief systems. Most of these NGOs receive funding from outside Ghana, raising questions about differences in worldviews. The quote below suggests the discord is due to NGOs and their staff (especially those with foreign backgrounds) not believing in witchcraft (see Riedel, 2017). Thus, their actions are influenced by worldviews that are different from those in northern Ghana. In this way disbanding communities of refuge becomes a viable option. However, disbanding such communities exposes the people accused of witchcraft to more danger, especially if they return home.

> They [NGO workers] do not understand that witchcraft is real. We don't know how we can explain it to them. I wish they were always in our midst and anytime it [witchcraft] happens they will see it for themselves. (Waju, thirty-four-year-old participant, 2016)

Some have also raised the point that although NGOs bring many interventions to the communities, the real beneficiaries are rarely people accused of witchcraft. The interventions are diverted to the non-accused who purport to represent people accused of witchcraft. For example, one opinion leader in the Gnani community said,

> You see those NGOs, what they bring goes into the hands of people who are not even accused of witchcraft. The distribution of goods and services goes into the hands of middle persons, with little going to the people accused of witchcraft. Check the farms which have been ploughed by the NGOs and see who owns them. A lot of them are owned by people who are not people accused of witchcraft.

During an interaction with one of the people accused of witchcraft, she noted that "they select those they like and give them gifts. It is not all of us. If you have anything to give to me, just give it to me. If you give it to anyone to give it to me, I won't get it." Her views were quite revealing and reflect the other views I had heard earlier, about how the interventions of NGOs do not actually reach the intended beneficiaries. There appear to be leakages along the line, but no one was ready to say where these occurred.

Another view the community members worried about was the rebranding of communities in northern Ghana. In interacting with my research participants, three main communities emerged as spaces where witchcraft discourses are discussed: communities of refuge, feeder communities, and general communities. The implicit consequences of the rebranding of communities set to categorize the communities significantly away from what is known by the local people. For example, the NGO's reference to some communities as "feeder" or "witch camps," where there is a collapse of all differences and such communities projected in some homogenized manner, is unusual. Although such communities may have banished people to seek refuge elsewhere, there are far more differences than one can imagine. Some persons accused of witchcraft and residing in the Gnani and Kukuo communities had even crossed international and regional borders. There is a man in Kukuo who moved from Togo into Kukuo and another woman who moved from Krachi in the Volta Region into the Tindang community in Gnani. However, this uniqueness is blurred in the totalizing categorization of communities into the feeder and non-feeder communities.

Despite skepticism about the role of NGOs within witchcraft discourse, a participant from Kukuo, another community, revealed that they had benefited from NGOs because of the resettlement of people accused of witchcraft into their community:

> Look at the school block, clinic, grinding mill, electricity and road. We got these through the NGOs' advocacy. They have made us visible and we have benefited a lot. Some of the accused told me they received support from NGOs and governments such as LEAP and NHIS. However, they were more concerned with the closure of witch camps than anything else. Simply put, members of the communities did not feel they would be safe if they were to return back to their original communities and if their communities were to be closed thus left with little if no alternatives.

CONCLUSION

In short, there are obviously many contestations, debates, and disjunctures in the accounts of what various actors contribute to the ameliorating of the manifold vulnerabilities, insecurities, and needs of individuals who are accused of witchcraft and subsequently evicted to resettle in Gnani.

This chapter engaged with the various stakeholders and the roles played in meeting the needs of people accused of witchcraft and residing in Gnani-Tindang. The chapter highlights that both state and non-state actors have played key roles in meeting basic needs such as food, accommodation, psychological and emotional, and economic needs to varying degrees. One of the interventions that stood out particularly due to the controversy surrounding it is that of shutting down communities of refuge and reintegration of people accused of witchcraft. Intervening in witchcraft-related issues, especially in debates about closing such communities exposes the complications of dealing with issues such as witchcraft in Ghana. Different actors, especially the state and non-state actors such as NGOs are inclined toward the closure of communities of refuge are considered human rights abuse with many terrible living conditions. It is important that the actors liaise with and listen to the concerns of people accused of witchcraft too. This will help give a balance to their well-being as well. There is a need for partnership between local authorities and experts. The reliance on external (external here refers to people outside of the local communities) expert knowledge and intervention inherent in international human rights organizations, states, and NGOs is problematic and inefficient to deal with witchcraft and the issue of communities of refuge in Ghana.

NOTES

1. Bonyase or Bonyasi are both spellings that have been used to refer to the geographical location in Savanah region that initially provided refuge for people banished from their communities on witchcraft accusation but was closed down in 2014.

Conclusion

Decolonization of Development Epistemes, Knowledge Bases, and Practices

This concluding chapter brings the various pieces of the argument in the book together. It highlights the tensions between development theory and practice and contests how local cultures, experiences and realities intersect with the standardized approaches of development that nominally include culture in their planning but often view it as a barrier to development. The chapter expands on the book's central argument and calls for a rethinking of approaches to development that do not fully consider the potential of culturally specific solutions to social inequalities, safety, and care. It also contributes to a better understanding of the limits of the neo-liberal paradigm of socioeconomic development that has overwhelmingly dominated the directions taken by states and development actors whereby little consideration is afforded to the continuities and disjuncture in how development, wealth, and equity might be differently conceptualized. In short, this book contributes to the decolonization of development epistemes, knowledge, and practices.

DECOLONIZING DEVELOPMENT STUDIES SCHOLARSHIP

It has become clear from the various chapters in this book that the theories that we produce as academics have a correlation with how development is conceptualized and practiced. In particular, the various development practice approaches are usually underpinned by development theories as I highlighted throughout the various chapters of the book. If this is the case, then, development studies scholars and other cognate disciplines have a role to play in theorizing in ways that valorises local specific approaches to development. Colonization as we know was not just the political, physical, or economic occupation of the colonized territories but also involved cultural violence. Independence struggle was therefore the first stage or type of decolonization (Nkrumah, 1965). That is fighting for political freedom. This has been argued to be successful in Africa as all countries gained independence, even if it were symbolic. Inasmuch as a lot has been done to decolonize direct colonization through independent struggle, indirect colonization, or what Dr Kwame Nkrumah of Ghana terms as neocolonization continue to exist and permeate every fabric of the former colonies. Some have also termed this continuous influence of former colonial powers on former colonies as coloniality (Ngugi, 1986, 1993; Ndlovu-Gatsheni, 2018, 2021; Talabi, 2021). It is important to state that even if former colonies have not lived up to the expectations, at least in principle, people have the agency to rule themselves, which is the right and just thing to do. Although this book does not contribute to the political independence struggle, it builds on it. Colonization and its relics will take a long time to be undone and as far as these are still in place, there is a need for the decolonial struggle to continue as well.

There are several issues that are still at stake in current former colonial territories. One such is the discounting of indigenous knowledge as irrational, mystical, or consigned to "the traditional." Like the colonial enterprise that sought or presented itself as a civilizing mission, with the West nominating itself as an epitome of superiority with the mandate to spread such civilization to other parts of the world, we must be careful as development scholars and practitioners to not perpetuate a similar narration through our works. This can easily be taken for granted especially when we assume that we know what people need and have the solutions to their needs. We need to consciously be reflective, and reflexive, and adopt a critical approach to our scholarship that informs practitioners' approach in the field. One way to do this is through *decolonization*.

With regard to development scholarship, the presumption for a long time was that with development, and modernity more generally, witchcraft would disappear (Kyriakakis, n.d.; Parrinder, 1958; Stenberg, 2010). That is why a number of countries adopted strategies to discourage witchcraft. For example, Benin in its quest to modernize adopted a nationwide exercise to prohibit witchcraft (Kahn, 2011). The Taita Highlands area in Kenya also employed the services of witch doctors to do away with witchcraft (Smith, 2005, 2008). This is complicated and these strategies to get rid of witchcraft are paradoxical as the people fall back on the expertise of local experts who are themselves considered powerful witches or at least distinguishing between a witch and witch doctor is blurred (Smith, 2005, 2008). As argued throughout this book, despite the spread of economic development and ideas of modernity, uncertainties remain regarding whether it has led to a decrease in witchcraft accusations. Indeed, the opposite would appear to be true, I would argue, which is also supported by established literature.

When considered within the context of Africa, development appears to have led to an increase in accusations and banishments, as people try to adjust to the changes that have arisen with modernity (see Indonessia, Bubandt, 2015; Kyriakakis, n.d.). In fact, Kyriakakis (n.d.) observes that belief and practice in witchcraft in West Africa is rising. Considering this, there is a responsibility for development studies—as a discipline leading the debate in advancing development in less-developed countries—to consider conceptual frameworks and theoretical perspectives that can navigate and champion a meaningful and beneficial development amid belief systems such as witchcraft. The persistence of beliefs and practices of witchcraft, despite development endeavors to eliminate them, exposes the weaknesses in a conceptualization of development connected to the spread of capitalism, which has benefited a few and thereby created and deepened inequalities. Admittedly, this task is a herculean one, but this issue is crucial for advancing development scholarship. This is where decolonization becomes an essential framework and draws our attention to local epistemologies and approaches to development.

The frequently argued position in anthropological and development scholarship that belief in, and practices of witchcraft, are irrational and archaic is undoubtedly connected to the framing of development, which is ostensibly a rationalist (economic) project (Green and Mesaki, 2005) any engagement with that deemed as magic or witchcraft seems to contradict such rationalist perceptions. The stranglehold of the idea that witchcraft beliefs and practices are primitive speaks to the lack of development or progress. The extent to which development scholarship could turn its gaze toward a deeper theoretical and critical engagement with witchcraft was a key motivation for engaging with the subject of this book, bringing to the fore the relevance of the theoretical framework, post-development and decolonization, which call for a detailed engagement with local contexts, and an exploration of how people in such contexts understand the development and seek to engender a development that is appropriate within their contexts (Escobar, 1995, 1999; Esteva, 1992).

Rather than a legitimate, persisting, and rational explanation for conditions in society, witchcraft is represented in development practice simply as a problem or challenge. This idea is undoubtedly connected to the ongoing, if not hegemonic, framing of the subject in much development practice as inherently connected to social evolution and thus the antithesis of modernity, development, and progress (see Green and Mesaki, 2005). On the contrary, throughout this book, it has been argued that witchcraft is not about people being backward or yet to develop. Rather, it is about a different mode of engaging with and accounting for, both personal and collective development as well as action. Of course, drawing on witchcraft as an explanation may seem irrational to outsiders, but it is also an aspect of how societies govern interpersonal tensions and conflicts associated with change (see Crampton, 2013). For this reason, a deeper understanding of witchcraft is not simply a call for accepting difference or reducing the divide between "self" and "other" by doing away with the discourse of exoticism. More importantly, it is a call for delving more critically into the very rationale of development as relating to change.

The conundrum is that "progress," as envisaged in the conceptualization of development, does not necessarily accord well across different societies. It sets in motion a stark contrast between individual and collective "progress," a tension between distinction or standing apart from others and the need to engage in a community as relative equals. Moreover, it sets in motion the categorization of societies around a particular set of variables or values that are not necessarily valued in the same way (see Green and Mesaki, 2005). For instance, development, as it is typically portrayed by external actors, suggests that it is "a community"-based, and yet it is often inadequately attuned to the nature of the community. This is an outcome most likely due to the competition for scarce resources for self, in contrast to the collective self (the collective self as defined—including its boundaries—by those practitioners of development rather than the community for whom the project is allegedly designed), as a structural construction of society in the supposed modern world where things are shaped by neoliberal policies as was discussed in chapter 3.

One core explanation for the continued presence of witchcraft is economic disparity. It has been argued by many authors that economic disparity in Africa has led to an increase in witchcraft accusations where often older people are accused of using witchcraft to unduly amass wealth and/or using witchcraft to destroy the wealth of others (see Ashforth, 1998; Comaroff and Comaroff, 1999b; Geschiere, 1997; Jensen and Buur, 2004; Mabefam and Appau, 2020). I found that it was poor, elderly women who are more likely to be accused, confronted, and ejected from their societies on the basis of witchcraft. There is an inherent fear by relatively successful people that the poor are jealous of their wealth and may bewitch them. As a result, poor, elderly persons, especially women—who have not been able to leap out of poverty or acquire some wealth over time as a cultural expectation may be considered social failures. They are therefore deeply suspected to be likely to use their accumulated knowledge, which some suspect to be witchcraft, to destroy the wealth of relatively younger successful people in the community (Mabefam and Appau, 2020). The reverse is also that people also use witchcraft accusations to eject the poor, elderly women out of their societies at the least suspicion. Thus, I argue that economically motivated accusations against the elderly are a cultural rebuke of their poverty, relative to their lived opportunities (Mabefam and Appau, 2020).

ONGOING SCHOLARSHIP ON THE EXISTENCE OF WITCHCRAFT

Witchcraft is not linear or static. Even in so-called "developed" societies, witchcraft is neither completely outdated nor irrelevant. The difference perhaps across societal contexts is in the meanings attached, and the forms of expression that emerge with witchcraft beliefs and practices. Irrespective of whether societies are labeled as "developed," "modern," or the antithetical "underdeveloped" or even "third world," the salience and adaptability of witchcraft is clear (Comaroff and Comaroff, 1999; Ezzy, 2001). Nonetheless, the politics involved in categorizing witchcraft as a problem in less developed or modern societies is critical to emphasize here. In contrast to the West, where witchcraft is now presumed to be a lifestyle choice or an identity for individuals (Ezzy, 2001), in supposedly less-developed societies it is taken for granted as "cultural" and "traditional" and communal (Green and Mesaki, 2005). For example, Green and Mesaki argue that witchcraft as modern is an anthropological construction (2005, p. 372). However, what both authors acknowledge is that witchcraft is on the increase (see Kyriakakis, n.d.; Smith, 2005; 2008). The question, therefore, is if witchcraft is a backward practice, why has it not disappeared with modernity? Taking into consideration Ghana, Tanzania, and Kenya, Benin as well as other countries that are just as modern as countries elsewhere. Such framing suggests a lack of capacity to differentiate or understand the "nature" of witchcraft among those deemed to reside within a less-developed context. That the context is important to consider is also quite clear and indeed, the difference between responses to lifestyle choices or identification in the West today as opposed to previous epochs of witch-hunting is evident.

Witchcraft beliefs and practices have been adapted or transformed to the changing landscape of policies, economic change, and local and global interactions (Comaroff and Comaroff, 1999a, 1993, 1999b, 2002). One of the key aspects of the argument presented in the book is that the case of Ghana highlights the importance of considering witchcraft in relation to the contemporary sociopolitical context. Social and political dynamics, as encountered by Ghanaians, alongside development and modernity shape the engagement with, and meaning of, witchcraft. As demonstrated in this book, witchcraft cannot be relegated to the past, as traditional, static, or primitive precisely because it adapts and accommodates new forms alongside development and modernity so to speak.

INTERSECTIONALITY: GENDER, AGE
WITCHCRAFT, AND DEVELOPMENT

A number of factors coalesce to make one more prone to witchcraft accusations and eviction. Gender issues stand out throughout this book. As was seen in chapters 1, 2, and 4, a disproportionate number of women are accused and banished from their communities to resettle elsewhere. Except for the Gnani, all other communities host only women accused of witchcraft. This suggests that more women are accused and banished from their communities based on witchcraft as compared to men. This allies with the global and historical fact that more women are accused of witchcraft than men (see Ben-Yehuda, 1980; Chaudhuri, 2012; Federici, 2008, 2010).

Again, in comparison to other contexts in Africa, women are also predominantly accused in Ghana. However, in addition to being a woman and predisposed to witchcraft accusations, being elderly increases a woman's chances. Age as an additional layer of witchcraft accusations has also been well documented in both Ghana and other places (Eboiyehi, 2017; Machangu, 2015; Miguel, 2005). For example, Miguel (2005) found that 3,072 accused witches were killed in Sukumaland, Tanzania, from 1970 to 1988. Out of these, about 80 percent of the victims were elderly women. Miguel argues that elderly women serve as scapegoats for the communities in Tanzania and are rejected in times of economic crisis and natural disasters. Machangu's (2015) study in the Fipa of Sumbawanga district of Tanzania between 1961 and 2010 found that the area was among the five top areas noted for the killing of elderly women based on witchcraft accusations. This is probably why Crampton (2013, p. 199) labeled witchcraft as an "old woman's problem."

Although more women than men are accused and banished from their communities in Africa, the plight of men who are also accused and banished into Gnani are equally important. However, the foundational approach in development work with regard to assisting people accused of witchcraft differs based on gender. For example, both local and international NGOs (nongovernmental organizations) working in the various communities of resettlement do not believe that men who live in such communities are actually accused of witchcraft. One staff member of one of the NGOs working in Gnani asserts that men who are claiming they are driven away are either lazy or want to benefit from the support given to women accused of witchcraft and residing in Gnani. This assertion downplays the consequences of witchcraft accusations and banishment on men in Gnani. This assumption might be due to the clothes, food and shelter. Based on the above, different non-state actors assist residents with what they can afford. For example, some NGOs have provided them with food, others have assisted them to acquire health insurance and helped them to renew their health insurance membership while the Catholic Church has provided them with pipe water.

The non-state actors sometimes employ partnership and participatory approaches. As will be discussed below, ActionAid Ghana has over the years partnered with Songtaba, a local NGO, to intervene in the case of people accused of witchcraft in northern Ghana. The closure of one of the Bonyasi refuge community in the Central Gonja district was also reported to result from a partnership between the Ghanaian state, ActionAid Ghana, and local community leaders. The next section details some of the specific issues and the lens through which NGOs look at the issues of witch camps and their mode of intervention. Essentially, their interventions can be categorized into *human rights awareness creation and protection, meeting the immediate needs of people accused of witchcraft, economic empowerment,* and *closure of communities of refuge and reintegration.*

Human Rights Awareness Creation and Protection

NGOs see the issue of communities of refuge and people accused of witch-craft as a human rights issue, and thus, their interventions are enmeshed in the human rights framework. The quotation below encapsulates the roles NGOs play in the various communities of refuge. The quote is culled from a focus group discussion (FGD) held with staff of ActionAid Ghana in Northern Ghana.

> The interventions we offer range from supporting them to meet their immediate needs. We support them with food, clothes and roofing of their houses. But over time, we realised such direct support was not sustainable. We started mobilising them to assist in advocating for their rights. We brought all the communities of refuge together. We believe there is strength in numbers. If it is only the Kukuo or Gnani community often speaking out, they might be ignored but when they (duty bearers) know that you are mobilising some women to also advocate for their rights on a large scale, they are likely to pay attention. We have therefore mobilised all the people accused of witchcraft at the various communities of refuge into one network with an executive who leads them in doing all the advocacy work. (staff of AAG at a Focus Group Discussion)

While in the field, I also interacted with another NGO, Songtaba, which is a partner organization to ActionAid, and their coordinator, had this to say:

> You know people accused of witchcraft come from different places and are seen as individuals. Because of their vulnerable situations, they are not able to fight for their rights as individuals. We there organised them into a group, so that they can have one voice that is loud enough to express their concerns for the government and others to help them out. We organise and train them on leadership skills, public speaking skills, and group management.

From the above, it can be seen that human rights underpin some of the works of NGOs, to the extent that everything depends on it. For example, while speaking to the staff of ActionAid, regarding the kind of interventions they do in the various communities, one of them said,

> For us as an organisation, we are not looking at whether there is witchcraft or not. That is not our focus. We are looking at how people's rights are violated, abused and discriminated against. For example, if you ask someone not to come to her community because of witchcraft accusations, you have exiled the person and it constitutes a violation of the person's rights. (staff of AAG at a Focus Group Discussion)

The abuse and non-recognition of human rights within the limits of the Ghanaian legal framework is one of the key areas in which NGOs are fighting to ensure that the rights of people accused of witchcraft are protected. While it is a fact that there is a conflict between culture and legal rights in Ghana regarding how people accused of witchcraft are treated, it is argued that banishing people from their own societies is an abuse of their rights (ActionAid, 2008b, 2008a, 2014; NCCE, 2010). Global development organizations such as the UN and others have sought to protect the rights of the vulnerable by developing legal frameworks. Beyond being signatories to these international legal frameworks, member countries are encouraged to develop local laws that ensure people's rights are protected. It is acknowledged though that although some member countries sign or rectify the laws, they lack the will to implement them to the letter (ActionAid, 2008b, 2008a, 2014; NCCE, 2010). This creates a gap where people's rights are being denied or abused and they suffer. It is in this landscape NGOs, both local and international, fill the gap by advocating for and on behalf of people accused of witchcraft. The above quotation from a staff member of ActionAid Ghana focuses on the rights of people accused of witchcraft. ActionAid Ghana does this by collaborating with other NGOs to champion the rights of people accused of witchcraft. They work with government departments, those accused, and community leaders to ensure that people accused of witchcraft enjoy their rights too. These development organizations argue that it is the right of every individual to decent accommodation, health, food, and clothing. Banishing people to unknown destinations deprives them of these basic rights. However, while fact that men are often considered the perpetrators of witchcraft accusations and violence and thus, it is unimaginable to think that men can equally be victims of accusation and eviction as well, and the case of Gnani proves so. Here, the ethnic dimension of people accused of witchcraft comes into play. Among the participants of my research, men in Gnani were of *Bikpakpaam* ethnic group. There was only one from the *Dagbamba* ethnic group. During our interaction, the man from the *Dagbamba* ethnic group mentioned that he left because he did not like the tensions that were brewing in his community due to him being alleged as a witch.

CATEGORIZATION AND BRANDING
OF COMMUNITIES

Another area to which this book contributes is the understanding of the construction of labels by development workers, media and government, and the impacts on development subjects. Inherent in media, NGO and advocacy work is a reference to some communities as "feeder" or "witch camps," where there is a collapse of all differences between accused and non-accused as I found from the field (Also see Mutaru, 2019, p. 126). This book departs from and complicates such labels by arguing that although such communities may have people banished to seek refuge elsewhere, there are far more differences than one can imagine, for them to be perceived as a homogeneous group. Some persons accused of witchcraft and residing in Gnani and Kukuo communities had even come from other countries or regions outside northern Ghana. There was a man in Kukuo who moved from Togo into Kukuo, and another woman who moved from Krachi in the Volta Region into the Tindang community in Gnani. However, this uniqueness is blurred in the totalizing categorization of communities into the feeder and non-feeder communities and with it, the nuances of each person's experience when they are accused of witchcraft.

Again, communities that accept to host people accused of witchcraft are not referred to as witch camps by the locals. Referring to such communities as witch camps is problematic as not everyone there is an accused or confirmed witch. It also continues to apply the stigma to people accused of witchcraft, already vulnerable, who seek to step beyond the categories and their victimization in their old communities and build lives and a sense of belonging as people with dignity. In addition, these communities existed before the integration of people accused of witchcraft. They were not created "just" for the sake of people accused as witches and seeking refuge.

In short, in development practice, professionals continuously create labels that essentialize communities, exoticize people, and the African continent more broadly, and the terms "witch camps" and "feeder communities" are key examples. Within Ghanaian society, this practice of politicism, inherent in development thinking, has exposed development subjects to further risks of exclusion and avoidance. For example, people from Gnani, whether accused or non-accused, are all labeled as witches by people outside the Gnani community. This is also the case for Kukuo and other communities that have resettled people accused of witchcraft. One woman told me that after mentioning to fellow passengers (in the car she was in going to Bimbilla) that she was from Gnani, these passengers distanced themselves from her to leave her alone in her row). Children from the community who attended schools elsewhere were shunned by their colleagues because they were perceived as witches or children of witches. Similarly, I received disdainful comments anytime I mentioned my research in Gnani, with people supposing that having been among people accused of witchcraft, I could have been infected with witchcraft as well.

The critical question that comes up from my analysis may be this: "How should we refer to such communities?" My suggestion is simple. Call them by the names the local people prefer or often refer to when speaking about such communities. Locals refer to such communities by names that do not suggest they are witch camps. Usually, they are called Gnani, Kukuo, Kpatinga, Gambaga, and Nabole. This allies with the work of Mutaru, where he argues that naming communities as "camps" is enmeshed in Western politics. He asserts that

> the term "camp," as used by ActionAid and other rights-conscious NGOs, is symbolically inscribed in a specific Western political tradition. Its usage in respect of the accused women's settlements referenced universalised notions of human rights violations that often occur in refugee and concentration camps. (Mutaru, 2019, p. 126)

The logic that a camp in the West has always been a place of abuse, exploitation, and lack or exception to the rule and hence deserves attention to liberate and save the vulnerable in such communities is underpinned by different actors' intervention to close such camps. Local people do not see such communities as places of exploitation or abuse.

Again, the people who live in these communities do not consider them as camps. All that the local people would tell you is that there are shrines in these communities that can help cleanse witchcraft, but this does not define the broader community identity in its entirety. The suffix "witch camp" as added to their original names is something the locals detest, as I gathered, due to the negative connotations. Furthermore, the local perceives these communities both as centers of protection for the most vulnerable in society such as people accused of witchcraft, who without such communities would have been abused and even killed. Indeed, clearly, there is a disjuncture between local understanding of witch camp communities and external-referring to NGOs, media, and the Ghanaian government.

DEBATE ON DISBANDMENT AND REINTEGRATION SCHOLARSHIP

The Ghanaian state, NGOs and other human rights activists often argue that the existence of communities such as Kukuo, Gnani, or Gambaga is an abuse of the rights of individuals accused of witchcraft (ActionAid, 2008b, 2008a, 2014; Government of Ghana, 1998; Wumbla, 2017; NCCE, 2010). Thus, there are ongoing debates about disbanding the communities of refuge and reintegrating people accused of witchcraft into their home communities or different communities of their choice. So far, two of such communities have been disbanded by partnerships between the government, ActionAid Ghana, and communities (Actionaid, 2014; Igwe, 2016a; Riedel, 2017). There are contentions about the actual closure of these communities as well. Riedel argues that it was staged for media attention and publicity that aimed to protect the image of Ghana, rather than the well-being of people accused of witchcraft (Riedel, 2017, p. 4). For example, it was reported that fifty-five persons were reintegrated into their communities after the closure of the Bonyase resettled community. But as was shown in the introduction of this book, it had only five people as accused witches at the time of closure (Riedel, 2017). The assumption, that once such communities are disbanded and people accused of witchcraft are reintegrated, the problem of witchcraft in northern Ghana would be solved, appears both overly simplistic and highly problematic. I do not encourage the banishment of people from their communities. But I do maintain that in the absence of any structured mechanism to protect the lives of people accused of witchcraft when reintegrated, it is safer to allow them to have a second life in communities of refuge that welcome them and offer an opportunity of belonging that is no longer possible in their original community of residence.

Evidence gathered in Gnani suggests that some people accused of witchcraft are unwilling to be reintegrated into their home communities (See Mutaru, 2019; Riedel, 2017; Igwe, 2016a). They feel that they will face repeating accusations, discrimination, downgrading, and sometimes violence. Of all the people accused of witchcraft I interacted with, only one was willing to go back home. She self-reported that she was sick and that there was no one in Gnani to take care of her as her children would. She, therefore, preferred to go back home where at least some family members could take care of her. This is in consonance with the findings of NCCE (2010) that 89.6 percent of people accused of witchcraft, when asked whether they wanted the camps closed, said no. A similar finding was revealed by CHRAJ (Commission on Human Rights and Administrative Justice) in 2008 when it ordered the Gambarana to close the Gambaga and for all the people accused of witchcraft to return home. The order was obeyed by the Gambarana and yet none of the accused went home. According to Naboo (2017, p. 99) when a women's parliamentary caucus visited Gambaga with the intention of clos-ing the camps, the women accused of witchcraft pleaded with the group to allow them to stay. Regardless of these pleas and concerns about the safety of people accused of witchcraft, government and development workers are fixated on the human rights frameworks of liberation and are determined to have the camps closed down (Riedel, 2017).

Rather than ensuring that the communities of refuge are disbanded, I am shifting attention away from communities of refuge as a critical point of focus to the general Ghanaian society. I suggest emphasis be focused on the general Ghanaian society by working on changing the perceptions and the deeper conviction that people accused of witchcraft are harmful, the convic-tion that justifies the abuse of their rights, and the violence, discrimination, and denial of opportunities. Attention, in my view, should be focused on the communities of refuge only if there are intentions to improve the well-being of people who are already resettled. Such communities will eventually not receive people if the general society adopts different mechanisms of coping with witchcraft and people accused of witchcraft, where those accused of witchcraft do not find themselves vulnerable within their original communi-ties. In this instance, a revisit to the management of witchcraft accusations in the past where people accused of witchcraft were cleansed at the chief's palace and allowed to stay in their communities before the banishment of people accused of witchcraft became the norm, can be beneficial. This could resurrect the practice of people accused of witchcraft had their witchcraft spirits cleansed and being allowed to stay in their communities, a common occurrence in other parts of northern Ghana.

In arguing against the closure of resettled communities, I highlight that witchcraft accusations are embedded in violence and abuse and as a result, the affected search for safer places for survival. Until such conflicts and violence are managed, it is dangerous and unfair to ask people accused of witchcraft to return home. Their banishment has foregrounded the conflictual interac-tions between an accuser and accused, which is strongly linked to many fac-tors such as power, status, gender, economic status, and inequalities. I argue that, in part, it is about gender conflicts, age, and economic differences, and how power is exercised. Those vulnerable are more prone to suffer overt witchcraft accusations and victimization. If it is insisted that they return to their original home, this could expose the accused to more danger and risks of death, mistreatment, discrimination, and starvation (Riedel, 2017; Igwe, 2016a). In any case, as explained to me by the shrine priest of Gnani, he does not force any of the accused to stay in Gnani. They are free to go home after going through the ritual cleansing process. My point is that effort should be made to improve the livelihood of those who are currently living there.

However, the ongoing pressure mounted on the Ghanaian nation by the media, NGOs, development partners, and human rights organizations to end witchcraft abuse, especially for those who are considered held hostage communities of refuge though has some merit, it is inadequate to address the problem of people accused of witchcraft. It also discounts the approach of providing refuge as a local development intervention as irrelevant. This is because, with a similar approach initiated by NGOs in Burkina Faso, it is considered a development approach to protect the victims of witchcraft accusations. There seems to be a double standard here. This is especially so taking into consideration that the signing of international protocols and the influence of Ghana's legal colonial legacy affects witchcraft issues. Although it may appear to be an indirect exercise of power, Roxburgh (2018, pp. 1–2) argues that the arrival of NGOs and other development actors from the West is a continuation of dominance and control by the West on Ghana. Thus, in her view, different NGOs and international development organizations are exercising the power of the West over Ghana, imposing a (Western-defined) ideological paradigm to attract funding.

The Ghanaian state has authority that is encapsulated in the 1992 Constitution of Ghana that gives the state power to regulate and control any practice in the country deemed dehumanizing. Chapter 5, section 32, article 2, of Ghana's constitution states that "all customary practices which dehumanise or are injurious to the physical and mental well-being of a person are prohibited." Witchcraft accusations and the mishandling of people accused of witchcraft are argued to fall within practices considered dehumanizing, including banishment. Accusing people of witchcraft is considered a civil case in which the charges could be defamation of character of the individuals accused. This is evident in Adinkrah's book where an entire chapter was devoted to witchcraft trials in Ghanaian courts (Adinkrah, 2015). But, where there is violence leading to death, it can be considered a crime. The example of Mr. Ndo in chapter 4 highlights the criminality that is associated with witchcraft accusations.

However, it appears that although the Ghanaian state has the authority and power, it does not have support at the grassroots level, as well as officials working in state offices mandated to govern such issues. The individuals working in the state offices are first social beings whose cultural beliefs are woven into the state fabric. Therefore, the actions of the state are often confronted and questioned by the local people, who assert that they have legitimacy over witchcraft control and not the government. Local community leaders, although not having the authority and power from the national perspective, do have the legitimacy of the grass root communities, and even the elites in state structures, to preside over witchcraft governance. This brings us back to the issue of local epistemologies and how they need to be paid attention to.

IMPLICATIONS FOR POLICY, PRACTICE, AND FUTURE RESEARCH

Implications for Policy and Practice

It is almost an expectation, especially in development scholarship, that every study has recommendations or implications for further practice. Despite the duty on my part to offer such recommendations, I admit that no matter how important my recommendations may be, they are not intended to be a "practice guide" or "saviour template" for the complex issues of witchcraft in Africa. Rather, they are a proposal for deeper consideration by stakeholders as we seek to decolonize development scholarship and practice. The complexities of the ongoing issues of witchcraft in Ghana make it difficult to capture in a single book all the tensions, conflicts, power dialectics, and dilemmas of witchcraft beliefs and accusations.

I intend to move away from such oversimplification of the issues by examining the complexity and diversity of lived experiences of people accused of witchcraft, their dependents, the fear in the community, and the relationship between the government, non-state actors, and community members. But the gaps in both "formal" and "informal" systems dealing with witchcraft in Africa, as illustrated in chapter 4, fall short, and often expose people accused of witchcraft to greater risks and danger. It is my intent for my research to affect, in one way or the other, the mindset and perceptions of Africans, state, and non-state actors who work with people accused of witchcraft and to encourage them to employ a more nuanced approach in their work, one that will improve the living conditions of people accused of witchcraft, rather than exacerbating their plight.

This book has illustrated the ongoing existence of witchcraft and the social impact of witchcraft beliefs in Africa, as told by those experiencing the effects firsthand, as well as those who dismiss witchcraft in the name of development and modernity. With these experiences in mind then, there is a need to revisit and reconceptualize development works and project designs. Both state and non-state actors (who are always at the forefront in either "fighting for" people accused of witchcraft, or to end witchcraft accusations and encourage reintegration of people accused of witchcraft back into their communities) need reexamination. The conviction among the government and NGOs, that the closure and reintegration of accused women into their original communities of residence will automatically lead to the disappearance of witchcraft and ensure a better life for those accused as witches, is simplistic.

It is my suggestion that people should be left to make that decision voluntarily, especially regarding which communities they want to move into, if their home communities are not safe for their return. It is argued that the "voluntariness" of people accused of witchcraft returning to their original communities, as it appears now, is always present. But I propose that this is typical of development intervention, which inherently seeks to invoke change. There are efforts to facilitate such "voluntariness" and hence the efficacy of it can be questioned. We can refer to the case of the two people accused of witchcraft who relocated to Gnani after the closure of Bonyase community of refuge. It was said that the closure and reintegration of people were voluntary and the same extension to the people who were accused. However, their relocation to Gnani and several scholars asserting that they denied such claims supports my point of questioning such "voluntariness." Life and living in the "witch camp" might not be the best possible solution for those that are accused, but when voluntariness is facilitated with an intent to empty communities of refuge and then close them down, it exposes people accused of witchcraft to more harm and danger, including discrimination, death, violence, and exclusion for the just-returned accused witch. I raise this concern and appeal that development scholars and practitioners take this point into consideration: that the sole aim of the government, to close down all communities of refuge without providing a safer or better alternative for those that have been accused, is undesirable. What value will life have for people accused of witchcraft, who have nowhere to go, when the state or the NGOs who have facilitated their reintegration do not provide security for them in their communities? Closing down "witch camps" without forward planning and work to offer an alternative "safe haven" may in fact leave a vacuum that exacerbates, rather than eliminates, the vulnerability of those accused as witches (see Mutaru, 2019; Riedel, 2017; Igwe, 2016a).

The employment of ethnographic strategies in exploring the relationship between witchcraft and development contributes to methodological issues in development. Deeper insights into witchcraft discourse revealed through this study are intended to encourage the development of scholarship, making it a point to understand people within their cultural context before assisting them with any intervention. This is because what people think about development agencies matters. It was surprising to learn from some people accused of witchcraft in the community, some NGO officials, and some long-term residents of Gnani that some development agencies exploit the vulnerability of people accused of witchcraft. These agencies use people accused of witchcraft to raise funds and do not appear in the community after the funds have been raised. This study also contributes to knowledge through the adoption of an ethnographic approach to theorize the issue comprehensively and deepen the understanding of witchcraft issues around development.

One key point noted from the study was the fact that none of the people accused of witchcraft had any form of education and thus were limited in terms of the avenues available to them to challenge their accusation. In contrast to previous scholarship that has argued that witchcraft will disappear with education and enlightenment, this book does not hold that view. Instead, it posits that when children are educated in formal schools, they become aware of the alternative ways available for contesting accusations and confrontations. Even though witchcraft is still prevalent among the educated in Ghana, they are unlikely to be accused, confronted, and banished from their societies. Ensuring that every Ghanaian child has access to education will be one of the ways of opening and rethinking the challenge of witchcraft labels in Ghana.

The government should also consider intensifying the support for the elderly and gender issues in Ghana. Taking into consideration that most people accused of witchcraft in the resettlement communities are elderly, to improve their livelihood, the government should extend social interventions such as LEAP, and National Health Insurance to everyone (see Mutaru, 2019). One of the arguments I gathered from the field was that improving the situation of such communities will attract more people to relocate. The argument being presented here is that the government has attempted to offer such services in other communities, and it is my assumption that if these accused elderly women and men were in their communities, they would have benefited like others in their original communities. It is therefore justifiable to propose that the Ghanaian government tries to reach every elderly person who is challenged with caring for themselves, regardless of their community of residence. Free health insurance registration will enable accused elderly persons to access health care without any difficulties.

There is also the need to rethink kinship relationships. It is quite disturbing that a family that cared for its members in times of hardship is fast abandoning that role. The danger is that without adequate support from the government for vulnerable people, such neglect exposes the vulnerable, such as people accused of witchcraft, to greater risks. The fundamental base from which every community is built is the family and thus, positive cohesion within the family unit is core to maintaining the emotional, social, and economic well-being of its members. Here again, capitalist modernity, with its emphasis on individuation, has obstructed the communal lifestyle and approach to development. Though simplistic, the complexities such as ongoing tensions, conflicts, jealousy, and even hatred that exist within kin and communities serve as key challenges.

Implications for Further Research

Regarding the link between witchcraft and development, I acknowledge that this book is not exhaustive, nor would I suggest any book could be exhaustive. Due to limited space and scope, there are still many issues that remain under-explored. One such area is the lived experiences of young girls and boys who move along with their accused parents or grandparents to offer some form of support because of their ageing status and sicknesses. A future or extended study of this topic is crucial as it will help unpack the kind of lifestyle these children live, and the implications for their adult life. My research suggests that these children may also be subjected to discrimination and prejudice in society or be at greater risk of witchcraft accusations themselves. They might also be deprived of some basic necessities of life, including quality education, better health care, and accommodation.

Another area that needs further research is the impact of the blanket labeling of communities that accept people accused of witchcraft as "witch camps." This will be crucial as it will focus on the non-accused in the communities and examine the impact that the presence of the accused has on them, especially as development subjects. This may involve undertaking a detailed analysis of the lives of people from such communities as they interact with others outside their communities and how the pivotal role of their position in Ghanaian society interacts with this.

One area crucial for a deeper understanding of the progress of development workers is to measure the impactful nature of development interventions on people accused of witchcraft. Further studies could consider a social and economic audit of the activities of NGOs and other civil society organizations. From my interactions with participants in the community, it emerged that some development organizations and individuals use the disturbing stories of people accused of witchcraft to make economic gains for themselves. As a staff member of one of the NGOs remarked, "When you went to the communities, didn't you see several billboards of different organisations presenting themselves as working to improve the lives of people accused of witchcraft?" I personally saw some of these billboards. The absence of a regular presence or the fulfilment of work by these same advertised organizations beyond their billboards is disturbing and could be a key concern that can be addressed in future research.

Finally, it is hoped that this study encourages future studies that deeply engage with witchcraft and feminism or gender issues and analyze the political and power dynamics that inform the everyday aspects of witchcraft, as well as the broader scholarship of this topic. Although this book touches slightly on this, it was more focused on general development implications. Particular and deep reflection on gender issues with regard to rethinking witchcraft and witchcraft accusations will be crucial to continue in further studies.

CONCLUSION

In summary, this book extends scholarly discussions on witchcraft across a range of issues within the context of Africa. Expanding on the more recent anthropological scholarship across the continent, many people in developing countries are perceived as engaging in occult forces and witchcraft to acquire wealth, property, and protection, which are key attributes of what is considered to be capitalist modernity. Yet, bypassing or overlooking such transformations, especially in local communities, does little to acquaint us with the reality of the effect witchcraft has on development in Africa. Based on the above premises, the focus on the impact of witchcraft on individual, social, and economic development in Africa, contributes to scholarship on how witchcraft fulfils its role as both a traditional and modern tool adapted to explain and intervene in social situations.

Finally, this book contributes to a critique of the boundaries set up between "traditional" and "modern." Such a binary obscures the dynamic processes of capitalist development. In relation to this tendency to separate practices as either modern or traditional, cultural or economic, it is important to realize the limits of development. Rather than reducing the consequences on people, governmental interventions that address witchcraft have in fact worsened the plight when seeking to close down witch camps. This highlights how state institutions respond to issues of witchcraft in Africa in ways that don't support their vulnerable populations.

Crucially, witchcraft accusations and eviction exclude people accused of witchcraft from broader societal participation and inclusion. This affects economic development as, for people accused of witchcraft and the people who depend on them, their responsibilities in their homes are changed. Both the accused and their dependents are often denied resources for education, parental upbringing and social belonging in a community environment. The inclusion of people accused of witchcraft in the participation of development at the community level is crucial for holistic development anticipation. In the absence of this, non-state actors can move into the communities of refuge to affect development in ways so that the excluded also benefit. Thus, the significance of witchcraft in Ghana is seen in the way non-state actors perform development; hence, this serves as a parameter for the measurement of the ongoing relevance of NGOs in Africa.

As complicated as it might be, witchcraft and its continued existence remind us of the complexities of capitalist modernity. As Brain noted, "the problem of the presence of evil in the world is one which humans have wrestled with since time immemorial. A belief in witchcraft is part of an attempt to solve that problem" (1982, p. 371). He argues that "a greater secularization of life combined with tool social mobility" is crucial as an "end to a belief in magic and witchcraft" (Brain, 1982, p. 384). Brain suggests that the way to decrease witchcraft lies in its collective benefit, in his case collective farming in Tanzania. He argues that

> material success, if achieved collectively, can be a matter for self-congratulation rather than being the source of envy and jealousy likely to be inspired by successful individuals. So far, however, the response of the public at large to calls for collective farming has been poor, in some measure due to pricing and marketing policies. Given the circumstances of many people living relatively close together yet without the anonymity of the large towns, the possibility for irritation, spite, hatred, suspicion and, above all, for envy, is very high. This is the ground in which witchcraft fears thrive. Of course, collective activities in which everyone does not take an equal part could also be productive of hatred. (Brain, 1982, p. 383)

Thus, this research points to the ongoing presence of witchcraft irrespective of economic development or development; that the desire for people is not simply to have a part of the collective wealth or opportunities, but rather that they are admonished precisely because they are assumed to act individualistically. That there is not simply a problem with those who stand out, but that individuals desire to stand out in some way from the collective is what is problematic.

In sum, this book has contributed to scholarship and development policy by critiquing witchcraft-centered development interventions by development workers and the government. The book argues that the act of closing down witch camps further victimizes people accused of witchcraft, leading to safety concerns and discrimination. In this case, the intention of development, which aims to improve the well-being of the vulnerable in the case of Ghana, the underlying assumptions as well as poor implementation and hence development workers and government instead compound the problem even as they attempt to solve it. It is therefore recommended that development workers pay serious attention to seriously incorporating local epistemologies.

Glossary

Biwadam: Shrine priests
Binyɔkdam: Spiritualists
Bibɔab: Diviners/soothsayers
Bininkpiib: The elderly
Bibɔrib: Chiefs
Bitindam: Landowners
Bikpakpaam: The local term for the Konkomba people of Ghana.
Borga: A Ghanaian who has travelled abroad.
Communities of refuge: Communities that people banished from their communities seek refuge
Dagbamba: Dagomba ethnic group
Dagbani: Language spoken by Dagbamba
Ilik aa nyɔk: Rituals for money making (occult)
Kisamook: Ritual performed to improve farm yields. It is usually the mixture of herbs and blood which are prescribed by a spiritualist.
Kisamowambiik: Ritual that is performed to help improve farm yield but can be considered as occult as it is perceived to demand for human blood as part of the ritual to make it work.
Kijaaŋ: Twin
Lipobipiln: Good heart
Liyimɔɔln: Good luck medicine especially for people engaged in small enterprises.
Likpakpaaln: Language spoken by the Bikpakpaam
Likpasiil: Lean season (a period of food shortage)
M-mumuun: Growth/Development.
Nagbatoo: It is a form of occult/witchcraft that is used to destroy people's farms
Sakawa: It is a Ghanaian term referring to internet fraud or cybercrime. It also refers to the manipulation of others by magical means causing them to give Sakawa boys huge sums of money.

Tibɔar: The process of divination

Ubɔa: Soothsayer/diviner

Ubɔr: Chief

Ugbaŋmar: Secretary

Unyɔkdaan: Spiritualist/jujuman/witch doctor

Unyɔkdaankpaan: Powerful spiritualist

Uteenbɔa: Public consultation with ubɔa. Uteenbɔa normally takes place when someone dies, and soothsayer has been consulted to find out the cause of the death. This is also intended to diagnose the community of its spiritual ills and what can be done to pacify the community.

Utindaan/Tindana: landowner

Uwadaan: Fetish/shrine priest

Witch camps: A politically contested term coined by NGOs and human rights organisations to refer to geographic areas where people displaced by witchcraft accusation seek refuge.

Bibliography

ActionAid. 2008a. Condemned without trial: Women and witchcraft in Ghana— Ghana. https://reliefweb.int/report/ghana/condemned-without-trial-women-and -witchcraft-ana.

ActionAid. 2008b. *The state and condition of alleged witches in northern region of Ghana.* https://www.africabib.org/rec.php?RID=394457854.

ActionAid. 2012. Condemned without trial: Women and witchcraft in Ghana - Ghana. https://reliefweb.int/report/ghana/condemned-without-trial-women-and-witchcraft-ghana. Accessed May 30, 2020.

ActionAid. 2014. *National conference on witchcraft accusations in Ghana 10th December, 2014,* Accra international conference centre. ActionAid International. https://nanopdf.com/download/summary-actionaid-international-5b20830e852f3 _pdf.

Adinkrah, M. 2004. Witchcraft accusations and female homicide victimization in contemporary Ghana. *Violence against women* 10, no. 4 (2004): 325–356.

Adinkrah, M. 2015. *Witchcraft, witches, and violence in Ghana.* Berghahn Books.

Adinkrah, M. 2019. Crash-landings of flying witches in Ghana: Grand mystical feats or diagnosable psychiatric illnesses? *Transcultural psychiatry* 56, no. 2 (2019): 379–397.

Adinkrah, M., and Adhikari, P. 2014. Gendered injustice: A comparative analysis of witchcraft beliefs and witchcraft-related violence in Ghana and Nepal. *International Journal of Sociology and Anthropology* 6, no. 10 (2014): 314–321.

Adu-Gyamfi, Y. 2016. "Thou shalt not suffer a witch to live" (Exod 22: 18) and contemporary Akan Christian belief and practice: A translational and hermeneutical problem. *Old Testament Essays* 29, no. 1 (2016): 11–32.

Adu-Gyamfi, S., and Owusu-Ansah, D. 2014. Do witches only fly? A historical narrative of the British colonial administration's clamp down on witch finding shrines amongst the Asante people of the Gold Coast (1907–1940). *EA Journals* 1, no. 2 (2014): 1–10.

Agamben, G. 1998. *Homo Sacer: Sovereign power and bare life. Translated by D. Heller-Roazen.* Stanford, CA: Stanford University Press

Agyekum, G. 2004. A witch is banished from Anufoland; What is the Christian response? In *The Witchcraft Mentality Seminars,* pp. 33–35.

Akurugu, C. A. 2019. Gender performativity in rural northern Ghana: Implications for transnational feminist theorising. *Feminist Theory* 22, no. 1 (2021): 43–62.

Alkire, S., Conconi, A., Robles, G., and Seth, S. 2015. Multidimensional poverty index. Brief methodological note and results. *OPHI Briefing* 27 (Winter 2014/2015): 1–3.

Ally, Y. 2014. Witchcraft Accusations in South Africa: A feminist psychological exploration. PhD diss., University of South Africa.

Apter, A. 1993. Atinga revisited: Yoruba witchcraft and the cocoa economy, 1950–1951. In *Modernity and its malcontents: Ritual and power in postcolonial Africa*, edited by J. Comaroff and J. Comaroff, 111–128.

Ardener, E. 1970. Witchcraft, economics, and the continuity of belief, 1.

Armstrong, A. 2011. "Sakawa" rumours: occult internet fraud and Ghanaian identity. Unpublished BSc. Working Report in Anthropology. London: University College.

Ashforth, A. 1998. Witchcraft, violence, and Democracy in the New South Africa (Sorcellerie, violence et démocratie dans la Nouvelle Afrique du Sud). *Cahiers d'études africaines*: 505–532.

Ashforth, A. 2005. *Witchcraft, violence, and democracy in South Africa*. University of Chicago Press.

Assimeng, M. 2010. *Religion and social change in West Africa: An introduction to the sociology of religion*. Accra: Woeli Publishing Services

Assimeng, J. M. 1999. *Social structure of Ghana: A study in persistence and change*. Tema: Ghana Publishing Corporation.

Baba, I. M. 2013. Life in a witch camp: Experiences of residents in the Gnani Witch Camp in Ghana. The University of Bergen, Department of Health Promotion and Development. https://bora.uib.no/handle/1956/7465.

Badoe, Y. 2005. What makes a woman a witch? *Feminist Africa* 5 (2005): 37–51.

Barbier, C. 2020. *Social exclusion of older Mossi women accused of witchcraft in Burkina Faso, West Africa*. Doctoral diss., University of South Florida.

Bartels, L. 1975. Dabo: A form of cooperation between farmers among the Macha Galla of Ethiopia. Social aspects, songs, and Ritual. *Anthropos* (H. 5./6), 883–925.

Bekoe, P. O. 2016. *Religion and human rights of women and children at the Gambaga witch camp in the Northern Region of Ghana*. Dissertation, Kwame Nkrumah University of Science and Technology, Kumasi, Ghana.

Ben-Yehuda, N. 1980. The European witch craze of the 14th to 17th centuries: A sociologist's perspective. *American Journal of Sociology* 86, no. 1 (1980): 1–31.

Bierlich, B. 2007. *The problem of money: African agency and western medicine in northern Ghana*. Berghahn Books.

Brain, J. L. 1982. Witchcraft and development. *African Affairs* 81, no. 324 (1982): 371–384.

Brown, A. 2014. The place of ethnographic methods in information systems research. *International Journal of Multiple Research Approaches* 8, no. 2 (2014): 166–178.

Bubandt, N. 2015. The empty seashell. In *The Empty Seashell*. Cornell University Press.

Cardinall, A. W. 1918. Some random notes on the customs of the Konkomba. *Journal of the Royal African Society* 18, no. 69 (1918): 45–62.

Chaudhuri, S. 2012. Women as easy scapegoats: Witchcraft accusations and women as targets in tea plantations of India. *Violence against women* 18, no. 10 (2012): 1213–1234.

CHRAJ. 2003. Commission on Human Rights and Administrative Justice. Annual Report. CHRAJ.

Ciekawy, D. 1990. *Utsai and the State: The politics of witchcraft eradication in post-colonial Kenya*. University of Chicago.

Ciekawy, D., and Geschiere, P. 1998. Containing witchcraft: Conflicting scenarios in postcolonial Africa. *African Studies Review* 41, no. 3 (1998): 1–14.

Comaroff, J., and Comaroff, J. 1993. *Modernity and its malcontents: Ritual and power in postcolonial Africa*. University of Chicago Press.

Comaroff, J., and Comaroff, J. 1999a. Alien-nation: Zombies, immigrants, and millennial capitalism. *Codesria Bulletin* 3–4 (1999): 17–28.

Comaroff, J., and Comaroff, J. 1999b. Occult economies and the violence of abstraction: Notes from the South African postcolony. *American Ethnologist* 26, no. 2 (1999): 279–303. https://doi.org/10.1525/ae.1999.26.2.279.

Comaroff, J., and Comaroff, J. 2000. Millennial capitalism: First thoughts on a second coming. *Public Culture* 12, no. 2 (2000): 291–343.

Comaroff, J., and Comaroff, J., eds. 2001. *Millennial capitalism and the culture of neoliberalism*. Duke University Press.

Comaroff, J., and Comaroff, J. 2002. Alien-nation: Zombies, immigrants, and millennial capitalism. *The South Atlantic Quarterly* 101, no. 4 (2002): 779–805.

Cooke, E., Hague, S., and McKay, A. 2016. The Ghana poverty and inequality report: Using the 6th Ghana living standards survey. University of Sussex, 1–43.

Crampton, A. 2013. No peace in the house: witchcraft accusations as an "old woman's problem" in Ghana. *Anthropology & Aging Quarterly* 34, no. 2 (2013): 199–212.

Darko, J. 2016. *37-year-old "witch" crash lands in Kumasi*. GhanaStar. https://www.ghanastar.com/news/37-year-old-witch-crash-lands-in-kumasi/.

De Certeau, M., 1984. *The practice of everyday life*. Berkeley: University of California Press

Dogbe, K. 1980. Concept of community and community support systems in Africa. *Anthropos* 75, no. 5/6 (1980): 781–798.

Dolan, C. S. 2002. Gender and witchcraft in agrarian transition: The case of Kenyan horticulture. *Development and Change* 33, no. 4 (2002): 659–681.

Eboiyehi, F. A. 2017. Convicted without evidence: Elderly women and witchcraft accusations in contemporary Nigeria. *Journal of International Women's Studies* 18, no. 4 (2017): 247–265.

Edelman, M. 1999. *Peasants against globalization: Rural social movements in Costa Rica*. Stanford University Press.

Escobar, A. 1992. Imagining a post-development era? Critical thought, development and social movements. *Social Text* 31, no. 32 (1992): 20. https://doi.org/10.2307/466217.

Escobar, A. 1995. Encountering development: The making and unmaking of the third world. *Princeton Studies in Culture/Power/History*. Princeton University Press.

Escobar, A. 1999. The invention of development. *Current History* 98, no. 631 (1999): 382–386.

Esteva, G. 1992. Development in *The Development Dictionary–*A guide to knowledge as power. London: Zed Books.

Evans-Pritchard, E. 1937. *Witchcraft, oracles and magic among the Azande*. Vol. 12. Oxford London.

Eves, R., and Forsyth, M. 2015. Developing insecurity: Sorcery, witchcraft and Melanesian economic development.

Ezzy, D. 2001. The commodification of witchcraft. *Australian Religion Studies Review* 14, no. 1 (2001): 31–44

FAO. 2012. *Gender inequalities in Rural Employment in Ghana—An overview* (p. 58). FAO. http://www.fao.org/3/ap090e/ap090e00.pdf.

Federici, S. 2008. Witch-hunting, globalization, and feminist solidarity in Africa today. *Wagadu* 6: 49–64.

Federici, S. 2010. Women, witch-hunting and enclosures in Africa today. *Sozial. Geschichte Online* 3: 10–27.

Ferguson, J. 1994. *The anti-politics machine: "Development," Depoliticization, and Bureaucratic Power in Lesotho*. University of Minnesota Press.

Ferguson, J. 1999. Expectations of modernity: Myths and meanings of urban life on the Zambian copperbelt. University of California Press.

Fisiy, C. F., and Geschiere, P. 1990. Judges and witches, or How is the state to deal with witchcraft? Examples from Southeast Cameroon (Juges et sorciers, ou Comment l'État traite-t-il la sorcellerie. Exemples du Cameroun du Sud-Est). *Cahiers d'études africaines*, 135–156.

Forsyth, M. 2016. The regulation of witchcraft and sorcery practices and beliefs. *Annual Review of Law and Social Science* 12, no. 1 (2016): 331–351. https://doi .org/10.1146/annurev-lawsocsci-110615-084600.

Fortes, M. 1945. The web of kinship among the Tallensi of Northern Ghana. Oxford: Oxford University Press.

Fortes, M. 1948. The Ashanti social survey: A preliminary report. *Rhodes-Livingstone Journal* 6 (1948): 1–36.

Fortes, M. (1969) 2017. *Kinship and the social order: The legacy of Lewis Henry Morgan*. Routledge.

Fortes, M., and Mayer, D. 1969. Psychosis and social change among the Tallensi of Northern Ghana. In *Psychiatry in a Changing Society*, by S. H. Foulkes and G. S. Prince. Tavistock Publications.

Frank, A. G. 1970. *Latin America and underdevelopment*. Vol. 165. NYU Press.

Gershman, B. 2016. Witchcraft beliefs and the erosion of social capital: Evidence from Sub-Saharan Africa and beyond. *Journal of Development Economics* 120 (2016):182–208. https://doi.org/10.1016/j.jdeveco.2015.11.005

Geschiere, P. 1997. *The modernity of witchcraft: Politics and the occult in postcolonial Africa*. Charlottesville: University of Virginia Press.

Geschiere, P. 2005. *The state, witchcraft and the limits of the law—Cameroon and South Africa*. https://dare.uva.nl/search?identifier=c82f1111-e0fb-4433-9737 -7c3ae7366812.

Geschiere, P. 2013. *Witchcraft, intimacy, and trust: Africa in comparison.* University of Chicago Press.

Ghana Statistical Service 2004. *Ghana demographic and health survey 2003.* GSS, Accra.

Ghana Statistical Service 2012. *Population and housing census. summary report of final results.* Ghana Statistical Service. Accra: Sakoa Press Ltd.

Ghana Statistical Service. 2013. *2010 population and housing census: demographic, social, economic and housing characteristics.* Ghana Statistical Service.

Gilbert, M. 1988. The sudden death of a millionaire: Conversion and consensus in a Ghanaian kingdom. *Africa* 58, no. 3 (1988): 291–314. https://doi.org/10.2307/1159802.

Goody, E. 1970. Legitimate and illegitimate aggression in a West African state. In *Witchcraft Confessions and Accusations*, pp. 207–244. Tavistock Publications.

Government of Ghana. 1998. *Round table conference on the treatment of suspected witches in Northern Ghana.* Tamale. Government of Ghana.

Gray, N. 2001. Witches, oracles, and colonial law: Evolving anti-witchcraft practices in Ghana, 1927–1932. *The International Journal of African Historical Studies* 34, no. 2 (2001): 339–363. JSTOR. https://doi.org/10.2307/3097485.

Green, M., and Mesaki, S. 2005. The birth of the "salon": Poverty, "modernization," and dealing with witchcraft in Southern Tanzania. *American Ethnologist* 32, no. 3 (2005): 371–388.

Gunder, A. F. 1969. *Latin America and Underdevelopment.* New York and London: NYU Press.

Hall, S., and Gieben, B. 1992. The West and the rest: Discourse and power. In *Race and Racialization: Essential Readings*, edited by D. G. Tania, 85–95. Second edition.

Harvey, D. 2005. *A Brief History of Neoliberalism.* Oxford: Oxford University Press.

Hayden, S. 2018. Gambia's dictator ordered a witch hunt. This village is haunted by it. *Washington Post.* Retrieved from https://www.washingtonpost.com/world/africa/gambias-dictator-ordered-a-witch-hunt-this-village-is-still-haunted-by-it/2018/05/27/bb8a4fc2-32a9-11e8-b6bd-0084a1666987_story.html. Accessed February 25, 2023.

Heerde, K. 2016. Witches and wizards are flying to the moon. Modern Ghana. https://www.modernghana.com/news/680052/witches-and-wizards-are-flying-to-the-moon.html.

Hord, F. L., and Lee, J. S. 1995. *I am because we are.* University of Massachusetts Press.

Hosokawa, F. 2010. *Building trust: Doing research to understand ethnic communities.* Rowman & Littlefield.

Igwe, L. 2016a. Do not close down "witch camps" in Northern Ghana. Modern Ghana. https://www.modernghana.com/news/713689/do-not-close-down-witch-camps-in-northern-ghana.html.

Igwe, L. 2016b. *The Witch is not a witch: The Dynamics and Contestations of witchcraft accusations in Northern Ghana.* University of Bayreuth. https://epub.uni-bayreuth.de/3377/1/THESISfinaldraft.pdf.

ISSER. 1991. *The state of the Ghanaian economy in 1991.* ISSER, University of Ghana.

Jensen, S., and Buur, L. 2004. Everyday policing and the occult: Notions of witchcraft, crime and "the people." *African Studies* 63, no. 2 (2004): 193–211.

Joseph, N. 2014. Critical role: How South African justice deals with witchcraft claims. *Index on Censorship* 43, no. 4 (2014): 47–50.

Kahn, J. 2011. Policing "evil": State-sponsored witch-hunting in the People's Republic of Bénin. *Journal of Religion in Africa* 41, no. 1 (2011): 4–34.

Kambala, M. I. 2022. Colonial origins of comparative development in Ghana. *The Journal of Development Studies* 59, no. 2: 188–208.

Kiely, R. 1999. The last refuge of the noble savage? A critical assessment of post-development theory. *The European Journal of Development Research* 11, no. 1 (1999): 30–55. https://doi.org/10.1080/09578819908426726.

Kothari, U. 2005a. Authority and expertise: The professionalisation of international development and the ordering of dissent. *Antipode* 37, no. 3 (2005): 425–446.

Kothari, U. 2005b. From colonial administration to development studies: A post-colonial critique of the history of development studies. In *A radical history of development studies: Individuals, institutions and ideologies*, edited by U. Kothari, 47–66.

Kpessa-Whyte, M. 2018. Aging and demographic transition in Ghana: State of the elderly and emerging issues. *The Gerontologist* 58, no. 3 (2018): 403–408.

Kroesbergen-Kamps, J. 2020. Witchcraft after modernity: Old and new directions in the study of witchcraft in Africa. *HAU: Journal of Ethnographic Theory* 10, no. 3 (2020): 860–873.

Kwasi Sarpong, P. 2004. Witchcraft, magic and dreams in the witchcraft mentality seminars: Applications to ministry and development, edited Jon P. Kirby, 9–13.

Kyriakakis, I. n.d. *The Political Economy of Witchcraft.* https://www.academia.edu/24053763/THE_POLITICAL_ECONOMY_OF_WITCHCRAFT_IOANNIS_KYRIAKAKIS?auto=download.

Lentz, C. 2000. Of hunters, goats and earth-shrines: Settlement histories and the politics of oral tradition in Northern Ghana. *History in Africa* 27 (2000): 193–214. https://doi.org/10.2307/3172113.

Lévy-Bruhl, L. 1952. A Letter to E. E., Evans-Pritchard. *The British Journal of Sociology* 3, no. 2 (1952): 117–123. https://doi.org/10.2307/587489.

Lewis, D., and Mosse, D. (Eds.). 2006. *Development brokers and translators: The ethnography of aid and agencies.* Kumarian Press.

Loxley, J. 1990. Structural adjustment in Africa: Reflections on Ghana and Zambia. *Review of African Political Economy* 17, no. 47 (1990): 8–27. https://doi.org/10.1080/03056249008703845.

Ludsin, H. 2003. Cultural denial: What South Africa's treatment of witchcraft says for the future of its customary law. *Berkeley Journal of International Law* 21, no. 1 (2003): 51.

Mabefam, M. G. 2017. Fear of witchery and the mental illness scapegoat: A discourse of an intersection between mental health and spirituality in Ghana. In

Complementary Medicine and Culture: The Changing Cultural Territory of Local and Global Healing Practices, edited by P. Cherniack. Nova Science Publishers.

Mabefam, M. G. 2019. *Witch camps in Northern Ghana: Contesting gender, development and culture*. Doctoral diss., University of Melbourne.

Mabefam, M. G. 2022. Limitless opportunities for wealth? Witchcraft as a strategy for (in)equality and economic (dis)empowerment. In *Forum for Development Studies* 49, no. 2: 233-260.

Mabefam, M. G., and Alexeyeff, K. 2023. Becoming a sakawa boy: Magic and modernity in Ghana. In *How to live with monsters: Imagined field guides*, edited by Y. Musharbash and I. Gershon, 201–214. California: Punctum Books. doi:10.53288/0361.1.00.

Mabefam, M. G., and Appau, S. 2020. Witchcraft accusations and the social exclusion of the elderly in northern Ghana: Understanding how cultural discourses and practices affect the wellbeing of the elderly. In *Measuring, understanding and improving wellbeing among older people*, by S. A. Churchill, F. Farrell, and S. Appau, 187–209. Palgrave Macmillan.

Machangu, H. M. 2015. *Vulnerability of elderly women to witchcraft accusations among the Fipa of Sumbawanga, 1961–2010*. Vol. 16, no. 2, 12.

Madden, R. 2010. *Being ethnographic: A guide to the theory and practice of ethnography*. Second edition. SAGE. https://doi.org/10.4135/9781529716689.

Mair, L. 1964. Witchcraft as a problem in the study of religion. *Cahiers d'Études Africaines* 4, no. 15 (1964): 335–348.

Martin, F. 2014. *Shrines, witches, and explanations on trial: The witchcraft cases of the Nae We shrine in Accra, Ghana*. Thesis, Mount Saint Vincent University.

Matthews, S. 2004. Post-development theory and the question of alternatives: A view from Africa. *Third World Quarterly* 25, no. 2 (2004): 373–384. https://doi.org/10.1080/0143659042000174860.

Mavhungu, K. 2012. Witchcraft in post-colonial Africa: Beliefs, techniques and containment strategies. Langaa RPCIG. https://muse.jhu.edu/book/21657.

Mayer, P. 1954. Witches, Inaugural Lecture, Rhodes University, Grahamstown, South Africa. In *Witchcraft and Sorcery*. Penguin Harmondsworth.

Mbugri, R. 2019. *ActionAid Ghana closes down alleged witches camp in Northern Region*. http://www.ghananewsagency.org/social/actionaid-ghana-closes-down-alleged-witches-camp-in-northern-region-161783.

McGregor, A. 2009. New possibilities? Shifts in post-development theory and practice. *Geography Compass* 3, no. 5 (2009): 1688–1702.

Mesaki, S. 1993. Witchcraft and witch-killings in Tanzania: Paradox and dilemma. PhD thesis, University of Minnesota.

Mesaki, S. 2009. Witchcraft and the law in Tanzania. *International Journal of Sociology and Anthropology* 1, no. 8 (2009), 132–138.

Meyer, B. 1998. Commodities and the Power of Prayer: Pentecostalist attitudes towards consumption in contemporary Ghana. *Development and Change* 29, no. 4 (1998): 751–776. https://doi.org/10.1111/1467-7660.00098.

Miguel, E. 2005. Poverty and witch killing. *The Review of Economic Studies* 72, no. 4 (2005): 1153–1172. https://doi.org/10.1111/0034-6527.00365.

Moore, H., and Sanders, T. 2001, Magical interpretations and material realities: An introduction. In *Material Interpretations, Material Realities: Modernity, Witchcraft and the Occult in Postcolonial Africa*, edited by H. Moore and T. Sanders. Routledge.

Morgan, L. H. 1877. *Ancient society: Or, researches in the lines of human progress from savagery, through barbarism to civilization*. Henry Holt & Co.

Muchie, M. 2004. Resisting the deficit model of development in Africa: Re-thinking through the making of an African national innovation system. *Social Epistemology* 18, no. 4 (2004): 315–332. https://doi.org/10.1080/0269172052000343321.

Musah, B. I. 2013. *Life in a witch camp: Experiences of residents in the Gnani Witch Camp in Ghana*. Doctoral diss., master's thesis, University of Bergen.

Musah, B. I. 2020. *Ambivalence of culture in Ghana's alleged witches' camps: A micro-level approach to human rights*. Vol. 39. Nomos Verlag.

Mutaru, S. 2018. An anthropological study of "witch camps" and human rights in northern Ghana. In *Religion, Law and Security in Africa*, edited by M. C. Green, T. J. Gunn, and M. Hill. Conf-RAP.

Mutaru, S. 2019. *Naming the witch, housing the witch and living with witchcraft: An ethnography of ordinary lives in Northern Ghana's witch camps*. Stellenbosch University.

Mutaru, S. 2022. Access to land in difficult times: An ethnographic study of morally compromised strangers in northern Ghana. *Social Dynamics* 48, no. 2 (2022): 314–337.

Mutaru, S., and Sekyi, N. A. S. A. 2023. Murder at Kafaba: Debating witchcraft and "witch camps" in Ghana. *Nordic Journal of African Studies* 32, no. 1 (2023): 28–49.

Naatogmah, A. B. 2017. Gov't to shut witch camps in Northern Region. Citi 97.3 FM. http://citifmonline.com/2017/08/govt-to-shut-alleged-witches-camps-in-northern-region/.

Naboo, E. W. 2017. The role of the Presbyterian Go-Home Project in addressing the challenges of the Gambaga witch camp. Thesis. http://ugspace.ug.edu.gh/handle/123456789/24679.

NCCE. 2010. *Research on witchcraft and human rights of women in Ghana*. https://www.nccegh.org/publications/view/123-Research+On+Witchcraft+And+Human+Rights+Of+Women+In+Ghana+-+September%2C+2010.pdf.

Ndlovu-Gatsheni, S. 2018. Rhodes must fall. In *Epistemic Freedom in Africa: Deprovincialization and Decolonization*, edited by S. Ndlovu-Gatsheni. Taylor & Francis.

Ndlovu-Gatsheni, S. 2021. The cognitive empire, politics of knowledge and African intellectual productions: reflections on struggles for epistemic freedom and resurgence of decolonisation in the twenty-first century. *Third World Quarterly* 42, no. 5 (2021): 882–901

Ngugi, W. T. O. 1986. *Decolonising the mind: The politics of language in African literature*. Nairobi: East African Educational Publishers Ltd.

Ngugi W. T. O. 1993. *Moving the centre: The struggle for cultural freedoms*. Oxford, UK: James Currey.

Niehaus, Isak. 2005. Violence and democracy in South Africa. University of Chicago Press. *African Studies Review* 48, no. 3 (2005): 170–171. https://doi.org/10.1353/arw.2006.0034.

Nkrumah, Kwame. 1965. *Neo-colonialism: The last stage of imperialism.* Lulu Com.

Nukunya, Godwin Kwaku. 2003. *Tradition and change in Ghana: An introduction to sociology.* Ghana Universities Press.

Nustad, K. G. 2001. Development: The devil we know? *Third World Quarterly* 22, no. 4 (2001): 479–489. https://doi.org/10.1080/01436590120071731.

Nyabwari, B. and Kagema, D. 2014. The impact of magic and witchcraft in the social, economic, political and spiritual life of African communities. *International Journal of Humanities Social Sciences and Education* 1, no. 5: 9–18.

Oduro-Frimpong, J. 2014. Sakawa rituals and cyberfraud in Ghanaian popular video movies. *African Studies Review* 57, no. 2 (2014): 131–147.

Ohene, A. 2016. Woman identified as a "Flying Witch" falls from the sky after experiencing electric shock. GhanaStar. https://www.ghanastar.com/uncategorized/woman-accused-of-being-a-flying-witch-in-kumasi/.

Onyinah, O. 2002. Deliverance as a way of confronting witchcraft in modern Africa: Ghana as a case history. *Asian Journal of Pentecostal Studies* 5, no. 1 (2002): 107–134.

O'Reilly, K. 2012. *Ethnographic Methods.* Routledge.

Osei, M. A. 2003. *Witchcraft in the religion of the Hlubi of Qumbu: Focussing on the issues of sickness and healing in the society.* Doctoral diss., University of South Africa.

Ouedrago, B. 2012. Burkina Faso moves to support banished women accused of witchcraft. Retrieved from https://www.theguardian.com/global-development/2012/may/14/burkina-faso-women-accused-witchcraft. Accessed February 25, 2023.

Palmer, K. 2010. *Spellbound: Inside West Africa's witch camps.* Simon and Schuster.

Parish, J. 1999. The dynamics of witchcraft and indigenous shrines among the Akan. *Africa* 69, no. 3 (1999): 426–447. https://doi.org/10.2307/1161216.

Parish, J. 2003. Antiwitchcraft shrines among the Akan: Possession and the gathering of knowledge. *African Studies Review* 46, no. 3: 17–34. https://doi.org/10.2307/1515040.

Parish, J. 2005. Witchcraft, riches and roulette: An ethnography of West African gambling in the UK. *Ethnography* 6, no. 1 (2005): 105–122. https://doi.org/10.1177/1466138105055664.

Parish, J. 2010. Circumventing uncertainty in the moral economy: West African shrines in Europe, witchcraft and secret gambling. *African Diaspora* 3, no. 1 (2010): 77–93.

Parish, J. 2011. West African witchcraft, wealth and moral decay in New York City. *Ethnography* 12, no. 2 (2011): 247–265. https://doi.org/10.1177/1466138110392467.

Parish, J. 2013. Chasing celebrity: Akan witchcraft and New York City. *Ethnos* 78, no. 2 (2013): 280–300. https://doi.org/10.1080/00141844.2012.690440.

Parrinder, E. G., 1958. *Witchcraft, a critical study of the belief in witchcraft from the records of witch hunting in Europe yesterday and Africa today.* Penguin Books.

Pieterse, J. N. 1995. The cultural turn in development: Questions of power. *The European Journal of Development Research* 7, no. 1 (1995): 176–192.

Pieterse, J. N. 2000. After post-development. *Third World Quarterly* 21, no. 2 (2000): 175–191. https://doi.org/10.1080/01436590050004300.

Pieterse, J. N. 2001. *Development theory (deconstructions/reconstructions)*. London: SAGE Publications.

Powles, J., and Deakin, R. 2012. *Seeking meaning: An anthropological and community-based approach to witchcraft accusations and their prevention in refugee situations*. UN High Commissioner for Refugees (UNHCR).

Prebisch, R. 1949. Growth, disequilibrium and disparities: Interpretation of the process of economic development. *En: Economic survey of Latin America, 1949-E/CN*. 12/164/Rev. 1–1951-p. 3–85.

Rahnema M., and Bawtree, V., eds. 1997. The post-development reader. Zed Books.

Rashid, T. 2022. What is in a name: How colonial patriarchies have contributed to breaking relationship between humans and nature. Retrieved from https://www.developmentstudies.asn.au/2022/01/26/what-is-in-a-name-how-colonial-patriarchies-have-contributed-to-breaking-relationship-between-humans-and-nature/. Accessed February 25, 2023.

Reeves, S., Peller, J., Goldman, J., and Kitto, S. 2013. Ethnography in qualitative educational research: AMEE Guide No. 80. *Medical Teacher* 35, no. 8 (2013), e1365–e1379.

Richter, R., Flowers, T., and Bongmba, E. 2017. *Witchcraft as a social diagnosis: Traditional Ghanaian beliefs and global health*. Lexington Books.

Riedel, F. 2017. Failing state-interventions and witch-hunts in Ghana. *The Witchcraft and Human Rights Watch Information Network*, 1–14.

Riedel, F. 2018. The sanctuaries for witch-hunts victims in northern Ghana. *Modern Africa: Politics, History and Society* 6, no. 1 (2018): 29–60.

Roberts, J. 2012. Shrines of Accra: Witchcraft trial records at Nai, Korle and Sakumo We, Accra, Ghana (EAP540). Retrieved from https://eap.bl.uk/project/EAP540. Accessed February 27, 2023.

Rostow, W. W. 1960. *The stages of economic growth: A non-communist manifesto*. Cambridge University Press.

Rowlands, M., and Warnier, J. P. 1988. Sorcery, power and the modern state in Cameroon. *Man* 23, no. 1 (March 1988): 118–132.

Roxburgh, S. 2018. Empowering witches and the West: the "anti-witch camp campaign" and discourses of power in Ghana. *Critical African Studies* 10, no. 2 (2018): 130–154.

Sachs, W. 1992. *The development dictionary: A guide to knowledge as power*. London and New York: Zed Books.

Sarpong, P. 2004. Witchcraft, Magic and Dreams. In *The Witchcraft Mentality Seminars: Applications to Ministry and Development*, ed. Jon P. Kirby, 9–13.

Sasu, D. D. 2023. Total land and water size area in Ghana as of 2021. Retrieved from https://www.statista.com/statistics/1227804/land-and-water-area-in-ghana/. Access February 27, 2023.

Searburn, P. 2016. *Witches are falling from the sky in Ghana | Mysterious Universe.* https://mysteriousuniverse.org/2016/08/witches-are-falling-from-the-sky-in-ghana/.

Sefa-Dadeh, A. 2004. The witchcraft mentality in Ghana: Attribution for emotional turmoil and assertion of power of mystery. In *The Witchcraft Mentality Seminars: Applications to Ministry and Development*, edited by J. Kirb, 98–101. TICCS.

Shaw, R. 1997. The production of witchcraft/witchcraft as production: Memory, modernity, and the slave trade in Sierra Leone. *American Ethnologist* 24, no. 4 (1997): 856–876.

Singer, H. 1949. Economic progress in underdeveloped countries. *Social Research* 16, no. 1 (March 1949): 1–11.

Smith, D. 2010. Ghanaian woman burned to death for being a "witch." *The Guardian.* https://www.theguardian.com/world/2010/nov/29/ghanaian-woman-burned-death-witch.

Smith, J. H. 2005. Buying a better witch doctor: Witch-finding, neoliberalism, and the development imagination in the Taita Hills, Kenya. *American Ethnologist* 32, no. 1 (2005): 141–158. https://doi.org/10.1525/ae.2005.32.1.141.

Smith, J. H. 2008. *Bewitching development: Witchcraft and the reinvention of development in neoliberal Kenya.* University of Chicago Press.

Stenberg, S. 2010. Modernity through the eyes of witchcraft: A radical critique of categorisation. *Global Discourse* 1, no. 1 (2010): 53–61. https://doi.org/10.1080/23269995.2010.10707838.

Stromberg, P. 2011. Women Still Accused of Witchcraft in Ghana. Witch camp report, 1–12.

Talabi, J. M. 2021. Philosophical discourse on the decolonisation of the African mind. *AIPGG Journal of Humanities and Peace Studies* 2, no. 2 (2021).

Tarp, F., and Aryeetey, E. 2000. Structural adjustment and after: Which way forward? In *Economic Reforms in Ghana: The Miracle and the Mirage*, edited by E. Aryeetey, J. Harrigan, and M. Nissanke, 344–365.

Tayo, S. 2010. *An Analytical assessment of the Konkomba Belief in witchcraft and the institutionalised witchcraft at Gnani (Yendi Municipality): A challenge to Christianity.* University of Cape Coast.

Tembo, M. S. 1993 (December). The witchdoctors are not wrong: The future role and impact of African psychology on individual well-being. In *Annual Meeting of the African Studies Association held in Boston.*

Tortora, B. 2010. Witchcraft believers in Sub-Saharan Africa rate lives worse: Belief widespread in many countries. Retrieved from https://news.gallup.com/poll/142640/witchcraft-believers-sub-saharan-africa-rate-lives-worse.aspx. Accessed February 16, 2023.

Truxler, L. A. 2006. *From wise woman to mutilated hag: Witchcraft violence in Ghana.* Florida Atlantic University.

Tucker, V. 1996. Introduction: A cultural perspective on development. *The European Journal of Development Research* 8, no. 2 (1996): 1–21. https://doi.org/10.1080/09578819608426662.

Turner, V., 1967. Betwixt and between: The liminal period in rites de passage. In *The forest of symbols: Aspects of Ndembu ritual*, edited by V. Turner, 93–111. Cornell University Press.

Turner, V., 1981. Social dramas and stories about them. In *On Narrative*, edited by W. J. T. Mitchell, 137–164. University of Chicago Press.

Tylor, E. B. 1871. *Primitive culture: Researches into the development of mythology, philosophy, religion, art, and custom*. Cambridge Core; Cambridge University Press. https://doi.org/10.1017/CBO9780511705960.

UNDP. 2019. Inequalities in human development in the 21st century: Briefing note for countries on the 2019 Human Development Report Ghana. UNDP. http://hdr .undp.org/sites/all/themes/hdr_theme/country-notes/GHA.pdf.

UNESCO. 2012. Culture: A driver and an enabler of sustainable development. Thematic Think Piece. UN System Task Team on the Post-2015 UN Development Agenda.

van der Geest, S. 1997. Coping with old age in a changing Africa: Social change and the elderly Ghanaian [Review of: N.A. Apt (1997) -]. Tijdschrift Voor Gerontologie En *Geriatrie, 28*. https://dare.uva.nl/search?identifier=bf9c405a-cd6f-4086-9b52 -ea0fd7f2cd55.

van Gennep, A. 1960. *The rites of passage*. Translated by Monika B. Vizedom and Gabrielle L. Caffee. London: Routledge and Paul.

Walter, R. 1972. *How Europe underdeveloped Africa, Dar es Salaam*. TanzaniaPublishing House.

Ward, B. E. 1956. Some observations on religious cults in Ashanti. *Africa* 26, no. 1 (1956): 47–61.

Wells, K. 2012. The gaze of development after the cultural turn. In *Social Research after the Cultural Turn*, edited by S. Roseneil and S. Frosh, 110–123. Palgrave Macmillan UK. https://doi.org/10.1057/9780230360839_7.

Whitehead, T. 2004. What is ethnography? Methodological, ontological, and epistemological attributes. Ethnographically Informed Community and Cultural Assessment Research Systems (EICCARS) Working Paper Series, University of Maryland. College Park, MD.

Willis, R. 1970. Instant millennium: The sociology of African witch cleansing cults. In *Witchcraft confessions and accusations*, edited by M. Douglas, 129–140. Tavistock Publications.

Wolf, E. R., and Silverman, S. 2001. *Pathways of power: Building an anthropology of the modern world*. University of California Press.

Wolfgang, S. 1992. *The development dictionary: A guide to knowledge as power*. London: Zed Books.

World Bank. 2019. *The World Bank in Ghana*. World Bank. https://www.worldbank .org/en/country/ghana.

Wumbla, I. 2018. Condemned without hearing: An intersectional analysis of the practice of branding, banishing, and camping of alleged witches in Northern Ghana. ISS Working Paper Series/General Series 633: 1–51.

Wyllie, R. W. 1973. Introspective witchcraft among the Effutu of Southern Ghana. *Man* 8, no. 1 (1973): 74–79.

Ziai, A. 2004. The ambivalence of post-development: Between reactionary populism and radical democracy. *Third World Quarterly* 25, no. 6 (2004): 1045–1060. https://doi.org/10.1080/0143659042000256887.

Ziai, A. 2007). *Exploring Post-Development: Theory and Practice, Problems and Perspectives*. Routledge.

Index

Page references for figures are
italicized.

Abdul, Sumaila, 16
accusations of witchcraft: assessing
and adjudicating, 38–41; assessment
and adjudication case study,
42–45; causative factors, 49;
community exclusion as a result
of, 5–7; confrontation stage,
72–74; development and increase
in, 151; dreams and, 52–53;
economic disparity and, 152–53;
as enslavement, 138–39; expert
approaches to validating, 54–55;
failure/success paradox, 53–54;
following an inquest, 45–46; gender
and, 27, 36, 38, 66, 72, 79–81,
154–55; gossip/rumor stage, 72,
97; illness and, 51–52; Jilma's
case study, 68–70, 72–73; killings
of the accused, 141; kinship and,
27, 35, 81; occult power leading
to, 54; protections for victims of,
3–4; reasons for, 36, 49–50; socio-
demographic characteristics of
the accused, 36–38, *37*, 79; state
handling of contested, 124–25; and
threats of violence, 73; Tiya's case

study, 70–72; Upinyaan's case study,
67–68, 72. *See also* inquests
ActionAid Ghana, 1, 16, 39, 40, 60,
133, 135–40, 143, 145–46, 157
Adhikari, P., 79
Adinkrah, M., 3, 39–40, 52, 66, 79, 159
adjudication process. *See* assessment
and adjudication process
Adu-Gyamfi, Y., 129
Agamben, Giorgio, 75–76, 78
age: and accusations of witchcraft, 27,
36, 79, 154; elder support, 162
Agyekum, G., 52
Akan ethnic group, 1, 2
Alhaji (interviewee), 92–93
Ally, Y., 79
anti-witchcraft shrines, 2, 12
Anufo people, 52
Appau, S., 74
Apter, A., 80–81
Ardener, E., 97
Ashanti people, 65
assessment and adjudication process:
case study, 42–45; by CHRAJ,
118–19; by the community, 38–39;
by court system, 39–40; by local
experts, 40–42, 49, 59–61, 127;
participation by the accused, 40–41;
role of traditional authorities in,

About the Author

Matthew Gmalifo Mabefam is a lecturer in anthropology and development studies in the School of Social and Political Sciences at the University of Melbourne.

Milton Keynes UK
Ingram Content Group UK Ltd.
UKHW012313230424
441636UK00003B/61